Shadow Wars

Also by David Axe

From A to B: How Logistics Fuels
American Power and Prosperity

David Axe

Shadow Wars

Chasing Conflict in an Era of Peace

Potomac Books   Washington, D.C.

Potomac Books is an imprint of the
University of Nebraska Press.

Library of Congress
Cataloging-in-Publication Data
Axe, David.
Shadow wars: chasing conflict in
an era of peace / David Axe.
pages cm
Includes bibliographical references and index.
ISBN 978-1-61234-570-3 (hardcover: alk. paper)
ISBN 978-1-61234-571-0 (electronic)
1. Low-intensity conflicts (Military science)—
Case studies. 2. Counterinsurgency—United
States—History. 3. Irregular warfare—United
States—History. 4. Drone aircraft—History.
5. Special forces (Military science)—United
States—History. 6. Terrorism—Prevention—
History. 7. Insurgency—Developing countries—
Case studies. 8. Developing countries—History,
Military—Case studies. 9. Strategic
culture—United States. 10. United States—
Military policy—Case studies. I. Title.
U240.A94 2013
355.02'15—dc23
2013013186

Printed in the United States of America on
acid-free paper that meets the American
National Standards Institute Z39-48 Standard.

Potomac Books
22841 Quicksilver Drive
Dulles, Virginia 20166

First Edition

10 9 8 7 6 5 4 3 2 1

Contents

Preface   vii

Acknowledgments   xi

Introduction   xiii

PART I

1. Tinkerers, Dictators, and Soldiers of Fortune   3

2. Disillusioned   25

3. Balkanization   41

PART II

4. Backwaters   61

5. Distracted   73

6. Empowered   91

v

PART III

7. Backlash   119

8. The American Way of War   133

9. Full Circle   165

Epilogue   189

Addendum   191

Notes   197

Index   227

About the Author   236

Preface

Reading the news, you might think the world is falling apart.

Rebels in the Congo. Improvised bombs in Afghanistan. Drone strikes in Pakistan and Yemen. Abductions in Somalia and, sometimes, dramatic rescues by U.S. Navy SEALs.

Piracy. Insurgency. Terrorism. If these events alone represented the course of civilization in the second decade of the twenty-first century, then we really would be a world at war.

But in reality, war and talk of war are, more and more, aberrations. What's missing from the headlines is any mention of the context that, in fact, makes a story about a single robotic air strike or an isolated commando action in Afghanistan even newsworthy in the first place:

Overwhelmingly, and with diminishing exceptions, the world is at peace.

In recent decades the scale and intensity of human conflict have steadily and rapidly decreased. Wars have become more geographically constrained and less bloody. Deaths attributable to warfare have dropped to historical lows. Increasingly, armed conflict is sequestered in the world's poorest, remotest regions.

Why this has happened is complicated and largely outside the scope of this book. I'm more interested in *what* than *why*, although I do highlight the growth of peacekeeping by the UN, NATO, the European Union, and the African Union, to name a few. The rise of international intervention and peacekeeping forces helps explain the decline of war as well as its changing face.

To be sure, what Americans mean by "war" is not what we meant just seventy years ago, when mechanized armies of millions smashed each other on battlegrounds gouged in the landscapes of the world's richest countries. Today, organized violence is largely limited to the abandoned places—the overlooked corners of busy, but marginal, societies. American drones and commandos strike terrorists and insurgents in their remote camps and in the teeming cities of the world's poorest countries. Our enemies are harder to separate from the everyday people among whom they hide. The unpleasant job of battling these foes falls to equally ambiguous warriors: mercenaries, commandos, and intelligence operatives whose deniability is coveted by a government that would just as soon pretend such murky professionals didn't exist and is doing everything it can to keep the shadow warriors out of view of the press.

Proxies, too, are the order of the day—although this is not strictly new. During the Cold War one superpower would back client states and rebel groups in battles against the other superpower, therefore avoiding a direct confrontation that could quickly go nuclear. Today the proxy conflicts are less binary. Instead of standing in for superpowers battling each other, clients front the world's only remaining superpower in its least popular fights. America no longer wages wars it can simply pay another country or some peacekeeping outfit to fight for it.

We're in an era of change. The wars of the past are diminishing. For America, the wars of the future are likely to be small, subtle, and waged by mysterious men of mysterious origin.

They're shadow wars. And thankfully, they're footnotes to a world increasingly at peace.

Acknowledgments

I would like to thank the journalists, analysts, and former military officers whose written work I utterly relied on to fill in the vast gaps in my own knowledge and experience. They include: Spencer Ackerman, James Bamford, Alan Boswell, Steve Coll, Steve Fainaru, Curtis Feebles, David Fulghum, Jeffrey Gettleman, Greg Goebel, Terry McKnight, Sean Naylor, Robert Young Pelton, Bill Roggio, Jeremy Scahill, Eric Schmitt, Noah Shachtman, William Shawcross, P. W. Singer, Kevin Sites, Barbara Starr, Jessica Stone, Bill Sweetman, Stephen Trimble, Samantha Weinberg, Craig Whitlock, Richard Whittle, and the researchers behind the *Human Security Report*, iCasualties.org, the Bureau of Investigative Journalism, and WikiLeaks.

Introduction

It started with singing.

I was in my room at a guesthouse in sweltering Abéché in eastern Chad on a Friday evening when I heard the women's voices harmonizing. My photographer Anne bustled over. "Do you hear it?" she asked. "I think it's a wedding."

It was June 20, 2008. As a freelance reporter for *Wired*, C-SPAN, and other media, I was on the Chad-Sudan border to cover Central Africa's escalating refugee crisis, one of the heartwrenching side effects of the region's many civil conflicts and, more recently, the Darfur genocide in western Sudan.

We hopped the guesthouse fence, audio recorders in hand, hoping to capture the sound for our radio reports. But the singing had ended. Anne pointed out that at traditional weddings in some parts of Africa the women greet the bride and groom with a brief song. We'd apparently arrived a moment too late.

When I heard the first *pop-pop-pop* sound, I figured it was from fireworks at the wedding. But Anne said it was gunfire. Sure enough, the next sound, closer this time, was the deep *booda-booda* of a machine gun. Something was happening—and it was coming our way. Soon we could see tracers stitching the darkness.

Singing or no singing, this was not a wedding. It was a battle.

Who was fighting whom and why, we didn't know. Chad has long been vexed by rebel groups backed by its longtime neighbor and rival Sudan, which itself has come under attack by rebels backed by Chad. Between the warring parties in 2008 lay a UN peacekeeping force in Sudan and an EU peacekeeping force in Chad. And not far away, Sudanese troops did battle with U.S.-backed forces from the breakaway South Sudan. And with American help the South Sudanese fought the Ugandan Lord's Resistance Army, a front organization for Sudanese attacks on the south. Local militias and armed criminal gangs complicated the already complex eight-way fight.

As gunfire enveloped us in Abéché, it was impossible to know for sure exactly why. There were too many possible actors with too many possible proxies. Responsibility for the violence was obscured, diffused, and layered. Some frightened teenage conscript might be the one pulling the trigger, but he was compelled to do so by strong, mysterious forces far beyond his control.

The battle playing out before me that night in Abéché was cloaked in literal and figurative shadows. Only later did I understand that was *by design*.

Soon the shooting was just outside our compound. Red tracers arced overhead. Rockets whooshed. I grabbed my cameras and joined Anne in her room.

I realized I had forgotten the battery for my video camera. As I raced across the courtyard back to my room, two dark shapes appeared at my side: young men, dressed in camouflage, toting AK-47s. "*Ça va?*" I asked in my rudimentary French. *What's up?*

Now I could see the whites of their eyes. They were scared. One of them was pleading for something, but I couldn't understand his rushed French. He plucked at my clothes. He wanted them.

As a rule I don't argue with men carrying guns, but I wasn't about to strip naked. I led the young men into my room and from my duffel bag dug out a spare shirt and pair of jeans. I flipped on my camera as the one soldier, breathing hard, tugged off his uniform and pulled on my clothes. They didn't fit—he was as thin as a rail—but still he was almost pathetically grateful. It occurred to me that the guy and his friend were army deserters, fleeing the fighting. Unwitting and often fickle combatants—another hallmark of Central African fighting that, much later, I would come to understand as part of a much wider trend.

I grabbed my battery and hurried back to Anne. I figured the deserters would disappear, find someplace to hide, but one of them pushed inside Anne's room behind me. He was carrying two AK-47s and begged us to hide them in Anne's bathroom. We said, "*Non.*" He cradled the weapons and shuffled out.

The sounds of shooting moved down the street. "Come on," I told Anne. I climbed atop a shed and glimpsed soldiers moving in the light of a few streetlamps. But the view was terrible. I needed to be out there. I needed to try to understand what was happening. I sensed, deep down, that I was seeing something profound, even world-altering, playing out on a tiny scale in this neglected desert town. Anne didn't want to come. Earlier I had promised her I would never let her out of my sight: I was about to break that promise. I climbed the fence. "Good luck," she said. Later I learned she spent three hours in her room, terrified and worried about me, as fighting raged around her.

I moved toward a broad intersection where I could hear machine guns chattering away. Army "technicals"—pickup trucks with machine guns on their hoods—roared past. Each time one did, I dove behind a bush or into a heap of garbage. In Chad, the army is as dangerous as the rebel groups, if not more so, and the last thing I wanted was a run-in with a truckload of desperate soldiers driven to the edge by a war they probably understood only slightly better than I did.

I saw a figure climbing over a wall to escape a nearby army compound. I could hear what sounded like a tank engine rumbling inside. The soldier dropped onto the street beside me. "*Ça va?*" I greeted him. His name was Ahmed. He asked me what the hell I was doing out there. I told him I was a journalist and showed him my cameras. He asked where I wanted to go, and I pointed in the direction of the gunfire. He said, "*Venez,*" and we set off toward the fighting.

We were intercepted by two technicals. A soldier in the first truck demanded to see my press credentials. As I reached for my badge, I mulled running away. There was almost no way an encounter with two technicals was going to end well: at the very least, they would seize my cameras.

But to my surprise and relief, another soldier in the back of the truck waved his hand impatiently. "*Laissez,*" he said. *Let him go. We have more important things to do.*

Sure, but what? We'd seen plenty of shooting and lots of soldiers, but no one who was obviously a rebel. Then again, what did a rebel even look like? With my flashlight for illumination, I shot video of a young man, dressed in a mix of army fatigues and civilian clothes, bleeding out on the road. Was he a rebel, or just some innocent bystander with a somewhat martial fashion sense? A machine gun opened fire, cutting short my bloody ruminations.

Ahmed and I ran. We ran deep into the Chadian night, dodging army patrols and technicals.

When I begged off, insisting that I should return to Anne and my guesthouse, Ahmed and the squad of fellow deserters he'd gathered refused to let me leave. Ahmed explained that he and his compatriots were traitors—no kidding—and that if I told anyone about them, "It would be bad." They took some of my gear. I saved the rest by shoving it down the front of my pants.

My captors dove into a ditch to dodge the headlights of a passing vehicle. I bolted. Ahmed gave chase, the knife he held glinting in the weak moonlight. Spotting an army foot patrol down the road, I ran wildly, waving my arms and calling out in English, "I'm American!"

The heavily armed soldiers gaped at the mad white man sprinting toward them through the darkness. Ahmed, the deserter, turned and fled in the opposite direction.

I told the soldiers I'd gotten turned around and asked how to get to the guesthouse. They said they weren't sure but pointed in the general direction. I said thanks and continued running.

Back in the guesthouse I hugged Anne tightly. She was relieved, and angry. She had decided I was either dead or arrested. She told me to take a cold shower. I must have looked like I needed it.

Two Chadian soldiers wandered onto the guesthouse compound, apparently looking to hide out until the fighting was over. Anne met them in the courtyard and gave them water. After that I made sure she locked the door.

All night, I lay awake on my bedroll on the floor, sweating from the intense heat and clammy from the aftereffects of two hours on the edge. I listened to the soldiers trying to break into the vacant room next to ours, looking for loot or shelter, I didn't know.

In the morning everyone rolled their eyes and shrugged like last night was no big thing. "Welcome to Chad," more than one person said, like gun battles were just part of the scenery.

As we headed out for a scheduled lunchtime interview with EUFOR, the European Union peacekeeping force, the young soldier to whom I had given my jeans walked up with his father and asked for his uniform back. The guesthouse proprietor made him promise to return my clothes first, which he did. In the daylight I could see that the kid couldn't have been older than thirteen.

The colonel at the EUFOR base told us that all the fighting had been a huge misunderstanding. Chadian soldiers had captured some rebel trucks and were bringing them into Abéché when the city's garrison opened fire. For two hours Chadian soldiers chased each other around town while the youngest troops stripped off their uniforms, hid their weapons, and ran.

I wasn't convinced. I'd been a lot closer to the fighting than EUFOR had been. The violence had been too sustained to be a mere accident.

But it wasn't until years later that I could even begin to make sense of the "Battle of Abéché." In the decade following 9/11, economic, military, and cultural forces converged to give shape to a new American way of war. I believe I saw this "shadow war" in primordial form that night in Chad.

As large-scale military occupations have proved more costly in lives, treasure, and political capital, it has become more common for the United States to "rent" the armies of poorer countries for the thankless work of war, just as Chad and Sudan each back rebel groups inside their neighbor's borders—and have done so for many years.

In the case of American proxy wars, the United States might provide the drones; Special Operations Forces (SOF); and other high-end, and often secret, capabilities while a poorer partner—Uganda, Somalia, Kenya, the Philippines, or Afghanistan, to name a few—offers up its legions of men to do the day-to-day fighting and dying.

In extreme cases armies-for-hire might even have their own proxies, in the form of militias and mercenaries.

Across many of the world's battlegrounds in the early twenty-first century, it has become steadily harder and harder to trace a conflict back to its source, especially if that source is American. The degrees of separation between the state and its combatants allow our leaders to deny any involvement and insulate themselves from the consequences of the violence.

On the ground where proxy forces clash, confusion reigns. The men in charge would have it no other way.

Even shadow war combatants don't always have a clear sense

of whom they're fighting and why; the voting, tax-paying publics in powerful countries have almost no chance of fully understanding their own nations' wars. The inability of everyday people to keep track of proxy conflicts allows leaders to wage war at their own whim—and to escape accountability if those wars go badly.

I never did figure out exactly who was fighting whom that night in Abéché. But at least now I understand the context for the battle. It matters less who fired the bullets or launched the rockets. What truly matter are the political forces behind such deadly acts, however many degrees removed from the actual battlefield.

The truth lies in the shadows.

This book represents my humble attempt to get at that truth. In planning it, I worked backwards. I began by identifying America's shadow wars in 2012, in places such as Somalia, Afghanistan, Congo, and the Philippines.

Next, I assessed the major components of the fighting: drones, Special Operations Forces, mercenaries, proxy armies, and the media (or lack thereof). Drawing on my twelve years of reporting plus the hard work of other journalists and researchers, I traced each back two decades or more, while at the same time making an effort to gauge the changes over time in the global scale of warfare: how many wars and how intense; how many deaths attributable to the fighting?

What I discovered is that the shadow wars of today have their roots in the late 1980s and early 1990s, an era of much bloodier and in many cases more overt conflict than the present age. The eighties and nineties represented a historical inflection point away from large-scale warfare and toward the smaller, shorter, and less bloody wars that are more common today. The Afghanistan war beginning in 2001 and the 2003–2011 Iraq War were, if anything, painful reminders that big wars are no longer consistent with the politics and strategy of the current age.

I concluded that the rise of shadow wars and the decline of

war in general are two sides of the same coin. In an age where more and more people flatly reject violence as a solution to the world's problems, those who would wage war do so in darkness.

This book does not pretend to be comprehensive or always totally infallible. Much of the most important information on America's current wars is obscured, classified, or simply inaccessible with the time and resources at my disposal. So sometimes I guessed.

And in attempting to draw broad conclusions about the state of warfare in the early twenty-first century, I necessarily smoothed out some of the outlying data points in favor of what I saw as the major trends. In other words, there are plenty of exceptions to the rules I attempt to describe within these pages.

And of course, all opinions and errors contained herein are mine and mine alone.

Shadow Wars

I

1

Tinkerers, Dictators, and Soldiers of Fortune

Abraham Karem was about to change the world, but he had no idea.

It was 1980 in Hacienda Heights outside Los Angeles. Karem, a then-forty-three-year-old aeronautical engineer born in Baghdad and raised in Israel, was spending much of his time in his garage. The garage doubled as headquarters for Karem's own aerospace design firm, Leading Systems, Inc. There Karem was building something. Something tube-shaped with wings. Sometimes Karem would sit in the living room tinkering with the circuits and black boxes of electronics.[1] A year later the project had grown and, according to a newspaper account, "spilled into the guest room." It was a remote-controlled airplane: a drone. Karem called it "Albatross." His wife called it funny.

So did the Pentagon, when Karem flew the Albatross in front

of a group of military observers at Dugway Proving Ground in Utah. Still, the drone managed fifty-six hours of flight between crashes—a big improvement over existing robot aircraft.

Since World War II the military had used rudimentary drones as aerial targets for air defense gunners, and sometimes as photo-reconnaissance craft. Previous drones had looked like miniature versions of manned planes. By contrast, Albatross wasn't much to look at. The military dismissed it as "skinny."[2]

And that would have been that, if not for an unlikely rescuer: the Defense Advanced Research Projects Agency (DARPA), the military's fringe science incubator.

DARPA was formed in 1958, in the months following the Soviet Union's successful launch of Sputnik, Planet Earth's first man-made satellite. DARPA was supposed to gamble a little cash on seemingly unlikely research projects, in hopes of occasionally scoring big with a major technological breakthrough.

Karem's skinny drone sure looked unlikely. It took a few years, but in 1984 DARPA ponied up $40 million for the robot. Karem rented office space in nearby Irvine and started hiring. His company would eventually grow to number 120. The seventh employee Karem hired was Frank Pace, an engineer then in his early thirties.

Two years after his DARPA windfall, Karem's improved Albatross was ready. "Amber," as he renamed it, was fifteen feet long, had a twenty-eight-foot wingspan, and weighed 740 pounds. Its four-cylinder, sixty-five-horsepower engine drove a tail-mounted "pusher" propeller. It carried enough fuel for thirty-eight hours of flight. It also included what were, for the time, sophisticated sensors.

"A high-altitude, long-endurance, high-Reynolds number type of airplane," is how Pace described Amber. In aviation, the "Reynolds number" is a way of quantifying how air moves over a wing. A high-Reynolds airplane has a long wing and flies slow.[3] This particular high-Reynolds plane was also *loud*—like "a lawnmower in the sky," according to one observer.[4] The noise isn't necessarily what killed Amber. But it certainly didn't help. After showing off Amber at the San Diego Air Show in 1988, Karem entered Amber into an army competition for a short-range reconnaissance drone.[5] By then he had built thirteen Ambers.[6]

"We lost that program," Pace recalled. Worse, "the company was essentially blackballed," he added.[7] Not only was Amber noisy, its creator could be "abrasive," according to aviation historian Greg Goebel.[8]

With Leading Systems, Inc., in trouble, Karem and his engineers designed a simpler, cheaper version of Amber they called the Gnat 750 and offered it to the Turkish government, but Ankara didn't bite. The CIA did, though. Agency director James Woolsey knew Karem personally and was eager to test the Israeli's new robot. The CIA purchased five Gnats.[9]

Foul-ups were frequent in the agency's early experiments with its new toys. One Gnat flew headlong into a gust of wind that reduced its airspeed to zero—it was, in essence, hovering—and convinced the onboard computer that it had landed. The computer dutifully shut down the Gnat's engine and it tumbled to the ground.[10]

With its DARPA money all spent and no further paying customers in the offing, in 1990 Leading Systems went into bankruptcy. Its drones and its people were up for grabs. In an act of profound industrial foresight, General Atomics, a San Diego company most famous for making nuclear reactors, snatched up all of Karem's robot designs plus ten of his engineers, including Pace. Karem himself signed on as a consultant.

In January 1991, during the bombing campaign preceding the ground war to liberate Iraqi-occupied Kuwait, U.S. Air Force and Navy warplanes searched in vain for Iraq's mobile Scud missile launchers, hiding out in the vast desert of western Iraq.

What the military needed was a reconnaissance system that could loiter for hours over the desert, patiently scanning for movement. The navy possessed a handful of Israeli-made Pioneer drones, launched from the battleship *Wisconsin*, but their endurance, and therefore their usefulness, was limited. So the Pentagon decided to give bigger, longer-range drones another chance and set up an office under navy supervision. Right before Thanksgiving in 1993 the office asked drone manufacturers for proposals. The deadline was in eight days, which Pace said was crazy.

What Pace apparently didn't know was that the CIA intended to send the new spy 'bots straight to the Balkans to monitor the rapidly deteriorating political situation in Bosnia. The agency needed drones *now*.[11]

The General Atomics team pitched Karem's Gnat 750, which barely survived as a viable project after Turkey finally agreed to purchase copies.[12] On a whim, the engineers added another option to their proposal. They sketched a larger Gnat 750 with a bulbous nose for more sensors and equipment. "That's the one they actually selected," Pace recalled.[13]

In January the navy-led office offered General Atomics a $5-million contract for two copies of the sketched robot, with a quieter and more powerful engine than that on the Gnat.[14]

And that's how the Predator, the world's leading "killer" drone—and a weapon that helped give rise to a whole new kind of warfare—was born.

Heart of Darkness

In the early 1960s the former Belgian Congo came apart at the seams. UN-backed Congolese troops battled the forces of the breakaway region of Katanga, which in turn was supported by hundreds of foreign mercenaries.

Among the pro-Katanga fighters was a tall, handsome, thirty-something French soldier-of-fortune named Gilbert Bourgeaud, better known by his nom de guerre "Bob Denard." The Frenchman was notorious for fearlessly manning a mortar while under heavy attack. The Congo crisis was the young Denard's first war-for-hire. He would later take part in conflicts in Yemen, Benin, Gabon, and Angola, among others.

The Katanga rebellion failed and Denard fled. In late 1965, the mercenary reappeared in Congo, this time fighting on the side of strongman Mobutu Sese Seko, a onetime opponent of the Katanga regime. Following the money, Denard had switched sides.

Mobutu consolidated power and declared himself president in November. Fearful of the mercenaries who had fought against him, then for him, and who still lingered in Zaire, as Mobutu had renamed the country, the new president asked Denard to help disarm one of the more notorious foreign fighters, a Belgian named Jacques Schramme. Instead, Denard switched sides *again*. He joined Schramme in trying to overthrow Mobutu.

The coup failed when the mercenaries ran into a platoon of North Korean soldiers accompanying their vice president on a visit to Pyongyang's African ally. The North Koreans did not hesitate to open fire on Denard's men. Denard was shot in the head and lay paralyzed for two days, as a woman, later to be his first wife, tended his wound with ice and herbs. Denard's men then stole a plane and evacuated their wounded boss.

Denard walked with a limp for the rest of his life. But the then-thirty-seven-year-old Frenchman was not done fighting. He returned to Congo for one more (ultimately failed) coup attempt before drifting into other African wars.

Denard's hasty attack on the leader of Benin in 1977 faltered after just three hours; he left behind living and dead mercenaries, weapons and other gear, and, most damning, documents describing his entire battle plan. Families of victims of the attack filed suit in France and Benin. In France, Denard was sentenced to five years in prison. In Benin, he was given the death penalty.

But by then Denard was far beyond the reach of either court.

He was on a boat, armed to the teeth at the head of a mercenary army, bound for the Indian Ocean island nation of the Comoros in the opening move of what would become a private war lasting nearly twenty years.[15] Denard's army in the Comoros would breed an entire generation of mercenaries who, three decades later, would find gainful employment waging war on behalf of a much wealthier client.

The United States.

War's End

The fall of the Berlin Wall and the end of the Cold War in 1989 marked the closing of a violent decade. The Iran-Iraq War and the Soviet occupation of Afghanistan, both of which ended in 1988, had boosted the overall number of high-intensity wars— in which battle deaths exceeded a thousand—to thirteen, compared to nine in the 1970s and eight in the 1960s.[16]

The wars of the eighties drove annual battle deaths to more than 250,000, nearly equal to the yearly toll during the post-colonial wars of the 1960s and just half the deaths that occurred every year during the Korea conflict in the 1950s. Between the mid-fifties and late eighties the world population doubled, meaning the *rate* of battle deaths declined by 75 percent.[17]

In 1989, another eight thousand people died in twenty-five one-sided campaigns of organized violence.[18] Militias and repressive governments in Sub-Saharan Africa were responsible for nearly half of those deaths.[19]

The decade's wave of violence in many ways represented a high-water mark—although only when *not* adjusted for population growth. Over the next thirty years, the overall number and intensity of wars and campaigns of violence would decline in absolute terms, albeit with occasional sharp reversals.

Not coincidentally, the number and scale of international peace operations—troop deployments to assist humanitarian efforts, protect threatened populations, or enforce cease-fires or treaties—grew exponentially.

In the UN's first four decades of existence, ending in 1988, the world body deployed just thirteen peacekeeping missions: fewer than four per decade.[20] Between 1989 and 1994 the UN Security Council approved twenty new peace operations—four per *year*—boosting the ranks of military peacekeepers from eleven thousand to nearly eighty thousand.[21]

With the Cold War receding into memory at the close of the 1980s, mankind stood on the threshold of a new era of global peace.

But not *all* mankind. Peace coldly skipped over some countries.

Rainy Days

In Somalia, the rain comes twice a year.

There's a small monsoon called the Dayr that lasts from October to December and helps sustain 10 million Somalis, their animals, and their crops through the dry season until the big monsoon, the Gu, drenches the arid East African landscape for three months starting in April. The Gu's torrential rains paint the desert green with vegetation.

The Gu also wreaks havoc on the impoverished country's poorly maintained roads. In 1986, the Gu's effects would have historical significance.

It was the evening of May 23, a Friday. Mohamed Siad Barre, Somalia's sixty-something president and dictator, was traveling by car with several other government officials thirty miles outside Mogadishu, the country's capital with its white beaches and picturesque Italian architecture. The rain was unusually heavy and the road was slick with mud. The driver lost control and slammed into the back of another vehicle. Three people died. Barre sustained serious head injuries.

On Saturday he was flown to Saudi Arabia for medical treatment. On Sunday Somali state radio assured its listeners that Barre's condition was "satisfactory."[22]

It was not. According to some sources, he'd sustained brain damage that would never heal.

An Italian-trained policeman from the Marehan clan, Barre had risen to command Somalia's army in the years following its 1960 unification and independence from Italy and Britain. When the president was killed by a rogue policeman in October 1969, Barre led the army in a bloodless coup.

Over the next seventeen years the square-jawed Barre courted first the Soviet Union, then the United States, offering access to Somali airstrips in exchange for weaponry and military training. In the late seventies he rallied his fractious countrymen in a bloody war against Ethiopia. The foreign arms, and his willingness to use them, allowed Barre to keep the clans in check.

When Barre weakened, rival clans grew stronger. In the aftermath of his accident, he was very weak.

The clans pounced. In the early 1980s dissidents from the Isaaq clan had formed the Somali National Movement, with backing from Ethiopia. After Barre's crash the rebels seized much of the country's north. Fighting between May and August 1988 killed 10,000 people and displaced 300,000 people. The Somalia National Movement seized several northern towns and repulsed government counterattacks.

Barre's legitimacy waned. A U.S. official predicted the regime's demise in "months, not years."[23] Government troops rounded up and executed 5,000 civilians, including at least 500 Isaaq men.[24] At a soccer game in Mogadishu in July 1990, fans threw stones at the still-wobbly Barre. Government troops opened fire, killing as many as 109 people.[25]

Barre's regime ended haltingly, clumsily, with Barre too impaired to appoint a successor. The Hawiye clan formed its own army and moved into central Somalia. Mogadishu slid into chaos, with running gunfights between opposing clansmen. Barre's presidential guard, fearsome in their blood-red berets, prowled the streets.[26] "It's a situation of everyone for themselves," another U.S. official said.[27]

In January 1991, Barre fled Mogadishu's hilltop presidential palace in a tank fifteen minutes before rebels seized the complex.[28] Bound for the United Arab Emirates, he left behind a ruined nation with no national leadership. "Bad government was replaced by no government," journalist William Shawcross wrote.[29]

The next year, 350,000 Somalis—nearly one in twenty—died of starvation. The rest of the world barely noticed. "At least at first, there was indifference," Shawcross wrote.[30]

Barre died of natural causes while in exile in Nigeria in 1995. Twenty-one years after Barre's overthrow, Somalia still lacked a functional central government.

The first al Qaeda terrorists arrived in Mogadishu in 1993.[31]

CNN Wars

Early on in Somalia's civil war few Americans paid much attention. Their appetite for battlefield news was fully satisfied by round-the-clock reporting on the Persian Gulf, where U.S. forces were laying waste to a hapless Iraqi army in Kuwait and southern Iraq.

The Gulf War from January to February 1991 was the first so-called CNN war, covered in breathless tone and numbing detail by an aggressive and highly technological media. It also marked the continuing evolution of military-press relations.

For 120 years the U.S. news industry and the military had skirmished. The press wanted free access to information during wartime. The military wanted control. The balance of power shifted with the terrain, politics, and technology.

In the American Civil War, both the Union and the Confederacy tried to control reporting on their armies. But there was no official censorship and, indeed, no consistent policy on either side. Instead, commanders attempted to limit reporters' access at the local level and at the officers' own whims.

It didn't work. The railroads allowed journalists to move at least as fast as the troop columns. The telegraph enabled the speedy filing of stories. When a *New York Herald* reporter traveling alongside Union general William Tecumseh Sherman gave away information about the general's movements, Sherman convened an impromptu and entirely unlawful court to "try" the offending scribe.

The federal government learned its lesson. In World War I the Espionage and Sedition Acts banned detailed reporting on military developments and made criticizing the troops and the generals punishable by law. Congress nationalized the radio networks. Military censorship of America's ninety approved war correspondents "was strict, if not overbearing," according to one account.[32]

Censorship continued in World War II and the Korean War. But in Vietnam everything changed. Attitudes in the press and the government were more liberal. Radio filing systems allowed reporters to bypass military censorship, although the Vietnamese government did review press cables.[33] In order to rein the media back in, during the 1989 invasion of Panama the Pentagon tried out a new concept: the press pool, a group of pre-approved reporters attached as a group to the military and frequently fed information by public affairs officers and senior officials.

Defense Secretary Dick Cheney, the future vice president, hoped the pool would partially supplant independent reporters on the ground in Panama, giving the military a greater degree of control over the flow of information. But the Pentagon botched the travel arrangements, and the pool arrived in Panama too late to cover the most critical events in the forty-two-day campaign.

When Iraq invaded Kuwait the following year and the U.S.

military mobilized for what would be a major air and ground campaign, the Pentagon's media handlers formed the pool early, convening seventeen print, TV, and radio reporters in Saudi Arabia just two days after the first U.S. forces arrived in the desert kingdom. The pool was subject to military censorship.

But the more than fifteen hundred American media personnel in Saudi Arabia who weren't in the pool weren't censored. The sheer number of journalists in the war zone was "overwhelming," Capt. Jon Mordan wrote in a military journal.[34]

And for good reason. In 1990, America's more than 600 newspapers, magazines, and broadcast media outlets employed more than 900,000 people—1 for every 278 people. The sheer number of reporters, and the resources available to them, would soon peak.[35]

The pressure was on for the Pentagon to devise some way of handling, if not outright controlling, the throngs of press that could descend on future battlefields. The system that evolved proved to have a beneficial side effect for the military. The media-relations machinery that enabled the military to grant press access could just as easily be used to *deny* it.

That would prove particularly useful as a shadow of secrecy descended over American wars.

Dog in Court

The U.S. military wasn't the only armed force with a strong interest in avoiding attention. In Africa entire wars raged largely unmentioned in all but local media. To many outside observers, these conflicts didn't even appear to be wars at all.

That was not an accident. A certain class of warrior deliberately obscured their origins, intentions, and methods. They fought not for nation or state, but for money. More often than not, they didn't even use their real names. They were mercenaries. In the 1970s and 1980s, Bob Denard was their king, and the East African island nation of the Comoros was their realm.

The three islands of the Comoros together represent Africa's third-smallest country, with just 863 square miles of tropical forest-covered mountains and hills, beaches and dense, seedy, labyrinthine cities for its nearly 800,000 people.

The Comorans are poor people in a poor land. They hunt, they fish, they grow vanilla for export. A quarter of the country's external trade is in the form of old, frequently toxic, decommissioned ships that the desperate Comorans dismantle and recycle or throw away—for a fee.

The islands were French until July 1975. Ahmed Abdallah, then fifty-six and the founder of his own political party, became the first president of the newly independent nation.

But not for long. In August he was overthrown. And so began one of the most bizarre, and grotesque, political successions in modern history. Abdallah's overthrower, Said Mohammed Jaffar, was himself overthrown in January 1976 by Denard, acting on behalf of a man named Ali Soilih.[36] Soilih's agents had found Denard in Paris, where he was bored and despairing. Africa's wars of decolonization in the1960s had been pretty good for the old "dog of war," as the press liked to call Denard. But several of the Frenchman's most ambitious gigs had ended in disaster. He found his reputation, and demand for his lethal services, waning.[37]

The future Comoran president's men offered Denard a $15,000 advance in exchange for his help raising an army against Abdallah. Denard called in some old cronies from Gabon and France; purchased ten tons of weapons, ammunition, and other supplies; and caught a commercial flight to Moroni, the Comoros' biggest city. There Denard equipped some overeager Comoran youths with unloaded weapons and sent them racing across the island in a show of force. There was one fatality: a young relative of Soilih who was decapitated by a machete-wielding guard.

Denard and his mercenaries flew to a neighboring island and

laid siege to Abdallah in his villa. The president surrendered. Soilih handed him a passport and a million dollars and made him swear to never re-enter politics. Abdallah left for Paris.[38]

Soilih held on for two years, himself surviving no fewer than four attempted coups. He was a terrible leader. His drug and alcohol abuse, and his tendency to look to his witchdoctor for strategic guidance, compounded his policy failures. Soon the treasury was empty, and the country was growing hungry. When the witchdoctor told Soilih he would be killed by a white man with a black dog, the increasingly mad president sent men to kill all the dogs on the island—an obviously fruitless task.

Deposed former president Abdallah watched Soilih's implosion from the comfort of exile in Paris. Abdallah allied with two wealthy Comoran businessmen. Together they came up with a suprising plan. They would hire the man who had overthrown Abdallah two years ago to restore the former president to power. They called Denard.

The old mercenary was a desperate man. His attempted coup in Benin the year before had left him with a bullet in his skull and prison and death sentences in France and Benin. He accepted Abdallah's contract—thus switching sides in a conflict for at least the third time in his career—and quickly spent millions of dollars of the conspirators' money recruiting and arming his troops. When the money ran out, a determined Denard sold a garage he owned and became a shareholder in Abdallah, Inc.

Denard bought a two-hundred-foot trawler he renamed *Masiwa*, stocked it with weapons, and brought aboard fifty of his best men and a pet German Shepherd—the black dog of Soilih's nightmares.

They sailed from France in March. On May 13, 1978, they slipped ashore wearing black uniforms, prophetic dog in tow. Killing four guards and cops en route to the presidential palace, they found Soilih drunk in bed with two young girls. "I should have known it would be you," Soilih said to Denard.

Abdallah resumed his interrupted presidency. Sixteen days later, the imprisoned Soilih was shot dead, allegedly by Denard's men.[39]

And Denard reaped the rewards. Installed as chief of the five-hundred-strong presidential guard—in effect, the military of the Comoros, equipped with machine gun–armed jeeps—Denard was widely considered the real power in the Comoros.

He recruited friends and fellow Europeans as guard officers. With his salary of more than $3 million a year, he built a luxurious estate on 1,800 acres. He married a hotel receptionist, his sixth wife, and had eight children. He converted to Islam. Or claimed to, at least.[40] Denard also claimed to have the support of the French government, which had been keen to retain some influence over its former colonies. If that claim were true, Paris never publicly confirmed it.[41]

But it seems Abdallah resented and feared Denard's power. The Frenchman had, after all, helped overthrow rulers in Nigeria, Angola, and Yemen. After eleven years of unofficial joint rule, in 1989 there were rumors Abdallah planned to replace Denard as chief of the guard.

The timing seemed right. All over the world, old alliances were weakening. The poor nations of the world were throwing off the chains of superpower conflict, ejecting its agents and realigning their interests.

But Abdallah never got the chance for his own version of the Soviet Union's perestroika, or "reform." On the night of November 26, the president was shot and killed in his bedroom.

Newspaper accounts, what few there were, varied wildly. At least one breathless article described a mercenary firing a rocket-propelled grenade into Abdallah's bedroom. The scant press actually paying some attention assumed Denard or his men killed Abdallah. Everyday Comorans believed it, too. They rioted in the capital city Moroni, chanting, "Assassin! Assassin!" when Denard appeared.[42]

But Denard, who fled to South Africa after Abdallah's death, later told a French court he was in the president's bedroom when Abdallah's personal bodyguard, Abdallah Jaffar, burst into the room and fired at *Denard*. Abdallah was hit by accident. Denard said he shot back and killed the assailant.

"I was a soldier," Denard said tearfully. "I was never a killer," he told the court.[43]

Said Mohamed Djohar, former head of the Comoros Supreme Court, succeeded the slain Abdallah and ruled until 1995, when he was overthrown by . . . Denard, again, out for one last adventure. That time, French troops swooped in to restore order. The old dog of war Denard, né Bourgeaud, was arrested and jailed. He died of Alzheimer's in Paris in 2007, at the age of seventy-eight. The truth concerning that bloody November night died with him.

The same year that Denard died, one of his former lieutenants, a man who had served under the self-styled warlord as an officer in the Comoros Presidential Guard in 1985, flew to Mogadishu, where he was to fulfill the destiny denied Denard.[44]

Richard Rouget, a.k.a. Colonel Sanders, was forty-seven years old when he helped conquer an African nation with the full but largely unspoken support of the United States, the UN, and other world bodies.[45]

Rouget fought for his own personal gain, but America was happy to benefit. And it didn't hurt that almost no one called Rouget a "mercenary." Decades after Denard's bloody heyday, mercenaries had learned to go by other names.

Contractors.

Balkan Predators

The shock of the Soviet Union's collapse starting in the late 1980s could be felt not just in the Comoros, but all over the world—and especially in the satellite states, clients, and friends of the once-mighty empire.

Yugoslavia, for decades a Soviet ally, could not stand without Moscow's support. The diverse country splintered into nine independent, largely mono-ethnic republics in 1991 and 1992. With the Republic of Bosnia and Herzegovina as the main battleground, Christian Serbs fought Christian Croats and Muslim Bosniaks. Croats and Bosniaks fought each other, too.

The fighting raged for forty-four bloody months. In 1992 the UN deployed an outnumbered, outgunned peacekeeping force. In 1993, NATO stepped up to enforce a no-fly zone. On February 28, 1994, U.S. Air Force F-16s shot down four Serbian Jastreb fighters attacking a Bosnian factory. In April, F-16s bombed a Serbian tank and a command post—the opening salvo in a concerted NATO bombing campaign that would expand into 1995 and, eventually, force the warring parties to the negotiation table.

Abraham Karem's drones helped provide the intelligence. In 1994 the CIA deployed one of its Gnats to Albania to keep watch over the war zone. The operators, seconded air force pilots trained at Nellis Air Force Base outside Las Vegas, Nevada, worked out of a trailer parked at the end of the runway. The drone was controlled by a line-of-sight radio until it flew over the horizon, at which point a rather clunky series of relays kicked in. A lightweight plane called an RG-8, which was so slow that it was referred to as a "powered glider," flew near the Gnat, picked up its signals, and relayed them to the ground station in Albania.[46]

From there, video streamed from the Gnat's nose-mounted camera was beamed via Ultra High Frequency satellite onward to CIA headquarters in Langley, Virginia, where agency director James Woolsey sat in his office, monitoring the feed like a night-shift security guard.[47]

The video was choppy, updating only every three or four seconds. "It basically made it impossible for the guy to steer the payload," recalled engineer Frank Pace, who worked under Karem. "He had to just point at places on the map to look."

The setup "didn't work very well at all," Pace said.[48] The RG-8 had limited endurance and could spend only two hours on station. Without the glider, the drone was useless, and coordinating the two required a lot of advance planning.[49] Plus, the Gnat was still vulnerable to high winds. Bad weather and rough terrain were problems, too.

Nonetheless, the CIA was impressed by the drone's performance. The air force was, too. Fortunately for both, the enlarged version of the Gnat had been on order for a navy-run office since January 1994.[50] It was big enough to carry its own satellite uplink, thus doing away with the clunky RG-8 relay plane.[51] "We had a goal to fly it in six months," Pace said. "That was extremely challenging."

Karem, Pace, and the other General Atomics engineers had to build new tooling for the Predator's larger fuselage. They still managed to beat the six-month deadline by four days. The Predator flew for the first time on July 3, 1994. A series of military tests culminated in a full-scale war simulation at the Pentagon's Roving Sands exercise in New Mexico in the spring of 1995.

In the summer of 1995, the Predator went to war.[52]

It had been fifteen years since Karem hand-built the first Albatross drone in his California home. The world had changed a great deal since then. The ungainly flying robot that military officials had once laughed at was fast becoming one of the most important weapons in the U.S. arsenal.

War would never be the same.

Eyes in the Dark

The Predator and drones like it represented an attempt to solve a fundamental military problem dating to ancient times. With its ability to loiter, look, and transmit data, it was meant to proverbially shine a light into the shadows, albeit only for a particular observer.

Drones were about seeing, so that the seer might understand.

Battlefield surveillance was fast becoming *the* defining need of a modern army or intelligence service. War was on the decline, but what conflicts remained were growing harder for outsiders to make sense of. And *not* making sense of them was not an option. For increasingly, outsiders were expected to intervene in almost *every* war.

In the decades following the Soviet collapse, the overall trend was toward fewer, shorter, less intensive, and less bloody conflicts—though there were plenty of exceptions to this rule. The Somali civil conflict represented a spike on the chart, as did the Balkan Wars and the violence in Rwanda and Congo.

Besides generally becoming less intense and bloody, the *nature* of the fighting was also changing. "Established patterns vanished," journalist William Shawcross wrote. "The world was now in a period of nonstructured or destructured conflict."[53]

Governments once propped up by one superpower or the other found themselves powerless to suppress long-building ethnic and religious tensions. Warlords challenged the very legitimacy of weakened states. Ethnic militias turned to criminal gangs to arm them in escalating battles with rival tribes; soon it was hard to tell the criminals from the nationalists. This description matched both Somalia and the former Yugoslavia in the early and mid-1990s.

And there were the terrorists. Stateless or sometimes state-supported. Islamic in many cases but not always. Few in number but capable of occasionally inflicting massive damage and, more to the point, attuned to societies' fear centers. They targeted airplanes, trains, and buses. They threatened to inflict death at random. And they made their bases in the same failing states that in the nineties produced most of the world's warfare. Bosnia. Somalia. Sudan. Chechnya. Afghanistan.

On February 26, 1993, agents of al Qaeda, a terror group with camps and cells in all of these countries, exploded a bomb in the parking garage of the World Trade Center in New York City, carving a crater a hundred feet across and killing six people in a prelude to the much more devastating attacks on the same building eight years later.

"Terrorism had arrived on American soil—with a bang," the FBI recalled in an official release.[54]

Terrorism, defined by U.S. law as "premeditated, politically motivated violence perpetrated against noncombatant targets by subnational groups or clandestine agents," was hardly new. In fact it was as old as civilization. But as major war faded in the aftermath of the USSR's collapse, terrorism seemed to loom larger.[55]

Terror was no more deadly than before on an annualized basis. It was just more prominent in the context of an otherwise increasingly peaceful world.[56]

In the late 1980s there were no fewer than five hundred terrorist attacks per year worldwide. Over the next two decades that number dropped by half, although each attack was more deadly on average, each claiming around five lives, up from one life per attack from the 1960s through the 1980s. Once a fast-growing world population was factored in, the trend was clear: terrorism, like war, was declining.[57]

But perceptions of terrorism are often at odds with the facts. People perceive a thing as dangerous only when it exceeds the level of risk they've grown accustomed to. In the 1990s, people's tolerance for even the remote risk of a terror attack shrank in parallel with war's decline, as it became more realistic to expect to live an entire life in peace and security.

Terrorists' methods accentuated their ability to spread fear despite the minimal—nearly nonexistent, even—threat they posed to the average person. Terrorists blended in. They struck suddenly. Where they came from, and what they wanted, were not always clear. In that way terrorists weren't all that different from the insurgents and warlords who were behind many of the wars of the nineties. And in that way, terrorists too represented a problem that drones were supposed to solve. Hence the CIA's strong interest in Ambers, Gnats, and Predators.

But it would take time for the technological solution to catch up to the sociological problem. And as it became harder in the first post-Soviet decade to clearly identify the combatants in a given conflict—and harder, by extension, to know for sure what the long-term damage might be—the United States and other big countries lowered their thresholds for intervention in small wars.

"This is no longer a world where you limit yourself to vital interests," U.S. Army general John Shalikashvili said in 1996. "Today, we protect our interests when they are threatened in order to shape the environment to ensure what develops is in accord with our goals." Hence Washington's willingness to send troops and drones to Somalia, Bosnia, and other violent backwaters.[58]

Moreover these conflicts offended people's sensibilities as well as their perception of security. Presented with the distant horrors of some war that otherwise had little obvious, direct effect on the wider world, people demanded someone intervene. War *anywhere* was becoming unacceptable to everyday people *everywhere*. "Today 'humanitarianism' often rules," Shawcross explained. "It becomes a sop to international concern."[59]

Popular revulsion at the new, more chaotic—though generally less bloody—wars of the 1990s was evident in the expanding authority of an increasingly activist UN. "Since the Gulf War the Security Council has consistently expanded what it regards as 'threats to peace, breaches of the peace and acts of aggression' to allow it to take action under Chapter VII, the enforcement chapter of the U.N. charter," Shawcross wrote.[60] In short, with strong public backing the UN's leaders gave themselves permission to intervene in more and more wars.

Not that the UN—"the indispensable institution," in the words of Kofi Annan, secretary general from 1997 to 2006—was always fully prepared for its new role as the world's peacekeeper. "The expectations of the secretary general were always great, but his ability to deliver was never as broad," Shawcross noted.[61]

Though it did broaden, one emergency at a time. Between 1987 and 1993, spending by the High Commissioner for Refugees (UNHCR), one of the world body's main bureaucracies for war response, swelled from $500 million to $1.3 billion. Over the same period the number of people UNHCR assisted every year more than doubled from 12 million people to 25 million.[62]

Still, by the mid-1990s, the International Committee of the Red Cross warned that the "human costs of disasters—mostly manmade—were overwhelming the world's ability to respond," Shawcross wrote.[63]

The shortfall was not indicative of any true increase in the number of desperate, war-affected people. Rather, it reflected the new international consensus: that in the event of war, it was everyone everywhere's responsibility to care for the sick, injured, orphaned, and displaced—and to cajole, coerce, or negotiate the warring parties toward peace. Intervention became the rule, and that only accelerated the downward trend in organized violence. But that was cold comfort to the people in lands still at war, as they awaited outside help—and then waited for outside help to actually *help*.

It was equally chilling to people in the developed world who expected intervention in the world's conflicts to immediately make them safer. And more important, make them *feel* safer. But for all the expanding scale of the UN and other interventionist bodies, for all the tens of thousands of U.S. troops deploying to Third World war zones, for all the CIA's growing technological prowess, for all the billions spent and lives expended, small wars still raged.

And failed states still sheltered terrorists, even if only a few.

For it was one thing to intervene. It was quite another to intervene successfully, and fast, in wars that the outside world did not understand. The drone era was dawning, and with it a new age of warfare defined by ignorance and knowledge, shadow and light. But in the early years the technology's promise exceeded its performance.

So for the time being, outside intervention in ugly, confusing, chaotic conflicts would be a matter of trial and error, with every mistake paid for in blood.

2

Disillusioned

By 1992 no fewer than twenty-seven different factions battled for control of Somalia. In Mogadishu the fiercest fighting was between Ali Mahdi Mohamed, nominally the appointed successor of deposed president Siad Barre, and Mohamed Farah Aidid, an accountant-turned-warlord who headed the United Somali Congress, the main rebel group in the city, built around the Habr Gedr clan.

A year of warfare had left 300,000 people dead and devastated roads, rails, ports, and other infrastructure. A million Somalis had fled the country, leaving crops to rot in the fields. Of the 7 million who remained behind, more than half were in immediate danger of starving. The UN assessed the humanitarian situation as "dire."

In early January 1992 UN Secretary General Javier Pérez de

Cuéllar y de la Guerra sent James Jonah, one of his undersecretaries, to Mogadishu to try to negotiate a cease-fire. Firefights still flared as Jonah and his team entered the ruined city, its Italian colonial facades pockmarked by shells, derelict armored vehicles littering the streets.

It's testimony to the severity of the emergency that almost all of the warlords favored a cease-fire. There was just one holdout: Aidid. But even Aidid agreed that the UN should play a role in repairing the country's fractured politics, even if he was unwilling to order his fighters to lay down their weapons just yet.

Incoming UN secretary general Boutros Boutros-Ghali kept pushing for a cease-fire, and in February 1992 he got his wish. At talks in New York from February 12 to 14, representatives of Aidid and Mohamed finally agreed to a cease-fire, to be monitored by forty UN personnel.

The monitors arrived in July. Tentatively, the UN laid plans for a bigger deployment of peacekeepers: five hundred at first, gradually expanding to more than four thousand.

Their mission: to protect the cease-fire monitors, secure Mogadishu's airport and seaport, and safeguard distribution of food aid from bandits and rebels. The need could not have been more acute. As many as three thousand Somalis were dying of starvation every day as food supplies piled up in warehouses for lack of secure distribution.

On December 3, the UN Security Council passed Resolution 794 (1992), authorizing the use of "all necessary means to establish as soon as possible a secure environment for humanitarian relief operations in Somalia." All means, including lethal force.

Two days later, U.S. president George H. W. Bush addressed the American public during primetime, announcing his decision to support the UN operation with troops, ships, and planes. "We will not stay one day longer than absolutely necessary," he vowed.

On December 9, U.S. Marines stormed ashore outside Mogadishu, their nighttime assault greeted by the glaring lights of

TV news crews. Four months later, the UN force had swelled to 37,000 troops from twenty-four nations, including 21,000 Americans.[1]

Rumors spread that the UN was eying Aidid's radio station, a vital link between the warlord and his followers in a city with few other news outlets. "They thought we were going to take it over," said army major general Thomas Montgomery, commander of U.S. forces in Somalia.[2]

At 10:00 in the morning on June 5, 1993, Aidid's gunmen ambushed a Pakistani UN force as they drove back to base after inspecting a weapons depot in Mogadishu.[3] Simultaneously, Aidid's fighters attacked another group of Pakistani troops guarding a food handout. "They put women and children at the front and just sort of let the crowd press in, and they pressed in around them and then disarmed them and then there were shooters in the crowd and they shot a couple of them [the Pakistanis]," Montgomery recalled. "A couple of them were literally taken apart by hand."[4]

In all, twenty-five Pakistanis died and more than fifty were wounded.[5]

All day, UN troops exchanged gunfire and grenades with Aidid's men at the central Kilometer Four roundabout. Eighty Pakistanis and ten Americans were pinned down and had to be rescued by Italian tanks. American Cobra gunship helicopters chattered overhead.[6]

The UN mission drifted from protecting aid efforts to capturing Aidid and dismantling his clan militia. On July 12, the Cobra helicopters fired missiles at what intelligence had indicated was a gathering of Aidid's lieutenants. In fact, the men inside the targeted house were clan elders meeting to discuss a possible peace deal with the UN.[7] Between fifty and seventy people died. When international journalists rushed to cover the carnage, an angry mob killed four of them.[8]

On August 4, a mine blew up a U.S. Army truck, killing four military policemen.[9] American reinforcements arrived in the form of four hundred U.S. Army Rangers and Delta Force commandos.[10] The fighting escalated. On September 23, a U.S. Army Blackhawk helicopter was struck by a rocket-propelled grenade, killing three men.[11]

In early October, the Rangers moved against Aidid. They did so lacking key supporting weapons. As a gesture of America's humanitarian intentions in Somalia, Maj. Gen. Thomas Montgomery, commander of U.S. forces in Somalia, had sent home his heavy air power, including four AC-130 gunships—old cargo planes fitted with batteries of side-firing guns. Worse, the Somalia contingent possessed no drones.

The latter omission would prove fatal after the Rangers got into big trouble on their October mission. "Unmanned Aerial Vehicles could have been employed to gather intelligence after [Task Force Ranger] had been pinned down," Maj. Clifford Day wrote in a paper for the Air Command and Staff College. "This intelligence could have been used to precisely locate both friendly and enemy forces which would have saved valuable time for the rescue team before they departed on their mission."[12] Instead, the botched Mogadishu raid turned into close-quarters melee as combatants on both sides blindly lashed out at each other over two days of furious fighting.

So much for humanitarian intentions.

Blackhawks Down

The mangled, smoking Blackhawk helicopter fell from the sky and crashed into a house just off National Street in downtown Mogadishu. Maria Osman and her three-year-old daughter were inside. The little girl died, smashed underneath the ruined helicopter, whose own pilot and copilot were also dead—and still trapped in the shattered cockpit.

It was October 3, 1993. A raid by U.S. Army Rangers and Delta

Force commandos, intended to capture top lieutenants of warlord Mohamed Farah Aidid, had gone horribly wrong. Aidid's fighters, armed with rocket-propelled grenades and allegedly trained by al Qaeda militants, shot down three Blackhawks—two of them over the city. By the time the fighting ended on October 5, eighteen Americans and two Malaysian UN troops were dead, along with hundreds, maybe thousands, of Somalis.

Osman saw the fighting firsthand from the ruins of her home, now a tomb for two Americans and her daughter. Eight minutes after the crash, another helicopter appeared overhead and more Americans roped down.

Militia fighters attacked, and in the crossfire Osman was shot in the arm—a nasty wound that took more than two years to heal and left the limb all but useless.

"I hate the Americans," Osman would say years later, while touring the overgrown battleground with U.S. journalist Kevin Sites. "I hate them for what happened to my daughter. If I saw one I would cut them up into so many pieces."[13]

Osman was not alone. Many thousands of Somalis felt the same way. An international mission meant to rescue a nation from starvation and civil war turned into a bloodbath. In total, forty-two Americans would die in Somalia, as would more than a hundred UN peacekeepers. The exact number of Somali fatalities disappeared into a running death toll that, over the next nineteen years, would climb into the hundreds of thousands.[14]

Eleven days after the battle, Sen. John McCain, an Arizona Republican, took to the Senate floor threatening to cut off funding for the Somalia mission. "It is time to come home," he said. "Our mission in Somalia was to feed a million starving [people] who needed to be fed. It was not an open-ended commitment. It was not a commission of nation building, not warlord hunting, or any of the other extraneous activities which we seem to have been engaged in."

McCain continued: "If the President of the United States cannot say, 'Here is what we are fighting for in Somalia, that more Americans may perish in service to the goals, and here is why it is worth that price,' then, Mr. President, we have no right—no right—to ask Americans to risk their lives in any further misadventures in Somalia."[15]

American troops pulled out in the fall of 1994.[16] The UN followed in early 1995.[17]

In their wake, the civil war raged on. But the famine, and the threat of mass starvation, *had* abated. What was quickly forgotten in the hasty retreat of foreign forces was that the United States and UN "actually stopped the famine," Somalia-based journalist Robert Young Pelton wrote.[18] Even among military professionals, the peacekeeping mission never really received the widespread credit it deserved for saving countless Somalis.

At Carlisle Barracks, a Revolutionary War–vintage outpost in Pennsylvania, the U.S. Army convened a panel of officers and civilian experts to weigh the lessons of the aborted intervention. It took them three months.

"There is a compromise that has to be made," said Montgomery, the U.S. commander in Somalia during the intervention's most violent phase. "Make sure that at the same time you're teaching people how to handle that peacekeeping environment you stay razor sharp so that if you have to fight in the desert or any place else, that you can do it without the loss of lives. And that's a tremendous challenge, I think, right now for the United States military."[19]

The warlord Aidid died in 1996 of gunshot wounds received in battle. But his war raged on.[20]

Shell Shocked

The Somalia debacle shocked then-sixteen-year-old U.S. Special Operations Command (SOCOM), the secretive umbrella organization for U.S. Navy SEALs, Army Rangers and Special Forces, and Air Force rescuers and special operations pilots—all of whom were present at the Battle of Mogadishu.

Most of the American combatants in the Mogadishu gunfight—and all but a handful of the U.S. casualties—were from SOCOM, which had been founded in response to another embarrassing bloodletting: the botched Iran hostage rescue in 1980 that claimed the lives of eight commandos.

Mogadishu soured the military on its own special warriors. That was evident in the next war. When NATO attacked Serbian forces in 1994, the commandos were held back.

"A great deal of Special Forces employment throughout the mid-1990s generally consisted of humanitarian-related missions," recalled army major Armando Ramirez in his thesis at the Naval Postgraduate School. "Policymakers chose to employ Special Forces units in non-offensive roles."[21]

America's elite warriors had lost their nerve. At least, their leaders had.

Retrenchment

The post-Somalia funk also engulfed the White House.

In May 1994, U.S. President Bill Clinton signed a Presidential Policy Directive—in essence, an executive order—that set forth "three increasingly rigorous standards of review for U.S. support for or participation in peace operations," according to one academic review of the classified document, "with the most stringent applying to U.S. participation in missions that may involve combat.

"The policy directive affirms that peacekeeping can be a useful tool for advancing U.S. national security interests in some circumstances, but both U.S. and UN involvement in peacekeeping must be selective and more effective."[22]

In other words, the United States would think twice before launching another major military intervention.

But in the seconds it took Clinton to sign the document, statistically speaking, several members of the Tutsi minority ethnic group in Rwanda were hacked to death by majority Hutus wielding machetes.

Between April and June 1994, an estimate 800,000 Tutsis died—a near-genocide born of long-simmering class and ethnic tensions and sparked by the assassination of the country's Hutu president, allegedly by Tutsis.[23]

The UN, spooked by its failures in Somalia and the Balkans, quickly pulled out a small force of peacekeepers. The bloodletting continued until a largely Tutsi rebel force attacked and pushed back the Hutu militia.

Millions of Hutus fled into neighboring Zaire, later renamed the Democratic Republic of Congo (DRC), setting the stage for repeated Rwandan incursions into that country that would ultimately help bring about one of the most terrible wars of the late twentieth century, a half-decade of fighting in the DRC that killed even more people than the Rwandan genocide.

Clinton had received daily intelligence briefing on the slaughter in Rwanda, but, still stinging from Mogadishu, he, and Congress, were in no mood to intervene. Years later Clinton would publicly express his remorse. "One of the greatest regrets of my presidency is that I did not send forces as a part of a UN mission to stop it," Clinton wrote.[24]

But there had been no strong UN mission for the United States to join. "The overriding failure in international community's response was the lack of resources and political will, as well as errors of judgement as to the nature of the events in Rwanda," the UN admitted in a 1999 inquiry.[25]

As the Rwandan genocide raged, the number of UN peacekeepers deployed worldwide had declined to barely 12,000, compared to 63,000 just four years earlier.[26] UN Secretary General

Annan expressed his "deep remorse" over Rwanda and vowed that the world body "would act to prevent or halt any other such catastrophe in the future," according to a UN summary.[27]

After a brief retrenchment, the UN doubled down on its post-Cold War intervention gambit. The lesson Annan and his lieutenants seemed to take from the wars of the early 1990s was that more, not less, intervention was needed. To that end, in the late 1990s and early 2000s the world body approved new peacekeeping operations in Angola, Bosnia, Burundi, Central African Republic, Chad, Côte d'Ivoire, Croatia, Congo, Ethiopia, Eritrea, Liberia, Guatemala, Haiti, Macedonia, Sierra Leone, and Sudan.[28] The total number of deployed UN peacekeepers rose from 12,000 in 1999 to 39,000 just a year later.[29]

Blinders

The U.S. media had done its part to encourage Washington and the world's inaction. The Bosnia war and the conflict in Rwanda overlapped: the media extensively covered Bosnia but essentially ignored Rwanda. One analysis found an average of two stories per month about Rwanda in six major U.S. newspapers between 1990 and 1994. Bosnia coverage amounted to two stories *per day* in the same papers.

"One way to shape stories about Africa to conform both to current policy objectives and to the acceptable understandings of most U.S. readers is simply *not* to report them," researchers Garth Myers, Thomas Klak, and Timothy Koehl wrote.[30] In short, the press did Washington a favor, effectively supporting the government's stance against intervention in Rwanda by rarely mentioning the country until the sheer scale of the bloodletting became impossible to ignore.

For insurgents, warlords, criminals, rogue governments, and other perpetrators of armed conflict, there was an important lesson in the media's blindness to Rwanda. It was still possible, though barely, to get away with a war, provided—among other things—that you avoided, suppressed, or at least manipulated reporting on the conflict. That could be achieved any number of ways. At one extreme, detaining or killing journalists. At the opposite extreme: embracing reporters while somehow convincing them that what they were seeing wasn't really a war and therefore wasn't the world's problem.

For governments intent on inflicting a little state-sponsored violence and eager to avoid widespread scrutiny, it helped if the men waging the war were not answerable to the voting (or protesting or rioting) public. It helped to outsource the fighting. That hands-off approach proved irresistibly attractive even to the most legitimate institutions.

Outsourced War

In the late 1990s there was a seismic shift in the way governments waged war in Africa and across the globe. Bob Denard's bloody antics in the Comoros had established a precedent. Men like Denard but perhaps a little less theatrical—and many of them South Africans—took the next logical step. They founded businesses with boring-sounding names but a deadly purpose: to fight Africa's nastiest conflicts on behalf of corrupt, inept governments, for profit.

They found willing customers in governments and international organizations increasingly unwilling to, or incapable of, waging war alone—inhibitions that only deepened following the Somalia bloodletting.

"In the post-Cold War era . . . this cross of the corporate form with military functionality has become a reality," security expert P. W. Singer wrote. "A new global industry has emerged. It is outsourcing and privatization of a 21st-century variety, and it changes many of the old rules of international politics and warfare."[31]

In 1989 former South African commando Eeben Barlow, a lanky, hook-nosed man with one blue eye and one green, founded Executive Outcomes, a UK-based company offering security training services to the South African military and businesses. Barlow was in his mid-thirties at the time. For five years he was Executive Outcomes' sole employee.[32]

Then, in March 1993, Angolan rebels seized Soyo, a major state-owned oil facility on the country's lawless coast. The Angolan army was busy battling rebels elsewhere, so the government approached Barlow with an offer the former commando could not refuse: $80 million to oversee the liberation of the captured oil facility.[33]

Barlow quickly assembled a strike team of fifty of his old Special Forces colleagues. With Angolan helicopters flying top cover and two chartered Cessnas shuttling in supplies, the Executive Outcomes strikers assaulted Soyo. In a week of hard fighting, the mercenaries liberated the facility. Three of Barlow's men were wounded.

The Angolan government was impressed. In June they offered Barlow an even more lucrative contract to train up an entire army brigade to fight the rebels. For this task Barlow recruited five hundred former South African commandos and chartered a small air force, including 727 jets.

Executive Outcomes' responsibilities gradually expanded. Soon the company was also providing pilots for Angola's Russian-made helicopters, propeller-drive attack planes, and MiG-23 jet bombers.

In November the Angolan brigade Barlow's men were training attacked the rebels, initiating what would be an eighteen-month campaign fought in equal parts by Executive Outcomes and its Angolan trainees, but with the South African company providing all the expertise and air power. The Angolan brigade was a front for a mercenary army. Two Executive Outcomes aircraft were shot down and several employees killed.

The battered rebels sued for peace and in January 1995 Barlow pulled his men out of Angola. They were not idle for long. The government of Sierra Leone, under pressure from rebels of its own, was Executive Outcomes' next client.

In April, a hundred of Barlow's mercs, led by a South African ex-commando named Duncan Rykaart, flew into the tiny coastal country in a chartered 727. Their plan: to evict the rebels from the capital, Freetown, and the country's diamond fields, then locate and destroy the rebel headquarters.[34]

Again with native troops fronting and Executive Outcomes' aircraft in support, Barlow's fighters advanced. A year later the rebels sued for peace. Riding high, Executive Outcomes alongside another security firm began negotiations with Mobutu Sese Seko, the dictator of the Congo facing a determined rebellion led by Laurent Kabila. "Neither firm took the contract, as the regime was on its last legs," Singer wrote.[35]

Instead, Executive Outcomes waited until after Mobutu fell and signed a contract with Kabila, now president of the Congo and facing rebellions of his own. In a daring operation, Barlow's commandos captured the strategic Inga dams. But Kabila failed to pay up, and so Executive Outcomes abandoned Congo, leaving Kabila and his ragtag army to fight on alone.[36]

In the wake of Executive Outcomes' successes, so-called private military companies (PMCs) sprouted like weeds. Nowhere were they thicker than in South Africa. The government in Cape Town moved to regulate the merc companies, and in 1998 Executive Outcomes folded. Its chief officers went to work for other PMCs or founded companies of their own. "Rather than truly ending its business, it appears EO simply devolved its activities," Singer wrote.[37]

Rykaart joined NFD, a security company with strong ties to Executive Outcomes and which was allegedly helping the Sudanese government in its battle with U.S.-allied southern rebels. Later, Rykaart worked in American-occupied Iraq for Aegis Defense Services. In 2009, while working in Somalia for yet another security company, he was killed when the plane he was riding in crashed shortly after takeoff.[38] The company's name was Bancroft Global Development. Among its roughly two dozen mercenaries was Richard Rouget, the former lieutenant of Bob Denard in the Comoros.

Sea Bandits

Mercenaries weren't the only shadowy figures behind the conflicts of the 1990s. Across the globe, civilians were taking up arms, organizing, waging what they saw as war against what they presumed was the creeping chaos of a new, lawless era. Depending on the point of view, they were rebels or militia, peacemakers or thugs.

In coastal Somalia, armed civilians fancied themselves civil defenders. The rest of the world saw them as something more sinister.

Pirates.

Before President Siad Barre's overthrow, Somalia possessed a reasonably powerful navy—Soviet-supplied missile boats and landing craft, mostly—and the will to use it. In 1970, the Somali navy even captured an American vessel that the government in Mogadishu accused of spying for Washington.[39] When Barre's regime collapsed, the navy did, too. Funding depleted and crews scattered, the missile boats rusted at their moorings in the port of Berbera. Suddenly Somalia lacked any ability to police its own mangrove-dotted coast and coral-lined inshore waters, which are rich in shark, tuna, mackerel, and lobster.

The navy's demise coincided with new restrictions on drift netting, which saw trawlers deploy free-floating nets as long as twenty-five miles that scraped up not only tuna and other desirable food fishes but also any passing shark, whale, or other large sea creature. The UN pushed a drift net ban; various treaties began to go into effect limiting the environmentally destructive practice. Nations' navies, coast guards, and environmental agencies sent air and sea patrols to monitor fishing fleets to ensure compliance.[40]

But not in Somali waters, which by 1991 were essentially ungoverned. Asian and European fishing fleets surged into the region with their drift nets, sweeping aside native fishermen who still worked from tiny motorboats.

Farah Ismail Eid, a twenty-one-year-old lobsterman in Boassasso, witnessed the assault. "They fished everything—sharks, lobsters, eggs," he said later. "They collided with our boats. They came with giant nets and swept everything out of the sea."[41]

While civil fighting raged ashore, for three years it was an oceanic free-for-all off Somalia's coast. In December 1993 a Dutch aid delegation flew over the coast and counted a dozen fishing vessels from Italy, France, Japan, Taiwan, and Korea within five hundred yards of shore.

Ali Ismail, a clan militia leader, was disgusted. "We've decided to defend ourselves using our own means and efforts," he told a reporter. "We have enough arms to defend our coastal areas." He threatened to send armed speedboats to intercept any foreign vessels plundering Somali waters.

Ismail made good on his threat. His self-styled coast guardsmen seized three Pakistani ships and two from Taiwan. The coast guardsmen kept the Pakistani vessels and sent the Taiwanese ones home. The fates of the Pakistani crews were not revealed, but they presumably returned home by other means.[42]

Soon clan groups up and down the Somali coast were calling themselves "coast guards" and performing their own maritime enforcement raids. In 1997, militiamen from the port of Hobyo seized ships from China and Kenya. From the Kenyan ship's owner they demanded a "fee" of $500,000. To some observers, this fine was something else—a ransom—and the militiamen were no better than pirates.

Not to Eid. "When I heard about this, I was happy," he said. His precious lobsters becoming rare from the relentless foreign plundering, Eid swapped his fishing tackle for some AK-47s and rocket launchers.[43]

3

Balkanization

The General Atomics team led by Abraham Karem had brought the Predator drone from blueprints to functional hardware in just six months, a feat that Paul Kaminski, the Pentagon's chief weapons buyer, later called "amazing."[1]

In July 1995 a team of U.S. Army and Air Force personnel deployed to Albania with four Predators. In neighboring Bosnia, militia under the command of pro-Serb commander Ratko Mladić were ruthlessly rounding up and executing Muslim men and boys in the town of Srebrenica—more than seven thousand in all. NATO bombers struck militia targets but could not stem the bloodletting.[2]

The Predators were able to observe Serb atrocities. But with no armament of their own, they were strictly passive. Nor could the drone operators easily guide other warplanes to attack targets they spotted—there were too many incompatible radios and too many bureaucratic hoops to jump through. Even if the channels had been clear, the Predator operators, hunkered in their trailers in Albania, didn't have the training they needed to oversee air strikes.[3]

The first Predator was lost on August 11.[4] It was an overcast day in Bosnia. The Predators were fitted only with video cameras and could not scan through clouds, as some radar-equipped planes can do. So that cloudy day the operators pushed their robot down to four thousand feet, just below the cloud cover, and let it linger there for an hour.

At that altitude, the drone was a sitting duck. Serbian troops opened fire and the Predator lost contact with its controllers, presumably destroyed. A second drone lost engine power a few days later. Rather than risk it falling into Serbian hands, the operators hit the self-destruct.[5]

"Growing pains," is how Secretary of the Air Force Sheila Widnall and Chief of Staff Ronald Fogleman described the accidents in their Senate testimony the following year.[6] In October the Pentagon pulled the Predators out of Bosnia and sent them back to Karem for upgrades, including a nose-mounted radar and de-icing gear to combat cold weather.

In March 1996 three upgraded Predators and fifty operators and maintainers returned to the Balkans, this time to an air base in Hungary, for continued operations over Bosnia. By then General Atomics had produced a total of eight Predators. A second drone unit was going through a ten-week course in Nevada with the goal of joining the Hungary-based squad in June. Over the next few years the Pentagon planned to expand the force to sixteen units, each operating four drones. They would lay the foundation for a global, round-the-clock surveillance network.[7]

At least, that was the vision. "Just as the United States possessed an overwhelming nuclear capability and extended a 'nuclear umbrella' over our allies during the Cold War, so too will the United States extend an 'information umbrella' over our coalition partners in the 21st century," Kaminski told Congress.[8] In 1996, a single Predator cost $3 million.[9]

Happy with the Predator's performance over Bosnia, in 1995 the Pentagon expanded on the drone concept. DARPA, the military's fringe-science wing, commissioned two new unmanned aerial vehicle (UAV) designs required to fly higher and farther than the Predator. The total cost: $400 million to develop and test fly several prototypes of each model within three years' time.[10]

The new drones included one type optimized for altitude and another that would fly lower but also include radar-evading stealth elements. Both were public efforts, routinely detailed in government press materials and widely discussed in the media.

San Diego–based aerospace firm Teledyne Ryan snagged the contract for the high-flyer, which it dubbed the Global Hawk.[11] Forty-eight feet long with the wingspan of a 737 airliner, the Global Hawk first flew at Edwards Air Force Base in California in February 1998. The next year, Northrop Grumman acquired Teledyne Ryan and, with it, the Global Hawk program.[12] Despite crashes, problems with the onboard sensors, and huge cost increases, the Global Hawk initiative endured. The huge drones spied on Afghanistan starting in 2001, Iraq beginning in 2003, and also mapped disaster zones. The navy decided to buy its own copies, and so did Germany and NATO.

But the Global Hawk's stealthy cousin was less blessed. Boeing and Lockheed Martin teamed up to produce the Dark Star prototype, which took off on its debut flight at Edwards in March 1996. On its second flight, in April, the drone malfunctioned and crashed. Boeing and Lockheed built several more copies, but in 1999 the Pentagon canceled the effort.[13]

Except not really. The Dark Star concept—and some of the technology—survived, in modified form. Lockheed quietly assembled the stealthy drone's high-tech successor in total secrecy. No outsiders would know anything about it until eight years later.

The only clue—and an oblique one at that—was a patent for

an unmanned aircraft filed in 1997 by the Texas plane-maker. A sketch included with the patent showed a single-engine, swept-wing robot with a bulbous body and the sharp wing edges associated with stealth designs.[14]

Messages by Missile

In the wake of the 1991 Gulf War the United States established a veritable military cordon around Iraq. Warplanes based in Saudi Arabia and Turkey and aboard aircraft carriers patrolled no-fly zones over southern Iraq—home to rebel Shi'ites—and northern Iraq, with its own rebellious Kurdish minority.

In the fall of 1996 the forces of Iraqi president Saddam Hussein overran the Kurdish city of Erbil in a bid to establish new local authorities loyal to Hussein. American retaliation was swift. On September 3, Clinton ordered two rounds of cruise missile strikes against Iraqi military installations in the south. At least five Iraqis died.

"Our missiles sent the following message to Saddam Hussein: When you abuse your own people or threaten your neighbors, you must pay a price," Clinton said.[15]

But in parallel, Washington was sending another, potentially more damaging message by more nefarious means. The Clinton administration hired the Rendon Group, a consultancy headed by longtime Democratic political operative John Rendon, to infiltrate Iraqi media with anti-Hussein propaganda. Rendon employees began asking around Harvard for a good Arabic speaker.

"Word got around the department that I was a good Arabic translator who did a great Saddam imitation," one Iraqi-born grad student recalled. "Eventually, someone phoned me, asking if I wanted to help change the course of Iraq policy."

Twice a week, the grad student took a taxi to a recording studio in Boston, where he was handed a script written in English.

They were *Saturday Night Live*–style bits mocking Hussein and his family. "We did skits where Saddam would get mixed up in his own lies, or where [Saddam's son] Qusay would stumble over his own delusions of grandeur," the student later told a reporter. "The point was to discredit Saddam."

The recordings were sent to northern Iraq and Kuwait and broadcast once a week. For his services the student was paid $3,000 a month for six years. "I never got a straight answer on whether the Iraqi resistance, the CIA or policy makers on the Hill were actually the ones calling the shots," the student said, "but ultimately I realized that the guys doing spin were very well and completely cut loose."[16]

It was not the Rendon Group's first time producing propaganda, nor would it be the last. The company had been on the payroll of the CIA and U.S.-allied governments and revolutionaries since the late 1980s. In 1991 it had shipped American flags to Kuwait for the natives to wave as U.S. troops liberated the country. The flag-waving was widely broadcast by unwitting international media.

"We've worked in ninety-one countries," Rendon himself told journalist James Bamford in one of his rare interviews in 2005. "Going all the way back to Panama, we've been involved in every war, with the exception of Somalia."[17]

After the 9/11 attacks the Rendon Group won several multimillion-dollar contracts to handle media relations for various U.S. military commands. In that way, the group's propaganda gradually shifted aim, away from the enemies of the United States and toward the free press of the United States.

Comedy of Errors

In Serbia in the spring of 1998, a long-simmering insurgency by ethnic Albanian separatists in the Kosovo region escalated. In

May, eighty-five NATO warplanes performed maneuvers over the Serbian-Albanian border, "an exercise intended to demonstrate the alliance's commitment to peace and stability in the region and [our] ability to project power into the region," in the words of U.S. Lt. Gen. Michael Short, the NATO air commander.[18]

It didn't work. Thousands of people died in ethnic fighting and entire villages were purged of either ethnic Albanians or ethnic Serbs.

NATO proposed to deploy peacekeepers. In March 1999 U.S. special envoy Richard Holbrooke met with Serbian president Slobodan Milošević in hopes of forging a peace deal. He returned to Brussels empty handed and told an audience of NATO officials that "the process now is handed both symbolically and formally back to you."[19]

On March 24, scores of NATO ships and more than a thousand warplanes attacked Serbian targets. The bombing continued into June.[20]

The Predator drones that had patrolled Bosnia now shifted to Serbia, this time under the sole control of the U.S. Air Force, which had formed two drone squadrons in Nevada. The drones were more numerous, more powerful, and equipped with better sensors than their predecessors from just three years earlier.

A crash five-week program by the fringe-science DARPA in April produced software and modifications that displayed GPS coordinates on the sensor screens inside the Predators' control vans. In theory, this update would allow Predators to spot targets for manned bombers.[21] But they still crashed or were shot down in prodigious numbers; in all, the air force lost four Predators in four months of combat. At least one was reportedly gunned down by Serbian troops firing from the open cabin of a helicopter flying alongside the drone.[22]

And the drone operators still could not reliably call in strikes on targets they spotted. The best they could do was read GPS coordinates off the sensor screen, radio an E-3 radar plane orbiting potentially hundreds of miles away, and read the coordinates to the radar plane's crew, hoping the crew would then pass the target location on to a strike plane.[23] "The command and control structures, procedures and lines of authority were complicated," U.S. Air Force Lt. Gen. Marvin Esmond admitted.[24]

"The result was a comedy of errors," aviation historian Greg Goebel wrote, "with one officer involved saying that with such clumsy methods it would take 45 minutes to get a strike aircraft into the same zip code."[25]

A laser designator, then in the planning stages, would give the drone the ability to guide bombs dropped by other warplanes, but what the Predator crews *really* needed was the ability to attack targets all on their own.

The flying robot spy practically screamed for a new role. It demanded to become a killer.

Startup

At the same time U.S. and NATO warplanes were converging on the Balkans, Michael Stock was graduating from Princeton University.

Stock's family had made a fortune in banking. In 1999 he used a portion of that fortune to found, in Virginia, a nonprofit organization called Landmine Clearance International. Its mission statement: to "rehabilitate populated areas in the aftermath of armed conflict through land-mine clearance and explosive ordnance disposal."[26]

Deliberate or not, the mine-clearing mission was misdirection. Soon Landmine Clearance International would have a new name—Bancroft Global Development—and a new purpose: to oversee mercenaries in a country most Americans hadn't thought about in half a decade: Somalia.[27]

Stock was just twenty-one years old. He was about to tap a

lucrative market of African warfare, one that had swelled with the collapse of every government, and the rise of every strongman. A market that, for all its richness, represented one of the few opportunities for profitable combat in an era of expanding peace.

Succession

For a third of a century, Mobutu ruled Congo like a king. For a third of a century, he held together a state whose fragility was due in great part to his own authoritarian rule. With every edict, every act of corruption or brutality, Mobutu planted seeds of conflict that would sprout only with his passing. Men like Stock would be there to reap what Mobutu had sown.

Starting in 1965 Mobutu crushed all political opponents and nationalized major industries in his schizophrenic drive to transform Congo from an exploited former Belgian colony into a modern, albeit authoritarian, state. Not accidentally, in the process Mobutu amassed a personal fortune reported to be as large as billions of dollars. Congo's roads, cities, and schools crumbled as Mobutu's personal ambitions hollowed out the modernization schemes. And when Mobutu died in 1997, Congo, a.k.a. Zaire, came apart at the seams. Just like Somalia after Barre. Just like the former Yugoslavia when the Soviet Union collapsed.

In Rwanda, a country still reeling from the recent genocide, resurgent Tutsi troops chased Hutu extremists over the border into Congo. There the Rwandans set themselves up in lucrative illegal mining operations. Rwanda and Uganda, another country with mining interests in Congo, threw their support behind Congolese rebel leader Laurent Kabila, whose troops captured the capital city of Kinshasa and installed him as president.

When relations soured between Kabila and his former allies, Ugandan and Rwandan troops invaded to bolster anti-Kabila rebellions. Angola, Namibia, and Zimbabwe all took Kabila's side.

The resulting conflict became known as Africa's World War. Between 700,000 and 3 million people died, according to the most reliable estimates.

Kabila was shot and killed by a bodyguard in 2001. His son, Joseph, took over on an emergency basis and in 2006 won the country's first democratic election in four decades. The younger Kabila's most important moves were to sign peace deals with Rwanda and, later, with several of the bigger rebel groups. As part of the latter deal, thousands of rebel fighters, some of them wanted war criminals, were invited to join the Congolese army in lieu of prosecution. "In Congo, peace must come before justice," Kabila famously said.[28]

In truth, for most of the population both peace and justice were years, even decades, away. Before peace, Congo had to endure its shadow war.

It was not alone.

Safe Haven

Al Qaeda operatives, smuggled in from Sudan, had helped train the militia fighters that shot down American helicopters over Mogadishu in October 1993.[29] Among them was Fazul Abdullah Mohammed, a native of the Comoros, Bob Denard's mercenary fiefdom.

Mohammed traveled across Africa and the Middle East: Mauritius in 1990, Pakistan and 1991 and 1992, Tanzania in 1994 and 995, Sudan several times in 1995, Yemen in 1995, and in 1993, 1994, and 1995, Kenya.[30]

At around 10:30 a.m. on August 7, 1998, bombs exploded at the U.S. embassy compounds in Dar es Salaam, Tanzania, and Nairobi, Kenya. Two hundred and twenty-four people died, including twelve Americans.

The FBI named thirteen suspects, including Mohammed and

al Qaeda founder Osama bin Laden, a man who until then was little known in the United States.[31]

With a $5-million bounty on his head, Mohammed fled to the last place U.S. agents would follow him: Somalia. "I came to Somalia after we carried out the explosions of American imperialist in 1998," Mohammed said later. He was offered shelter by Aden Hashi Farah Ayro, one of Somalia's top Islamists.[32]

On October 12, 2000, two al Qaeda operatives directly supervised by bin Laden and several lieutenants, including Qaed Salim Sinan al-Harethi, steered a motorboat packed with up to seven hundred pounds of explosives alongside the U.S. Navy destroyer USS *Cole* while the five-hundred-foot-long vessel was moored in Aden, Yemen, for refueling. The operatives "made friendly gestures to crew members, and detonated the bomb."[33]

The blast tore a gash in the side of the ship, nearly sinking it. Seventeen sailors died, and forty were injured.[34] Expecting U.S. retaliation, the planners went to ground: bin Laden shuttled between Kandahar, Khowst, Jalalabad, and Kabul in Afghanistan. Al-Harethi hid out in a remote region of Yemen, a country that like Somalia had suffered from post-Soviet neglect, weak central government, and deep tribal divisions.

Yemen was, in the words of the *9/11 Commission Report*, a "safe haven" for terrorists.[35] The U.S. government's presence in the country was small and mostly confined to Sana'a and other northern cities. To find al-Harethi in the remote, lawless southern tribal region would require extraordinary measures. It would require drones. Drones that were on the verge of being armed.

Big Safari

It was April 1999, and John Jumper was frustrated. A Vietnam War fighter pilot now commanding U.S. Air Forces in Europe as they pummeled Serbia, Jumper was finding that one of his most promising weapons was proving to be his most disappointing. The

Predator drone, which had promised to revolutionize America's ability to spot and track targets, was instead something of a tease.

Developed on a shoestring budget and rushed into production, the Predator lacked many of the systems that the crews of traditional warplanes took for granted. For one, the Predator was unarmed, meaning it could not attack the enemies it located. Moreover, it even lacked systems for swiftly and accurately guiding in other attack planes.

A laser designator, for example, would have allowed the Predator to "paint" a target with focused light. A bomber could fly in behind the Predator and lob a laser-guided bomb. Instead, the drone was limited to merely watching. "You would have a Predator up there looking at targets, but you had no way to get that information, other than verbally, to the airplanes that were going to attack those tanks," Jumper vented.[36]

In the second month of the air war, Jumper commissioned the air force's legendary Big Safari engineering team in Dayton, Ohio, to fit the Predator with a laser designator. Big Safari had previously produced sophisticated, manned surveillance planes based on the Boeing 707 airliner—and in 1994 had briefly resurrected the flying branch's Mach-3 SR-71 spy planes, originally retired in 1989.[37] In 1998 Big Safari had established a field office alongside General Atomics' air division in California. It was this office that handled the laser designator addition.[38]

Within three weeks, Big Safari and General Atomics had identified, installed, and tested a new ball turret carrying a laser designator and an infrared camera to replace the Predator's older turret, containing both a daylight and infrared camera.

Two modified drones were rushed overseas. And on June 2 one of the laser Predators painted a Serbian military vehicle, and an A-10 attack plane dropped a five-hundred-pound, laser-guided bomb that pulverized the vehicle. The air war ended the next day.

In the aftermath of the Kosovo war, some air force officers expressed doubt over the Predator drone, which had ballooned into a $600-million program but had betrayed serious flaws. "So many combat limitations that its long-term viability remains in question," is how Col. Thomas Ehrhard assessed the Predator in a 2000 PhD dissertation.[39]

Air Combat Command, which owned the service's Predators, still viewed the drone strictly as a reconnaissance platform and removed the laser designators Jumper had had installed. Jumper was "furious," according to Richard Whittle in his study "Predator's Big Safari." To Jumper, the solution wasn't to strip Abraham Karem's robot plane of its new gear or, worse, abandon it entirely. Jumper wanted to double down on the Predator's abilities.

Fortunately, Jumper was in a position to make that happen. In February 2000 he assumed leadership of Air Combat Command—and promptly ordered the laser designators reinstalled. Going one step further, he also instructed Big Safari to add weapons to the Predators. A new kind of small, guided bomb was considered, but it was rejected in favor of the tried-and-true Hellfire missile, which had been in service since the mid-1980s and came in several versions, including a laser-guided model.

Big Safari also devised an enhanced communications system that allowed the Predator to be controlled via satellite by operators thousands of miles away. Another control team sitting in a trailer at the Predator's forward airfield—in Albania, Hungary, or another friendly country—would still launch and land the drones using a line-of-sight datalink with minimal lag, but, once airborne, control passed to the remote operator.[40]

Soon, air force drone pilots would fly combat missions from the comfort of their Nevada bases, while CIA controllers sat in trailers in the parking lot of agency headquarters in Virginia. These so-called "split" operations kept the size of drone deployments small: just a few dozen people to launch, land, and maintain several robots. This meant there could be more of them—and ensured the deployed drone units more often than not flew below the radars of the U.S. and foreign press.

With a designator and Hellfire, a drone would be capable of finding, painting, and striking targets all on its own. At first, engineers weren't sure the missiles would even work on the lightweight Predator. They worried the ignition of the missile's rocket motor would cause the robotic aircraft to tumble out of control. Engineers dialed back the motor's power. A test in February 2001 confirmed the Predator could handle the launch.[41]

The CIA was, if anything, even more eager to get missiles on its Predators than the air force was. "We would have a capability to accurately and promptly respond to future sightings of high value targets," agency director George Tenet explained.[42] By 2000 the agency had established a drone base in Uzbekistan. The mission: to infiltrate Afghan airspace and find and track Osama bin Laden, whose al Qaeda group was behind the devastating 1998 embassy bombings in Africa.

On September 7 and again on September 28, 2000, CIA drones had bin Laden in their sights near Kandahar, but lacking weapons could do nothing but watch "the man in white" stroll around.[43]

The CIA hoped a Predator would eventually be able to track bin Laden long enough for the navy to position a warship and launch cruise missiles.[44] But Afghanistan's ruling Taliban regime was getting better and better at detecting the drones.

In the fall of 2000, the Taliban scrambled a fighter jet to chase down an agency Predator. Shortly thereafter, the CIA pulled its drones from the region. Cofer Black, the top U.S. counterterrorism official, argued that the Predator should not rejoin the hunt for bin Laden until it had missiles of its own.[45]

The White House, responding to the CIA's urgency, leaned on the air force to rush the armed Predator into service, but problems with the new hardware slowed the pace of development. In early September 2001, National Security Adviser Condoleezza Rice projected the armed drone would be ready to take a shot at bin Laden in the spring of 2002.[46]

"The ability to target individuals or fleeting targets with precision from an aircraft flown from total safety on the other side of the globe was a phenomenal capability—and a technological tipping point," Whittle wrote.[47]

Hunter Killer

The accelerating transformation of the Predator from a surveillance tool to a weapon of war and assassination occurred at a portentous moment in American history. But the drone's transformation happened too late to *prevent* that portentous moment. The man the CIA Predators failed to kill initiated an operation long in the planning.

On September 11, 2001, bin Laden's operatives hijacked four airliners over Boston; Washington, D.C.; and Newark and flew three of them into New York City's World Trade Center and the Pentagon. The fourth crashed into a field in Pennsylvania after the passengers fought back. Two thousand nine hundred and ninety-six people died, including the nineteen hijackers.

That morning, in the homes of Special Forces soldiers all over the United States and Europe, phones were ringing. "Tom," a young Special Forces officer, was at his then-girlfriend's house in Washington, D.C., sleeping off the accumulated fatigue of a long peacetime deployment. He hung up the phone without answering.

Then his girlfriend, a government employee, called to say "they" were attacking New York. "They blew up the State Department!" she kept saying, according to Tom. He had to reassure her that, whatever was happening, it was certainly not a nuclear war. Driving to pick her up, Tom saw smoke billowing from the Pentagon.[48]

For years America's commandos had been hamstrung by senior officers and politicians terrified of a repeat of the 1993 bloodbath in Mogadishu. That was about to change.

"Right after 9/11, the immediate impact was, how do we get a force to Afghanistan?" commented Eric Schmitt, a war reporter for the *New York Times* who would go on to cover drone and commando campaigns all over the world. "The only force capable of going in quickly were the small number of American Special Operations Forces."[49]

Tom and his fellow Green Berets immediately went on a war footing. With equal urgency, the air force completed the installation of missiles on the Predators. Now armed, the CIA's drones immediately returned to Afghan airspace. Air force Predators eventually joined them, flying from a base in Uzbekistan.

The robots were the vanguard of an invasion force. They orbited overhead on October 7 as U.S. Special Operations Forces landed in Afghanistan and began mobilizing resistance to the Taliban. That night, a CIA Predator tracked Mullah Omar, leader of the Taliban, traveling near Kandahar. With permission from Gen. Tommy Franks, in charge of U.S. Central Command, the drone fired a missile, missing Omar but killing two of his bodyguards.[50]

On the ground in northern Afghanistan, Tom's friend Capt. Mitch Nelson, leading a twelve-man Green Beret team, found himself practicing one of Special Forces' unique and long-dormant skills: "unconventional warfare." That is, molding local fighters into guerrilla forces and leading them into battle. Nelson helped an Uzbek warlord named Abdul Rashid Dostum lead fifteen hundred Northern Alliance cavalry in thundering charges against the Taliban's much more modern army.[51]

When a senior officer impatiently demanded an update on Nelson's progress on October 25, the sleepless Green Beret testily relayed a now-famous message: "I am advising a man on how to best employ light infantry and horse cavalry in the attack against Taliban T-55s [tanks], mortars, artillery, personnel carriers and machine guns—a tactic which I think became outdated with the invention of the Gatling gun."[52]

But it worked. Under assault from drones overhead and Special Operations Forces and their local allies all around, the Taliban collapsed. For now.

Soon tens of thousands of U.S. soldiers, Marines, and airmen were en route to Afghanistan, initiating what would be an open-ended occupation and land campaign lasting more than a decade. Drones and commandos remained, but their pinpoint strikes were subsumed by the much more massive maneuvers of regular army and Marine formations and powerful air attacks by bombers, jet fighters, and attack helicopters.

The era of big American ground wars had begun.

In response, Taliban and al Qaeda survivors, secure in their Pakistani safe havens, reorganized as an insurgency. They had the weapons, the training, and the will. If the Americans wanted a major war, a major war they would get.

Inflection Point

The so-called War on Terror is largely understood as a reaction to the attacks of September 11, 2001. But 9/11 was just the most devastating of a chain of attacks on U.S. and allied interests by Islamic terrorists, including al Qaeda, going back years. The 1993 World Trade Center bombing. The Battle of Mogadishu. The attempted destruction of America's African embassies. The *Cole* blast.

Even before 2001 the U.S. government had ramped up its counterterrorism efforts. The development and deployment of drones alone represented a profound improvement in the military and CIA's ability to find and neutralize terrorists. In that context, it's clear the War on Terror had been slowly coalescing for nearly a decade before hijacked airliners slammed into buildings in New York City and Washington, D.C., and a field in Pennsylvania.

But 9/11 *was* an inflection point. For the better part of a decade since the Somalia debacle, America had been reluctant to wage protracted ground war. *After* the September 2001 attacks, the

United States seemed all too eager to send tens or even hundreds of thousands of troops at a time on open-ended campaigns with the vaguest of aims and sketchy intelligence.

America became a major war-making nation. Ironically, it did so at a time when much of the rest of the world was swearing off organized violence entirely. By 2000, Bosnia, Kosovo, and Rwanda were at peace. The worst of the bloodletting in Somalia and Congo was over.

The number of state-on-state wars dropped from a post–Cold War high of fifty in 1991 to just thirty in 2001. Over the same decade, battle deaths in state conflict, in which at least one warring party was a government, declined from around 125,000 to just 25,000. (Battle deaths had hovered over 200,000 per year throughout the 1980s.)[53] Deaths from civil fighting reached a post–Cold War peak of around 10,000 in 1993, then dropped to 2,500 in 2001.[54]

Fatalities in one-sided violence—genocide and ethnic cleansing, for example—spiked twice in the 1990s. In 1994, half a million Rwandans died. At least twenty-seven thousand Congolese were killed in the related conflict in neighboring DRC in 1996. The annual death toll from one-sided fighting settled at a low of five thousand in 2001 and stayed there.[55]

The decline in war deaths was most striking when adjusted for a growing world population. In the mid-1940s, as many as twenty-two of every hundred thousand people died in combat every year. By the mid-1970s the rate was around seven per hundred thousand, ebbing to five for every hundred thousand in the 1980s, around two in the 1990s, and fewer than one starting in the early 2000s.[56]

In short, at the time of the 9/11 attacks the world was entering a period of unprecedented global peace. America's land wars would skew the statistics, partially masking the downward trend in violence elsewhere—but, all the same, doing nothing to arrest the steady, overall decline in organized violence.

Which is not to say that the U.S.-initiated interventions in Iraq and Afghanistan compared in terms of brutality to the Somalia civil war, the Rwandan genocide, or the bloody fighting in the DRC. Even the most intensive U.S. campaigns were less bloody than the African wars. And in a few years, U.S. military strategy conformed to the overall trajectory of world armed conflict.

When America soured on the high cost, confusion, and lack of progress evident in its ground wars in Iraq and Afghanistan, it shifted to a lighter, less bloody method of intervention, one relying on secretive drones and commandos to do most of the fighting quickly, quietly, and—where possible—at a distance. Scalpels instead of sledgehammers.

In doing so, the United States in essence returned to the strategy that had briefly guided its actions in the days and weeks following 9/11, when drones struck terror suspects and Special Forces mobilized foreign militias to fight America's war by proxy. The big U.S. wars of the early 2000s weren't just a global, historical aberration. Even for America, they proved to be costly, years-long exceptions to a rule written by decades of expanding peace.

Backwaters

For years following the end of the UN peacekeeping mission in Somalia, Washington—and most foreign governments, for that matter—all but gave up on trying to influence events in the ruined country. In a decade of isolation, a new form of government arose in the war-torn country. With everyday Somalis becoming more radicalized, a loose system of Islamic judges arose in Mogadishu. Their courts merged into a highly legalized but rudimentary government known as the Islamic Courts Union (ICU).

The ICU was a mix of hard-line and moderate Islamists. It was fairly popular and enjoyed a high level of support from Eritrea, which has long viewed Somalia as a proxy in its ongoing feud with neighboring Ethiopia. The hard-liners, and Eritrea's patronage, together represented the seeds of the ICU's destruction. But for a few years, there was relative calm in Somalia under the ICU's reign—and, by extension, calm in the region.

It did not last. The Americans were coming.

After the destroyer *Cole* was nearly sunk while refueling in Yemen, the U.S. Navy diverted its vessels to nearby Djibouti, an impoverished but stable nation in the Horn of Africa just north of Somalia. It was the first U.S. overture to a country that would become critical to American war aims.

In September 2002, eight hundred Americans—a mix of Special Operations Forces, pilots, and support personnel—flew into Djibouti's Camp Lemonnier, a former French base adjacent to the international airport.[1] A CIA team with Predator drones joined them, though exactly when is not clear. And in December, the command ship USS *Mount Whitney* moored in Djibouti's main port with hundreds more personnel on board, including troops from every branch of the military.[2]

Next came a battalion of fifteen hundred Marines aboard three assault ships. They stormed ashore for training. Helicopters and Harrier jets from the assault ships fired guns and rockets and dropped bombs. "We are getting heavy weapons ashore and firing," Col. John Mills told the *New York Times*. "I am preparing my unit to operate in a high-intensity conflict."[3]

For six months, *Mount Whitney* was a floating base for the main U.S. contingent as army engineers worked on facilities at Camp Lemonnier, transforming a former backwater outpost into a major operational hub for the military and intelligence agents. In May, the troops on *Mount Whitney* moved into their new barracks. By then the American force in Djibouti numbered three thousand. They looked south to Somalia . . . and north to Yemen.

Eavesdropping

For two years, the National Security Agency (NSA) listened for the distinctive voice of Qaed Salim Sinan al-Harethi, one of the men who had organized the October 2000 attack on the U.S.

Navy destroyer *Cole* in Aden, Yemen. The NSA had recordings of al-Harethi's voice, so it knew what the terrorist mastermind sounded like. The agency had acquired a partial list of the phone numbers al-Harethi used. Automated systems tied to the global network of commercial communications satellites would alert NSA analysts if one of the numbers were used. An analyst would listen to the conversation essentially live, hoping to recognize al-Harethi's voice.

As described in James Bamford's book *The Shadow Factory*, the alarm went off on November 3, 2002. One of al-Harethi's numbers was in use. An analyst cross-referenced the signal with the GPS constellation and pinpointed its source: the remote, lawless Mar'ib Province of Yemen. The analyst called a CIA Predator drone team in Djibouti. As luck would have it, the agency already had a missile-armed Predator on patrol near Mar'ib. The drone angled toward the GPS coordinates the NSA analyst provided.

Meanwhile, the analyst tried to match the voice coming over the satellite with what he knew al-Harethi sounded like. It didn't feel right. It was al-Harethi's number all right, but the man speaking was not the terrorist. "All of the sudden [the analyst] hears like a six-second conversation and it's the guy, he's in the backseat [of a car] and he's giving the driver directions," a source told Bamford.

The analyst recorded the call and quickly played it back for another analyst, who confirmed it: the second voice on the phone was al-Harethi, apparently in a car en route to somewhere in Mar'ib, with his driver handling the phone. The CIA Predator was already on its way. Now it had the authority to strike.

The Hellfire missile blasted the car, killing al-Harethi and avenging the *Cole*'s seventeen dead.[4]

Al-Harethi was the first major terrorist to die by drone assassination. He was not the last.

The drones did not stay in Djibouti long. In late 2002 they were drawn away, diverted to a new conflict—in Iraq.

Back in Action

Starting in 2003, U.S. Special Forces and CIA agents returned to Somalia to track down and kill or capture al Qaeda and affiliated operatives hiding out in the lawless country. There were no Predators to support them. Most were in Iraq.

In 2003, Joint Special Operations Command, the operational wing of the U.S. Special Operations Command, the holding organization for all Special Operations Forces, resorted to spending six months sneaking SEALs into Somalia by submarine to painstakingly plant disguised surveillance cameras—all to capture just a fraction of the images a drone could acquire in a single mission.

"If we're having to go to that extreme, it's because we lack other capabilities because they're drawn elsewhere," a senior intelligence official told *Army Times* reporter Sean Naylor. "Instead of doing it like that, you'd want to have more Predators."

The drone shortage also represented a huge risk for CIA agents attempting to build an intelligence network for tracking suspected terrorists in Somalia.

The agency used cash payments to Somali warlords as a "carrot" to draw them to the American side. U.S. air power was supposed to be the "stick" that helped motivate the Somalis, but for years the intel agency didn't actually possess any stick. So it lied, telling the warlords there were drones overhead when in fact there weren't. It was a risky bluff. "But it worked," an intelligence official told Naylor.[5]

Special Strategy

Washington's heavy reliance on Special Operations Forces in Somalia in the early 2000s was part of a larger trend. Having kept them on a short leash in the years following the Battle of Mogadishu, after 9/11 America cut loose its commando forces to fight terrorists using the bad guys' own tactics: secrecy, subtlety, and, where necessary, swift brutality.

All over the world, commandos were settling into hidden bases alongside the CIA. They concentrated in low-intensity war zones where their subtle methods could be most effective. Soon they were present in some sixty countries.[6] American Special Operations Forces included troops from all the main military branches plus agents working directly for Special Operations Command: Navy SEALs; Army Rangers, Special Forces (a.k.a. Green Berets), and Delta Force commandos; Air Force para-rescuemen and air controllers; and—relative latecomers to the exclusive club—recon Marines.

Their specialties varied. The U.S. Navy SEALs were long-range scouts and close-in killers. Army Rangers were elite infantry trained for the most dangerous, high-end military tasks: seizing airfields, for example. Delta Force rescued hostages. U.S. Army Special Forces trained and led militias. Air force commandos retrieved shot-down pilots and helped guide air strikes. Recon Marines, obviously, were best at recon. SOCOM's own intelligence agents and drone operators supported the commandos.

These Special Operations Forces gathered intelligence. They rescued journalists, aid workers, and ship crews kidnapped by militants, international criminals, and pirates. They found, tracked, and killed or captured terrorist leaders. They dropped into lawless territory in impoverished countries, made contact with sympathetic villagers, and organized them into makeshift armies dedicated to fighting a common foe.

Between 2001 and 2011 SOCOM grew from thirty thousand personnel to sixty thousand. Its budget swelled from less than $2 billion to nearly $10 billion.[7] The number of SOCOM's people within Joint Special Operations Command, the forward-deployed, combat-oriented division of SOCOM, ballooned from 1,800 to 25,000—nearly half of the command's overall payroll.[8]

"The reliance of senior policymakers and DoD leadership

upon Special Forces was unprecedented in its scope, ushering in a new era in Special Forces employment and operations," army major Armando J. Ramirez wrote.[9] That reliance applied not just to army commandos, but to other Special Operations Forces as well.

In some remote corners of the expanding War on Terror, entire campaigns were executed almost solely by SOF, backed up by small numbers of regular troops plus the CIA and other intelligence agencies. A turning point came in 2003, when the Defense Department drafted a new policy for the expanding use of Special Operations Forces. The Al Qaeda Network Execute Order, or AQN ExOrd, simplified the bureaucratic and legal processes for U.S. troops deployments, allowing commandos to "move into denied areas or countries beyond the official battle zones of Iraq and Afghanistan," according to *The Nation*'s Jeremy Scahill.

"The ExOrd spells out that we reserve the right to unilaterally act against Al Qaeda and its affiliates anywhere in the world that they operate," a Special Operations Forces source told Scahill.

Then–defense secretary Donald Rumsfeld signed the order in 2004, but it wasn't until years later, under President Barack Obama, that SOCOM fully flexed its new policy muscles.

"The Pentagon is already empowered to do these things, so let JSOC off the leash," is how Scahill's inside source characterized Obama's thinking. "That's what this White House has done. JSOC has been empowered more under this administration than any other in recent history. No question."

Obama sent American commandos into another nineteen countries on top of the sixty they were already in. Scahill drafted a partial list of the SOF's deployments since 2008. It included Belgium, France, Spain, Mexico, Colombia, Bolivia, Ecuador, Paraguay, Peru, Iraq, Iran, Turkey, Georgia, Ukraine, Yemen, Afghanistan, Pakistan, Somalia, and the Philippines.[10]

Southern Front

The U.S. military battled Islamists in the Philippines beginning in 1899, when the islands—the spoils of the Spanish-American War—became an American territory. The fighting raged in fits and starts for the next hundred years, mostly in the southern region of Mindanao.

By 2001 Mindanao was a haven for a shifting alliance of Islamic groups dominated by the Moro Islamic Liberation Front (MILF), Jemaah Islamiyah, and Abu Sayyaf—the latter two al Qaeda affiliates. In December of that year Jemaah Islamiyah plotted an attack on the U.S. embassy in Singapore, but Singaporean authorities intervened.[11]

Remote and rugged, the southern Philippines were the tropical analogue of the mountains and deserts favored by Islamic militants elsewhere. "Pretty much nothing but jungle and mountains and rice paddies," is how Rocky Zeender, a former Special Forces soldier who spent three years in the region, described the terrain. "It was extremely dense jungle, extremely dense forest, very steep terrain, and very difficult to travel, sometimes impossible to travel, by vehicle, only by foot."

In January 2002, Special Operations Command deployed Joint Task Force 510 to fight the Islamists alongside the Philippine military. The task force would soon change its name to Joint Special Operations Task Force–Philippines and grow to include six hundred soldiers, marines, sailors, airmen, and civilians operating trucks, gun-armed speed boats, helicopters, C-12 cargo planes, and U-28 spy planes.[12]

Under the cover of a training exercise in March 2002, Washington sent Gnat drones—the smaller, slower, older brother of the Predator—to the Philippines.[13] Comments by a military spokesperson created the impression that the Gnats were Pentagon assets, but in fact the military didn't take possession of its own Gnats until the following year. The Gnats in the Philippines were apparently CIA models, purchased in parallel with the agency's initial contingent of more powerful Predators.[14]

A photo snapped at Edwin Andrews air base near the southern city of Zamboanga, where TF-510 was based, showed men in civilian clothes—probably General Atomics contractors—fussing over a Gnat before or after a mission, with Philippine Air Force OV-10 Bronco attack planes hunched in the background.[15]

The "training" fig leaf stuck. Philippine law barred foreign forces from conducting military missions on the islands, so the U.S. task force was officially limited to advising native forces. The Americans stretched that definition as far as it would bend. In fact, the U.S. military was at war in the Philippines, a reality reflected in the drumbeat of American dead.

Accidents were the biggest killer. On February 22, 2002, an army MH-47 helicopter exploded and crashed into the sea off the southern Philippines while returning from a nighttime mission, killing ten of the eighteen people on board.[16] Four more troops died in accidents between 2004 and 2007.[17] Enemy ambushes also claimed lives. On October 2, 2002, a bomb packed with nails exploded outside a café in Zamboanga, killing a Special Forces soldier.[18] Seven years later, on September 28, an improvised explosive device (IED) struck a Humvee. Two American commandos died.[19]

With that being said, Philippine troops did most of the fighting on the ground, at sea, and in the air. With American assistance—valued $15 million a year initially, gradually increasing to no less than $30 million—the country's ragtag military grew leaner, smarter, and more lethal.

The OV-10s, numbering a couple dozen at their peak, were the backbone of the tiny air force and bore the brunt of the intensive bombing campaign against the southern militants. In May 2000, four Broncos dropped 500- and 750-pound bombs on a MILF encampment, clearing a path for army soldiers to seize the base. Forty-three MILF fighters died along with four government troops.[20]

But the two-seat, twin-propeller attack planes, armed with machine guns and unguided gravity bombs, were of Vietnam War vintage and badly in need of upgrade. Lt. Mary Grace Baloyo, then one of the Philippines' few female Bronco pilots, was returning from a training flight when one or both engines apparently failed. Baloyo's copilot ejected, but Baloyo stayed in the plummeting bomber long enough to steer it away from populated areas—and died when it slammed into the ground.[21] Baloyo's March 2001 crash was just one in a tragic litany of accidents that gradually cut the Bronco force in half.

While it's not clear that the United States provided funding *specifically* for the OV-10s' enhancement, it was only after the Pentagon began underwriting Manila's military that the air force, in 2004, finally signed a $6-million contract for upgrades. American firm Marsh Aviation provided new engines, each with four propellers instead of the usual three, and set up a better maintenance program. The changes "enhanced the operational capability and readiness of the Air Force," the Department of National Defense crowed.[22]

And that was just a first step. A second round of upgrades seven years later would transform the Broncos into high-tech, precision bombers capable of pinpoint raids in the dead of night. Combined with an expanding force of U.S. drones, the ancient bombers became the Philippines'—and by extension America's—most lethal weapon in the fight against al Qaeda's Southeast Asian arm.

And almost no one beyond the jungle battlefield even noticed.

Drone War

From humble beginnings, America's drone force in the Philippines grew in size and sophistication—although the expansion was rarely officially acknowledged. An offhand mention in 2002 by a military spokesperson of the Gnat drone was one the U.S.

government's few comments on the robot arsenal in the Philippines in anything but an emergency context.[23]

Instead, the drone escalation was marked mostly by its failures and the destruction it wrought—that is, the damage from robotic strikes plus crashes and alleged shoot-downs of the flying 'bots. When missiles exploded and the shattered hulks of downed drones began turning up, officials were sometimes compelled to explain. And when governments held their tongues, the drones' prey—the Islamic militants—did not hesitate to speak.

In March 2002 a Gnat plunged into Caldera Bay, ten miles west of Zamboanga City. In full view of local seafarers, U.S. Navy SEALs and Philippine divers recovered the robot "almost fully intact," U.S. Army Brig. Gen. Donald Wurster, commander of Special Forces in the Pacific, told local media. "Nobody got hurt. The pilot is safe," Wurster joked.[24]

Four years later on February 10, 2006, an unidentified UAV described as having a one-meter wingspan—possibly a hand-launched model used by U.S. Special Operations Forces—crashed into villagers in the mountains on Jolo Island, a MILF stronghold.

Muslim villagers, sympathetic to the rebel group, told a TV crew they would return the white-painted robot to the U.S. or Philippine government for 100,000 pesos—around $2,000. Media reports called it a "ransom."[25] There is no indication it was ever paid.

According to the *New York Times*, sometime in 2006 U.S. Predators fired a "barrage" of Hellfire missiles at a militant encampment thought to harbor Umar Patek, an Indonesian member of Jemaah Islamiyah suspected of helping orchestrate the 2002 bombing of a Bali nightclub that killed more than two hundred people.[26]

Patek survived. Five years later in January 2011 he was arrested in Abbottabad, Pakistan, not coincidentally the same town where Osama bin Laden was killed by U.S. Navy SEALs in May of the same year. An Indonesian court sentenced Patek to twenty years after he admitted making the Bali bomb.[27]

Col. David Maxwell, commander of the U.S. Joint Special Operations Task Force–Philippines at the time of the alleged attack, denied the *Times*' report. "In all my time in The Philippines in between 2001 and 2007, there has never been a Predator or Reaper deployed, and there have been no Hellfire missiles, let alone 'a barrage of Hellfire missiles.'"[28]

The October following the supposed drone-launched missile barrage, U.S. Marines from the 31st Marine Expeditionary Unit arrived in the Philippines for a training exercise. They brought along an experiment Silver Fox drone built by Advanced Ceramics Research, based in Arizona. The twenty-five-pound UAV with the eight-foot wingspan could support "a wide variety of missions, ranging anywhere from route reconnaissance, rear-area security, search and rescue, to battle-damage assessment," said Cpl. Jesse Urban, one of the drone's operators.

"This is an important asset for us," Urban said, adding a note of caution that was already common knowledge among American UAV operators. "The environment here consists of weather that is less than favorable."[29]

In part for that reason U.S. drones continued dropping out of the sky over the southern Philippines. An unspecified UAV with an eight-foot wingspan—possibly a Silver Fox—struck a coconut grove near Maguindanao on October 18, 2008, and crashed. U.S. and Philippine officials tried to cover up the incident, but local reporters broke the news.

Two weeks later another UAV went down in Talayan, outside Maguindanao—MILF territory. Rebels claimed they shot it down. A photo posted online was unambiguous: the 'bot in question was another Silver Fox.

"The spy plane is still in good condition and intact and we will not give it back to the U.S. military," rebel leader Mohagher Iqbal told a reporter. "It is now the property of the MILF."[30]

Not to be outdone by their American comrades, Philippine troops began crashing their own homegrown UAVs in rebel territory. Manila's navy modified hobbyists' radio-controlled helicopters for video surveillance. One of these apparently flew overhead during a "fierce firefight" between government troops and rebels in Maguindanao in June 2009.

"Commander Wahid Tundok ordered one his sharpshooters to zero in on the pestering air vehicle," MILF told reporters. "And with one shot, it crashed down in a hillside."

The army reportedly tried to buy back the wreckage for 400,000 pesos—$8,000—but the rebels rejected the offer. Manila denied even operating the drone.[31] But the evidence of drone warfare outweighed years of sporadic denials from Manila and Washington. And the best evidence was in the increasing scale, accuracy, and deadliness of government strikes on MILF and other militant groups in the Philippines.

With commandos on the ground, upgraded OV-10 bombers overhead, and a veritable armada of robots in support, U.S. and Philippine forces squeezed and bled the militants over a decade of covert combat.

5

Distracted

In early 2003 the White House under President George W. Bush provided Secretary of State Colin Powell with a list of intelligence claims purporting to tie Saddam Hussein's Iraq to international terrorism.

"He came through the door . . . and he had in his hands a sheaf of papers," Powell aide Col. Lawrence Wilkerson said of his boss. "He said, 'This is what I've got to present at the United Nations according to the White House, and you need to look at it.'"

Powell, Wilkerson, and CIA chief George Tenet spent four days going through the documents, weighing their believability and deciding which claims to use in the UN speech.

There was a problem. The list "was anything but an intelligence document," Wilkerson told CNN two years later. "It was, as some people characterized it later, sort of a Chinese menu from which you could pick and choose."

And unknown to Wilkerson or Powell, some of the information in the dossier was provided by a CIA source that the Defense Intelligence Agency—the Pentagon's in-house spy shop—had labeled a liar.[1]

On February 5, Powell stood before the UN and made the case for a military campaign. He displayed slides depicting what he claimed were Iraqi mobile biological weapons labs. "What you will see is an accumulation of facts and disturbing patterns of behavior," Powell said. "The facts on Iraq's behavior demonstrate that Saddam Hussein and his regime have made no effort—no effort—to disarm as required by the international community."[2]

Bush doubled down on the lies and bad intelligence in a March 6 press conference. "Iraq is a part of the war on terror," Bush said. "It's a country that trains terrorists; it's a country that could arm terrorists. Saddam Hussein and his weapons are a direct threat to this country."[3]

The Bush administration was determined to go to war, whatever the rationale. The U.S. news media were more than happy to help. For starters, they themselves were in shock following the 9/11 attacks. In an interview with late night talk show host David Letterman on September 17, 2001, CBS's Dan Rather famously addressed the president. "Mr. President if you need me, if you need me to go to Hell and back for my country, I will do it." As Rather broke down on camera, Letterman cut to commercials.

The press had on patriotic blinders, but their failure was not simply an emotional one. Since the 1980s the media had been increasingly, and subtly, managed by the Pentagon and the government at large. The creation of the pool system during the Panama War, the tight controls over media accompanying U.S. troops in Iraq in 1991—these were constraints on a free press that too many editors and reporters simply shrugged and accepted, in no small part because they represented cost savings compared to truly independent reporting.

The bottom line is that most reporters did not question Powell's claims. The mea culpas would come later. "I don't think there is any excuse for, you know, my performance and the performance of the press in general in the roll up to the war," Rather said in 2007. "Overall and in the main, there's no question that we didn't do a good job."[4]

Embedded

The U.S.-led invasion kicked off two weeks after Bush's March press conference, but preparations for the war had already been underway for more than year. In October 2001, the Defense Department awarded the Rendon Group—John Rendon's secretive PR firm—a $16-million contract to target Iraq with propaganda aimed at destabilizing Saddam Hussein's regime.

Under a previous contract with the CIA, Rendon had assembled a goup of Iraqi exiles, dubbed them the "Iraqi National Congress" (INC), and advised them in planning an uprising against Hussein. Ahmad Chalabi, the head of the INC, embraced his role as the manufactured leader of a secular, pro-U.S. Iraqi opposition that, in reality, barely existed. Chalabi presented the CIA with carefully groomed sources claiming firsthand knowledge of Hussein's efforts to acquire nuclear, biological, and chemical weapons of mass destruction (WMDs).

One Iraqi expat, Adnan Ihsan Saeed al-Haideri, an ethnic Kurd, was coached by INC spokesman Zaab Sethna to testify that he had helped the Iraqi government conceal stocks of WMDs.

The CIA subjected al-Haideri to a polygraph in his safe house in Thailand. The Kurd failed the test: he was a liar. But before the agency could disseminate the results of the lie detector, the INC pushed the story.

Sethna called Paul Moran, an Australian freelance TV reporter who had been on the Rendon payroll as an "information operations" specialist. Chalabi, working in concert with his spokesman, contacted Judith Miller at the *New York Times*.

Moran (who would later die in a suicide bombing in Iraq in 2003) and Miller both interviewed al-Haideri. "The story . . . was soon being trumpeted by the White House and repeated by newspapers and television networks around the world," Bamford wrote. "It was the first in a long line of hyped and fraudulent stories that would eventually propel the U.S. into a war with Iraq—the first war based almost entirely on a covert propaganda campaign targeting the media."[5]

Rendon's efforts were the covert half of a two-front campaign of media manipulation. The overt half was a new process for granting reporters access to the military—and in that way establishing a framework for managing the press throughout a war zone.

On October 30, 2002, Secretary of Defense Donald Rumsfeld unexpectedly showed up at a meeting of news bureau chiefs at the Pentagon. The chiefs expressed their fear that, in the event of war with Iraq, their reporters might lack access to the troops.

"Secretary Rumsfeld, charming, impish and in command, had something to tell us," wrote the *Weekly Standard*'s Kim Hume, who was present. "He was on board with the public relations strategy of embedding media with warriors."[6]

What was Rumsfeld thinking? Media critic Bill Katovsky had a theory. "The Pentagon outflanked the media by taking to heart Michael Corleone's godfatherly advice, 'Keep your friends close and your enemies closer.'"[7]

The embed system placed reporters inside frontline combat units—but only after being vetted by the Pentagon and agreeing to be subject to a long and constantly changing list of ground rules: no depicting casualties, no detailed descriptions of unit strength or movements, no mention of "electronic warfare," no photographing air bases, etc.

Embedded reporters enjoyed close contact with military sources and, piggybacking on the military logistical and transportation system, saw their own direct expenses shrink. Editors loved that, even if it came at the cost of the reporters' independence. On the other hand, embedded press went only where their hosts wanted them to go, and saw only what their hosts wanted them to see.

For the military, embeds were the next logical step after the press pool. The same control, but over a much greater number of reporters: some 600 during the early weeks of the war, or a quarter of the roughly 2,400 media representatives covering the conflict. The military began using the term "unilateral" to describe non-embedded journalists—as though *they* were the exception.

For the Pentagon, embeds weren't without risk—and it was prepared to "disembed" any reporter who violated the ground rules or otherwise pissed off the hosting troops. But military flacks justifiably had high hopes that embedding would result in sympathetic reporting—a sort of organic propaganda. "How detached could the press expect to be with troops who were also, as ABC News' John Donovan put it, 'my protectors'?" Katovsky asked.[8]

At the bureau chief meeting in October 2002, the always self-confident Rumsfeld blithely described the embed system from the military point of view with a word that should have sounded alarms in the minds of the attending news bosses. He called it "self-serving."[9]

Dogfight

As the Rendon Group drummed up support for the war, America's killer drones converged on Iraq. They hunted Iraqi troops formations and Scud missile launchers, among other fleeting targets. The UAV operators were in for a nasty surprise. In the 1990s the drones had faced stiff resistance from Serbian troops, and several were shot down. But in the years since, over Afghanistan, Yemen, Somalia, and the Philippines, the Predators hunted essentially defenseless enemies. The Pentagon and CIA had grown accustomed to total freedom of action.

But Iraq was not Somalia. It possessed a functioning army and air force and the will to use them. On many occasions when U.S. drones crossed into Iraqi air space, Iraqi jet fighters rose to intercept. Saddam Hussein's MiGs were making it hard for the drone crews to complete their missions. The United States sought a temporary fix while it worked on a longer-term solution to the drone vulnerability problem.

In fall 2002 James Clark, a highly regarded air force troubleshooter, approached Gen. John Jumper, chief of staff of the flying branch, with the idea of adding heat-seeking Stinger air-to-air missiles to existing Predators. The thirty-four-pound Stingers were used by U.S. ground troops and helicopters to defend against air attacks. The Stingers were small and short-ranged, and adding them to a Predator meant removing the drone's Hellfire air-to-ground missiles.

The Stingers were better than nothing—barely. "A Predator crew would find it hard, if not impossible, to spot an Iraqi fighter and launch a Stinger quickly enough to have a chance of hitting it, given the speed of a jet," Richard Whittle wrote. "At the very least, though, giving the Predator a way to shoot back might spook Hussein's pilots, Jumper and Clark agreed."

Big Safari, the same organization that had installed the Hellfires on the Predators a year earlier, awarded drone-maker General Atomics a contract to integrate Stingers in September 2002. By October a drone was flying mock dogfights against a Cessna. Four Stinger test firings resulted in two hits and two misses.

In November the Stinger-armed Predators deployed to the Middle East and were soon going up against Iraqi fighters, albeit apparently without launching missiles. Then on December 23, 2002, an Iraqi MiG-25 intercepted one of the Predators, and, for the first time, the two planes exchanged fire.

Video of the battle, shot by the drone, was obtained by CBS

News. "The engagement began when the MiG turned to attack head-on and fired a missile," Whittle wrote. "The Predator crew fired a Stinger back. The video shows the smoke trails of the missiles crossing, then the Stinger starting to dive, coming nowhere close to the MiG. Then the Predator video suddenly ends."

The drone fell to the ground in ruins. The MiG was reportedly undamaged.[10]

When U.S. forces invaded Iraq just over three months later, Hussein ordered the MiG-25s and the rest of the Iraqi air force buried rather than have it face American F-15s in what was certain to be a suicidal last stand.

The U.S. Air Force decided to strip the Stingers from the Predators. "Bottom line is there are systems better suited to defend our assets from other aircraft if we decide we need to do that," Lt. Col. Tadd Sholtis, an air force spokesman, explained years later. Sholtis didn't say, but it's possible he was referring to stealth: a drone that can't be detected can't be shot down.

The air force had been secretly working on a radar-evading UAV since the mid-1990s. Very few knew it, but by 2002 the stealth drone was almost ready for combat. It would greatly expand the reach of America's robotic strike force in Iraq and across the globe, laying the groundwork for future robotic warfare and, by extension, the shadow wars that would follow America's disastrous ground campaigns in Iraq and Afghanistan.

Silent Partner

One alleged participant in the invasion of Iraq was never officially acknowledged. But it *was* seen.

The pilots of high-flying U-2 spy planes, based in the United Arab Emirates for reconnaissance flights over Iraq, complained of nearly colliding with unidentified but obviously U.S.-origin drones flying along similar paths as the venerable U-2s.

David Fulghum, a reporter for the trade publication *Aviation Week*, caught wind of the U-2 pilots' gripes and managed to eke a few anonymous comments from Pentagon sources. An air force official told Fulghum that the air force possessed a new, secret UAV, built by Lockheed Martin using parts scavenged from the defunct Dark Star drone and other aerospace programs.

"It's the same concept as Dark Star," the official told Fulghum. "It's stealthy, and it uses the same apertures and data links.

"The numbers are limited," the source added. "There are a couple of airframes, a ground station and spare parts."

The new drone's sensors reportedly included a radar, a daylight camera, and an infrared imager. It could fly for up to eight hours at a time. Its ability to absorb or deflect radar energy away from ground-based emitters meant it could fly deep inside enemy defenses where other reconnaissance aircraft dared not venture.

Fulghum speculated that the secret drone was based at Al Udeid Air Base in Qatar, where the air force had roped off some hangars to keep inquisitive reporters away. He did not, however, speculate as to the new robot's designation. That would not be revealed for another seven years.[11]

War by Contract

The veil of secrecy surrounding the new UAV was not unique. Much of the Iraq War was waged in the shadows by men and equipment unknown and unaccountable to the American public. The massive expansion of American mercenary forces starting in 2003 was both a symptom and driver of this secrecy. If the bush wars of the 1990s sparked the explosive spread of private security companies, then the U.S-led invasion and subsequent eight-year occupation of Iraq was fuel poured directly on the fire.

"In the early days of the Iraq war, there weren't enough

troops," Steve Fainaru explained in his book *Big Boys Rules*. "As the situation deteriorated, a parallel army formed on the margins of the war: tens of thousands of armed men, invisible in plain sight, doing the jobs that couldn't be done because there weren't enough troops."[12]

In just the first eighteen months of the war, the U.S. government spent $766 million on security contracts with private companies. The governments of Iraq and various U.S. allies added untold millions to the total.[13]

In July 2005 the Government Accountability Office estimated there were at least sixty major security companies operating in Iraq with 25,000 employees. In those first two years of the war, no fewer than two hundred contractors died in combat.[14]

It was apparent that the Pentagon could no longer—or *would* no longer—fulfill its national security responsibilities without the assistance of mercenaries. That raised some profound questions, not the least of which was accountability.

On September 16, 2007, private soldiers from Blackwater, a North Carolina firm that provided security for the State Department, gunned down seventeen civilians in Nisoor Square in Baghdad. The mercenaries later claimed they had come under attack, but the U.S. Army found no evidence of insurgent fire. "The incident almost certainly would have been buried but for the sheer number of people whom Blackwater killed," Fainaru wrote.[15]

The Iraqi government protested. Blackwater attempted to settle the issue with payments to victims' families. In the United States criminal and civil suits were filed. At least one of the shooters got off on a technicality. Another pleaded guilty to manslaughter and agreed to cooperate with investigators. As of early 2013 four cases were still open, with the defendants facing manslaughter and weapons charges.[16]

Blackwater was barred from Iraq but held on to its State Department contract.[17] The company changed its name twice in an attempt to distance itself from the killings.

The Nisoor Square shootings shone a light on the shadowy world of security companies but did nothing to reverse the trend toward more and more corporate involvement in America's wars. Nor did the killings and the subsequent legal cases necessarily resolve the confusion over accountability. At worst, a few of Blackwater's employees could go to prison for manslaughter. But the business itself survived and even thrived, as did other companies like it.

"Public militaries have all manner of traditional controls over their activities, ranging from internal checks and balances, domestic laws regulating the activities of of the military force and its personnel, parliamentary scrutiny, public opinion and numerous aspects of international law," P. W. Singer explained in *Corporate Warriors*. Security companies, he added, "are only subject to the laws of the market.

"Who can and should be punished for these crimes?" Singer asked. "It is very clear that privatizing security actions only complicates the issue."[18]

But that was the *point*. The more the Pentagon relied on hired guns, the greater the distance between the government and the conduct and consequences of the wars it waged.

Quagmire

By the summer of 2003 Iraq was in the throes of a full-blown insurgency. A series of sweeps by occupying U.S. forces in the Sunni-dominated areas of north-central Iraq netted scores of insurgent fighters killed or captured but did not stem the swelling tide of gun attacks and improvised bombings.

Washington lost control quickly. What had been imagined as a lightning campaign to topple Iraqi regime became a bloody slog through Iraq's teeming cities and impoverished towns. The death toll mounted: 172 U.S. and coalition troops had died during the invasion phase of the conflict in March and April. Soon coalition fatalities exceeded two per day. In total, 580 died in 2003, 906 in 2004, 897 in 2005, 873 in 2006, and a staggering 961 the following year.[19]

Iraqis died in much greater numbers as religious sects turned against one another amid increasingly sophisticated attacks on coalition and Iraqi government forces. According to one count relying on vetted media sources, no fewer than ten thousand insurgents and fifty thousand civilians died between 2003 and the departure of U.S. forces in late 2011. The actual numbers could be much, much higher.[20]

As the insurgency worsened, leaders in Washington were desperate to insulate themselves from accountability. That meant controlling the press. As usual, the government turned to the Rendon Group to do the PR dirty work.

Having spent the years 2001 to 2003 helping convince Americans to support an unnecessary war, in 2005 Rendon shifted gears. Among other lucrative business deals related to the deepening conflict, Rendon won a $1.5-million Pentagon contract for "news analysis and media assessment" in Iraq. Rendon had sold the war, now it had to *keep* it sold. The embed system with its hundreds of sympathetic journalists was helping, but not enough. More and more embedded reporters were getting kicked out of Iraq for violating the ground rules or simply crossing U.S. commanders.

Under the terms of Rendon's new contract, which remained a secret for four years, the group was responsible for screening reporters who requested embeds, rating each journalist's work as "positive," "neutral," or "negative" toward the military. A negative assessment could lead to a reporter being denied access.[21] Rendon performed the same service in Afghanistan, advising U.S. commanders there on which reporters were most likely to write favorable stories.

In previous American wars, government censorship had been

overt, as had efforts to corral reporters roaming the battlefield. Rendon and its clients were instrumental in a new era, in which military suppression of the media occurred in secret. Control of the media was an obvious attempt on the part of the government to get ahead of, or at least mitigate somewhat, the inevitable public backlash against America's twin land wars of the post-9/11 era.

But it would also serve a more subtle purpose in parallel to the Iraq and Afghanistan wars—and beyond. The media tactics pioneered by the Rendon Group would become standard practice in the Pentagon's numerous small-scale, but long-term, interventions in places many Americans could not even locate on a map.

In Iraq and Afghanistan, the government had tried to skew the news. In Somalia, the Philippines, Congo, and other conflict zones, the Pentagon managed to completely block or otherwise evade the media. Manipulation and suppression of the press cast the shadows in shadow wars.

Disembedded

In early February 2006, I went to Iraq to cover the then-three-year-old conflict. It was my sixth trip to Iraq since launching my freelance war correspondence career in January 2005. I was embedded with a U.S. Army unit at a remote Iraqi training base in north-central Iraq, interviewing an American officer about the development of Iraqi security forces. A sour-faced sergeant pulled up in a Humvee. He ordered me to put away my cameras and get in.

"You're in violation of regulations," he said. I thought it was a joke. So did the officer. But the sergeant persisted. So I apologized to my interviewee, stowed my gear, and climbed into the Humvee. Over the next thirty-six hours, I was shuttled from base to base and finally to Kuwait—under armed guard for all but the final leg.

I'd been disembedded.

I never found out who ordered my disembedding. I never got an official explanation for what rule I'd violated. From my guards and others, I gleaned that I had published supposedly sensitive information allegedly endangering U.S. forces.

As a freelance Iraq correspondent for C-SPAN, the *Village Voice*, *Salon*, the *Washington Times*, and others, I'd been to Iraq six times, five times embedded with U.S. or British forces. Never had anything like this happened. I'd been bombed, shot at, and mortared many times, but in the protective embrace of Western armies, I'd never really been afraid. But this . . . this was plain scary.

It turned out that the "classified information" in question concerned radio jammers that the army used to defeat IEDs, the biggest killers in Iraq.

My editors were interested in the military's efforts to counter IEDs. I got the info in an on-the-record interview with a young army lieutenant who apparently didn't know it was supposed to be secret. Also, I had checked the info against public websites, which led me to believe that there was nothing sensitive about it.

The army's claim that I put U.S. troops at risk by betraying their secret weapons didn't hold up too well. But then, it didn't have to. For embedded reporters, the army was the highest authority.

The climate for journalists in Iraq could not have been worse. American freelancer Steve Vincent was murdered in Basra in August 2005. Jill Carroll, another American freelancer, was kidnapped in Baghdad in January 2006. ABC anchor Bob Woodruff was badly injured in a roadside bombing of an Iraqi convoy in north-central Iraq the same month. Scores of Iraqi journalists had also been killed since the beginning of the war. "There are levels of risk that often seem beyond reason," John Burns, the *New York Times*' Baghdad bureau chief, told me. In 2003, Burns had been briefly abducted by Iraqi gunmen.

In that context, embedding with U.S. troops made sense. But it was a false comfort. The embedded reporter traded his journalistic freedom for a measure of safety from certain kinds of attacks. Certainly, embedded press were still vulnerable to bombings and gun attacks on the units they traveled with—as Woodruff found out first hand.

Embedding also meant serious limitations. Routinely, you only saw what U.S. forces saw: the insides of armored vehicles, the passing faces of frightened and angry Iraqis, and the muddy landscapes of walled bases, mostly. Plus, embedding meant working within the rubric of the military public affairs operation, which encouraged self-censorship in addition to coming down hard on journalists who offended its sensibilities.

In mid-February, CBS correspondent David Martin had to admit to self-censorship, also surrounding the IED issue. He had finished a network news segment on the counter-IED tactics but pulled it an hour before airing it after a senior military officer told him it contained information that might be helpful to the enemy.

"I didn't find his argument about how it would help the enemy very persuasive," Martin wrote, "but because there's a war on I decided to give him the benefit of the doubt. I've done that a number of times over the years, and each time it's turned out that going with the story wouldn't have caused any harm.

"So how do you decide that a story contains sensitive information that shouldn't see the light of day?" Martin continued. "In war, you can make an extreme case that almost any accurate information about the U.S. military is news the enemy can use. ... So how do you decide that a story contains legitimate secrets? It's like the famous definition of pornography—you know it when you see it."[22]

Former L.A. Times reporter Monte Morin, later an Iraq correspondent for Stars and Stripes, told me he had run afoul of army public affairs on several occasions, at times being threatened with eviction from the country. One notable incident in the days before one of Iraq's contested elections saw him hauled through the rain to a confrontation with an angry officer. Morin had quoted a soldier talking about stockpiling body bags for the inevitable bloodshed. In the army's eyes, the quotation was an unforgivable offense—*by Morin*.[23]

He might have irritated host officers hoping for good news from the front, but never did he violate the code of conduct that mattered most for any reporter, whether embedded or not: our shared journalistic ethics. Morin announced his intentions as a reporter, quoted his sources accurately, and told the truth as he saw it. But to the military, journalistic ethics were beside the point. The embed system wasn't about facilitating good journalism. It was about controlling journalists, limiting their access, and turning off the spotlight in order to preserve the shadows cloaking a new era in warfare.

Secret Squadron

But the veil could not hold. The silence and darkness surrounding U.S. methods and weaponry in Iraq could not last forever. In increments, both intentional and imposed, the air force allowed its secret drone warplane—the one initially spotted by U-2 pilots over Iraq in 2003—into the daylight.

The revelation began with a name.

On September 1, 2005, at the highly secure Tonopah Test Range in Nevada, a base that had once housed the air force's secretive fleet of F-117 stealth fighters, the flying branch quietly reactivated the 30th Reconnaissance Squadron, an aerial photography unit that had been defunct since the 1970s.[24]

The air force kept the revived squadron's existence a secret for seven months. In a March presentation to a group of civilians at nearby Nellis Air Force Base, 1st Lt. Justin McVay flashed a slide listing air force Predator squadrons. The 11th, 15th and 17th Reconnaissance Squadrons and the 3rd Special Operations Squadron had all been previously disclosed, but the slide also referenced the "30th RS."

After the presentation, reporter Keith Rogers asked McVay about the 30th RS and was told its operations were classified. What McVay did not say, and may not have even known, was that the 30th was the operating unit for the new, stealthy spy drone that Lockheed Martin had salvaged from the ruins of the canceled Dark Star UAV and which had nearly collided with manned U-2 recon planes over Iraq two years prior.[25]

On July 17, 2007, just short of a year after McVay's admission, the air force approved a new uniform patch for the 30th RS that featured a predatory bird perched atop a globe of the world, its claws straddling Afghanistan, Pakistan, and Iran.[26] Sometime the same year, a photographer on assignment to cover French army operations in southern Afghanistan was on the flightline at Kandahar Air Field, NATO's major base in the region, when he spotted something curious: what appeared to be a flying-wing drone, flying overhead and taxiing along the runway.[27]

The photog apparently knew enough about UAVs to realize that the vehicle before him was of a type that had never been reported before. Under the embed rules, no picture-taking is allowed on the Kandahar flight line, but the photographer took a chance, and snapped several long-range shots, and then sat on them for no less than a year.

In April 2009, one of the photos was shown to Darren Lake, a reporter for *Unmanned Vehicles* magazine. Lake published a story hailing the debut of "a new, advanced but as yet undisclosed UCAV," or unmanned combat air vehicle.[28]

In May, the French magazine *Air & Cosmos* published one of the blurry photos depicting the drone in flight and provided another, similar image to *Aviation Week*, where veteran aerospace reporter Bill Sweetman dubbed the mysterious machine the "Beast of Kandahar."[29] Seven months later the French newspaper *Liberation* published yet another snapshot, this one much clearer and showing the Beast on the ground.

"Gotcha," Sweetman wrote.[30] Three days later, on December

4, 2009, the air force responded to *Aviation Week*'s queries with the biggest aviation scoop in years. The Beast of Kandahar was really the RQ-170 Sentinel, "a stealthy unmanned aircraft system to provide reconnaissance and surveillance support to forward deployed combat forces."[31] The Sentinel was flown by the 30th Reconnaissance Squadron, the air force admitted.[32]

The aviation media went wild speculating on the drone's origins, capabilities, and purpose. Sweetman zeroed in on the most compelling question. The air force seemed to imply the Sentinel was being used against the Taliban and al Qaeda in Afghanistan. "Why use a stealth aircraft against an adversary that doesn't have radar?" Sweetman asked.[33]

In truth, the Sentinel wasn't being used against the Taliban at all. For the radar-evading drone, Iraq had been a sideshow and Afghanistan was a front; its *real* targets were some of the most hidden and heavily protected in America's expanding shadow wars.

6

Empowered

Kenyan Kennedy Mwale was a fisherman, plying the waters off Kenya and Somalia in search of tuna and other big fish. But with piracy taking root in lawless Somalia, fishing and the sea trade were becoming riskier and less profitable by the day for the small operators.

One of the final straws for Mwale was a close call in 2002 with a band of fourteen pirates that sneaked up on the eleven-man refrigerator ship where the then-twenty-six-year-old Mwale was the chief engineer. The reefer ship followed behind the fishing boats to store fresh catches.

They came at night, as the ship was anchored near Mdoa Island, surprising the sleeping crew and their one Somali body-guard. When the pirates failed to wrestle away the guard's rifle, a standoff ensued. The pirates demanded the crew's money and possessions, plus all the diesel fuel stored on deck—and wanted the ship sailed to the Somali port of Kismayo. If the crew didn't comply, the pirates would start killing people, they said.

The crew coughed up all their cash—just a few dollars for most, but around $700 in the case of the ship owner's secretary—and handed over possessions, including a new boom box stereo. But the captain refused to give up the diesel or to sail to Kismayo. He would not allow the ship to enter into captivity, nor strand it at sea. The captain had only as much leverage as was afforded by his one armed guard, but it was enough. The pirates compromised. They agreed to go to Mdoa and continue negotiations.

That apparently was a clever bit of strategizing on the captain's part, for he had called at Mdoa earlier, seeking the ruling committee's permission to fish Somali waters. The committee had endorsed the expedition. And when the pirates rolled in with Mwale and his shipmates in tow, the committee immediately branded the captors criminals and had the local militia seize their weapons and return everything they'd stolen. They gave back the boom box, but denied taking anything else. The penniless Kenyans now were free to sail home.

This story has a happy-ish ending, but for Mwale, it was another near-miss in a career full of them. Every day the arguments mounted against working at sea. Already, three of his friends had been killed by sharks. And with piracy making profitable fishing a dicey venture, Mwale soon decided he'd had enough. He went ashore, for good, and for five years was unemployed on Mombasa's sweltering streets.[1]

Piracy was about to get worse—because *Somalia* was about to get worse. The long-suffering country's late downward turn dovetailed with the rise in secret U.S. warfare—and revealed a key weakness in American strategy.

Miscalculation

The hard-line Islamic Courts Union enjoyed a few years of loose control over almost all of shattered, scarred Somalia. An Ethiopian-backed secular regime called the Transitional Federal Government (TFG) held onto a splinter of northern territory. The ICU's ruling judges issued decrees based on sharia law that were enforced with swift brutality by the young thugs of Al Shabab, a militant Islamist group with links to al Qaeda.

No music. No dancing. No movies. Petty crimes could be punished by flogging, mutilation, or death. Somalia wasn't a pleasant place to live under the ICU, but it was more lawful and orderly than it had been for most of the previous decade.[2]

But the ICU, like the Taliban in Afghanistan, miscalculated hugely. It offered safe haven to members of al Qaeda and other terror groups. In the early 2000s no major terrorist attacks were launched from Somali soil—in sharp contrast to what occurred in Afghanistan—but the mere *potential* for attacks set the stage for a period of renewed upheaval in Somalia, instigated by the United States, but executed by a new and close American ally: Ethiopia, Somalia's neighbor to the west.

What happened when the Americans and Ethiopians targeted Somalia for its second major intervention in fourteen years revealed both the greatest strength and deepest flaw in the emerging U.S. shadow war construct.

For two years, Ethiopia acted as the main U.S. proxy in Somalia, waging a war that Washington desired but stood no chance of undertaking alone—not after 1993, and not with more than two hundred thousand American troops plus thousands of U.S.-paid mercenaries already on the ground in Iraq and Afghanistan.

To the extent that Washington relied on other countries such as the Philippines and Ethiopia to provide the manpower for large-scale ground fighting in remote battle zones far beyond the American consciousness, the U.S. government also surrendered a large measure of control over the results of the fighting. For all the American money, expertise, and specialized forces—drones and commandos—that underpinned shadow wars in Somalia and elsewhere in the 2000s, Washington's proxies exercised tremendous power . . . and could corrupt American efforts that weren't terribly noble to begin with.

In Somalia starting in 2006, the United States and Ethiopia plotted a joint invasion aimed at destroying the ICU. Washington considered the Courts a quasi–state terror sponsor, like a Somali Taliban. Besides fearing Somali-based terrorists, Ethiopian leaders were also possessed of territorial ambitions.

Ethiopia had fought a bloody civil war in the 1990s that had resulted in Eritrea breaking away and taking with it all of Ethiopia's coastline and sea ports. To keep up pressure on Ethiopia's right flank, Eritrea funneled arms to the ICU, setting them up as a proxy against Addis Ababa's own interests in Somalia.

The UN and United States closely monitored the Ethiopian-Eritrean cease-fire. Somalia was the only place left for the two countries to fight each other, albeit indirectly. Moreover, Somalia possessed in abundance what Eritrea had taken from Ethiopia: access to the sea.

And Somalis knew it.

Confab

The meetings that would launch a war took place in Addis Ababa in the summer of 2006.

On June 24, 2006., Jendayi Frazer, the top U.S. State Department official in Africa; Rear Adm. Richard Hunt, commander of the Horn of Africa task force; and U.S. ambassador to Ethiopia Vicki Huddleston, plus other lower-ranking military officials and diplomats, met in the sweltering capital to summarize previous discussions between U.S. and Ethiopian leaders.

Frazer called the situation in Somalia "uncertain." She laid out best- and worst-case scenarios. In the best case, the ICU would forge a peace with the rival TFG. "Moderates would emerge thus leading to stability," according to Huddleston's diplomatic cable detailing the confab. In the worst case, the TFG would collapse and the Islamists would gain total control over Somalia. "This would have a major negative impact on the Horn" and "would pull in Ethiopia," Frazer explained, according to Huddleston.

Frazer went on to say the United States feared Ethiopian involvement in Somalia, but in the same breath she vowed the United States would "rally with Ethiopia if the jihadists took over"—a message she had apparently already communicated to Ethiopian president Meles Zenawi. Frazer mentioned Eritrea's support for the ICU, calling it a "red line" that Ethiopia and the word could not ignore. "They will pay," she said of the Eritreans.

Indeed, Hunt and the other military official present had already assessed Ethiopia's ability to send troops into Somalia while maintaining adequate forces along the demarcation line with Eritrea. Hunt said it would be difficult but not impossible for Addis Ababa to muster the troops.

"If Ethiopia intervened in Somalia, it would be a mistake for the international community to condemn it," Huddleston recalled Frazer saying, in an echo of the Bush administration's rhetoric while drumming up support for the U.S.-led invasion of Iraq nearly four years prior.

In summary, "Any Ethiopian action in Somalia would have Washington's blessing," Huddleston concluded.[3] Not to mention direct support. Separately from the June meeting, Washington offered Ethiopia "intelligence sharing, arms aid and training" for an attack on Somalia.[4] With this backing, plus air cover provided by U.S. AC-130 gunships and carrier-based fighters and assistance on the ground by U.S. Special Operations Forces, the Ethiopian army launched a blitzkrieg-style assault on Somalia in December 2006.

Blitz

The Ethiopians fired their opening salvo on December 24, 2006. Sukhoi Su-27 Flanker fighter-bombers, most likely flown by Ukrainian mercenary pilots, hit strategic targets and Al Shabab ground troops while at least three thousand Ethiopian soldiers supported by tanks, helicopter gunships, and artillery rolled southeast across a countryside still drying from the Dayr rains.

The Flankers hit airports, roads, ammo dumps, Islamic militia camps, and convoys—disrupting transport, communications, and emergency resupply—while T-55s sporting external fuel tanks crawled south ahead of self-propelled howitzers. Hind gunships flew top cover, dropping 250-kilogram gravity bombs. Mi-17 medevac choppers evacuated wounded troops. Helicopters kept pace with the ground advance by way of forward operating bases. U.S. drones, AC-130 fixed-wing gunships, and Special Operations Forces accompanied the Ethiopians.

These heavy forces faced just a few thousand militants boasting nothing heavier than "technicals"—pickup trucks hauling heavy machine guns. There were reports of Eritrean forces aiding the Islamists and even swapping artillery barrages with the invaders; if true, this resistance hardly slowed the Ethiopian advance.

The Ethiopian government claimed a thousand Islamist fighters killed while declining to cite its own, surely lighter, losses.

In just a week the Ethiopian column covered the more than 150 miles to Mogadishu. By the first week of January, Islamic forces had fled to Kismayo and surrounding areas in the southern tip of Somalia. On January 8, the last militant holdouts came under assault by U.S. and Ethiopian forces, signaling the imminent end of large-scale military resistance.[5]

"The Somalia job was fantastic," Abu Dhabi Crown Prince Sheikh Mohammed bin Zayed Al Nahyan told then-U.S. Central Command boss Gen. John Abizaid in 2007.[6] The White House agreed with that assessment, at least initially. And the proxy approach to African security challenges quickly became central to Washington's policy for the continent. In 2007, the Pentagon formed a new regional command called Africa Command (Africom) to oversee operations in most of Africa.

The command would possess just a few thousand permanent staff and only one major facility—the steadily expanding complex in Djibouti. Proxies were central to the command's mission. "U.S. Africom most effectively advances U.S. national security interests through focused, sustained engagement with partners in support of our shared security objectives," the command announced.[7]

It would take a full year for Africa Command to stand up, but Africans did not wait to protest. The State Department sent diplomat Geoffrey Martineau to reassure the parliament in Abuja that the Pentagon did not plan to build any bases on Nigerian soil.[8] The Pentagon made similar promises in Botswana.[9]

And in January 2008, Bush himself was in Ghana telling the local media that the United States had no intention of building new bases anywhere in Africa. "I know there's rumors in Ghana—'all Bush is coming to do is trying to convince you to put a big military base here.' That's baloney. Or as we say in Texas, 'that's bull,'" the president said.[10]

Martineau, Bush, and other American officials did not mention the facility in Manda Bay, Kenya, where U.S. Special Operations Forces and contractors had been based since around 2004—and from where some air strikes had been launched in support of the Ethiopian attack on Somalia.[11]

As with the Taliban in Afghanistan, the defeat of the ICU's main forces by Ethiopian troops was only a prelude to even more bitter insurgent fighting.

On December 30, Sharif Sheikh Ahmed, chairman of the ICU, urged the scattered Al Shabab fighters to keep fighting. "I call on the Islamic Courts fighters, supporters and every true Muslim to start an insurgency against the Ethiopian troops in Somalia," said

Ahmed, an English-speaking former teacher widely considered a religious and political moderate. "We are telling the Ethiopians in Somalia that they will never succeed in their mission," Ahmed continued. "By Allah, they will fail."[12]

In January 2007, just four Ethiopian troops died in Somali combat. None died in February as the insurgency got organized. Fighting spiked in March and April: thirty-seven Ethiopians were confirmed killed along with more than four hundred insurgents and twelve hundred civilians. The bloodletting would continue as long as the Ethiopians remained.[13]

But the Ethiopian invasion *had* weakened the Islamists and, however briefly, shaken up the country's political dynamics. The ICU was out as a governing power; the TFG, though still weak, was nominally in charge of the country.

The UN, for one, saw opportunity in the tumult. After visiting Mogadishu in January, UN envoy François Lonseny Fall said he sensed "a small window opening for peace and reconciliation."[14] The Security Council, then a decade into an intervention binge, quickly authorized a fresh peacekeeping mission to be fronted by the African Union (AU), rather than the UN, though the world body would help support the force.[15]

Uganda offered to lead the military mission and European governments and the United States—*especially* the United States—pledged to pay for it. Over the next five years, the AU Mission in Somalia, or AMISOM, would ring up $1.7 billion in expenses; more than half of the bill would be footed by the United States.[16]

In essence, America was lining up another proxy in Somalia in the event the Ethiopians failed to restore peace and stability. But the proxy, whoever it might be, would not do all the fighting. Covert U.S. drone and commando activity in Somalia only escalated after the Ethiopian invasion.

The Somalia job had barely begun. And the *true* test of America's new shadow war strategy had yet to occur.

Under Fire

I was determined to see for myself the country that had, in short order, drawn Ethiopia into a bloody insurgency, inspired the AU and UN to establish a pricey new peacekeeping mission, and justified a brand-new U.S. military command built around the twin concepts of proxy armies and shadow warfare. After stints in Iraq, Afghanistan, Lebanon, and East Timor, I went to Somalia.

I was lucky to survive. The country was well on its way to earning a reputation for eating journalists. Between 1993 and 2007 no fewer than twenty-one reporters, both Somali and foreign, died covering conflict in Somalia—most of them murdered by government, militia, or insurgent forces or killed in crossfire. The number of dead journalists would more than double in the following five years, making Somalia arguably the most dangerous place in the world for media.[17]

The threats to journalists, while hardly condoned by the United States, dovetailed neatly with Washington's desire to keep Somalia—and U.S. activities there—out of the news. The suppression of reporting from Somalia, regardless of who was doing the suppressing, was central to the shadow war's conduct.

I checked into the Shamo Hotel. The Shamo's jovial manager, Ajoos, doubled as my "fixer"—a sort of combination interpreter, driver, and guide. Ajoos arranged for a squad of government soldiers to protect me during our forays into the city. I paid these impoverished soldiers $10 a day, which they immediately spent on khat, the narcotic leaf they brewed to make addictive tea.

The eldest of the guards was a toothless veteran with the nom de guerre Sleeper. One day he'd come crashing down from an intense khat high and had slept right through a brutal street battle raging all around him. Awakening, he'd looked around at the smoke, wreckage, and dead bodies and concluded he was the last man left alive on earth. Later, his surviving comrades doubled back and retrieved him.

I liked my guards, but I did not trust them. My suspicion was not off base. The August following my trip to Somalia, two freelance reporters and their fixers—Canadian Amanda Lindhout and Australian Nigel Brennan and Somalis Abdifatah Mohammed Elmi, Mahad Isse, and Marwali—would be kidnapped by militants after the Shamo guards gave them up. The Somalis were quickly released, but Lindhout and Brennan would endure 460 days of torture before their families paid a ransom to free them.[18]

I faced my own share of danger in Mogadishu, including narrowly escaping an armed mob that swarmed me, my fixer, and my guards while I conducted a street interview.

The Shamo was situated near Mogadishu's Kilometer Four, a key road juncture that, along with the nearby seaport, airport, and presidential palace, represented what Capt. Paddy Ankunda, the spokesman for the UN peacekeeping force, called the city's "strategic areas."

The roughly 5,000 Ugandan troops had arrived in February and established a defensive perimeter containing all of Ankunda's strategic areas. Furious street fighting had claimed five Ugandans—the first of nearly 150 peacekeepers to die over the next four years.

With Ajoos, I borrowed body armor and a helmet and climbed into the open crew compartment of a white-painted, four-wheeled armored vehicle for a quick tour of Ugandan lines, with the tall, smiling Ankunda as my guide.

We visited a forward position commanded by a startled-looking officer and his sullen gunners. Sweeping his muscular arm across the teeming streets on all sides of the machine-gun nest, Ankunda boasted of the growing numbers of refugees streaming through Ugandan lines, seeking safety from Al Shabab. And why wouldn't the Somalis flock to the peacekeepers, Ankunda asked. "We have the firepower."

We wandered the dilapidated seaport, where crane operators hooked sacks of donated grain and cooking oil from the stinking holds of UN-chartered cargo ships whose crews had braved pirate-infested waters to deliver the lifesaving aid. Trucks would come to whisk the supplies along roads patrolled by peacekeepers out to Afgoye, a refugee town on the outskirts of Mogadishu where the Ethiopian army *and* Al Shabab had both set up checkpoints.

We linked arms with Ugandan soldiers at the hilltop presidential palace—long ago abandoned by the government—and posed for pictures in front of their old Soviet-made tank.

Two years later, during one of many AU offensives, the tank and others like it would crawl through the ruined city streets, mowing down Al Shabab fighters as the insurgents' bullets bounced harmlessly off its steel hull.

Electrified and overwhelmed by my whirlwind tour of the world's most dangerous city, I was looking forward to a day off at the Shamo. When Ajoos told me I had visitors, I almost said, "I'm not here."

Downstairs in the hotel conference room, most of the city's best journalists had assembled. The roster of twenty-five or so media heavyweights included Mohamed Farah Italy, a popular talk-show host for Radio Simba; *New York Times* stringer Mustafa Haji Abdiner; reporter Mohamed Omar Hussein from the popular news website SomaliWeyn; plus Shabelle Radio boss Moqtar Hirabe and Ahmed Tajir, his senior producer and close friend.

The journalists had converged on the Shamo from every quarter of the embattled city, some risking their lives on roads that had become shooting galleries. Others had spent every shilling they had to buy gas or hire drivers. They had come to tell me their stories, in the hope that I might help relay them to the wider world. People did not understand, or appreciate, what was happening in Somalia, they said.

With Hirabe presiding, one by one the journalists recalled years of violence, oppression, and despair. Italy described helming his call-in show on the evening of November 11, 2007. The phone rang. The speaker claimed to be Moqtar Roboow, a spokesman for Al Shabab. "His views were aired that night," Italy said. "The government themselves listened to the interview. And in the morning they stormed the station and forced the radio off the air."

Italy and his director Abdullah Ali were arrested, imprisoned, and interrogated by government agents. Six days into his imprisonment, the leaders of Italy's clan intervened and secured his and Ali's release. But Radio Simba remained shuttered.

Italy's story was typical, though the oppressors varied. Government agents shut down a news agency they accused of colluding with Al Shabab . . . or simply not cooperating closely enough with the government. Defiance invited violence. In September, government armored vehicles had shot up Shabelle Radio's offices during a staff meeting, injuring several people.

Al Shabab and other extremist groups applied pressure from the opposite side, and by shadier means. After Ahmed Tajir refused to broadcast Al Shabab propaganda, he began receiving twice-a-day death threats via text message and phone. Al Shabab was suspected in several killings of journalists, the government and rival clans in others.[19]

The deaths represented a tiny proportion of the tens of thousands of Somalis who had died as a direct result of warfare every year since the early 1990s, but the killing of journalists by both sides in the fighting had a disproportionate effect on the conflict. Threats against reporters shut down the flow of information within and from Somalia.

The effect in the United States was to limit the public's ability to hold the government accountable for its role in the conflict. And while it is unfair to blame media suppression in Somalia directly on Washington, it's undeniable that the U.S. government benefited from reporting blackouts imposed by its proxies in Somalia. In just one chilling example, it was 2010 before anyone reported that U.S.-funded Somali army units had been forcing boys, some as young as twelve, to enlist and fight—a practice that had been going on for years and had helped bolster the waning strength of Somali units.[20]

The Somali journalists stayed at the Shamo for a couple hours. Exiting one by one, they shook my hand and thanked me in advance for telling their stories. Hirabe and Ahmed Tajir, the elder statesmen of this makeshift clan of reporters, lingered longest.

Ahmed Tajir spoke softly. His English was good but his accent was thick. His was a memorable voice. He asked for my phone number and email address. I wrote them on my notebook and tore out the page for him.

It was two years before I heard that voice again. The call came early one morning in 2009 at my home in South Carolina—evening, Somali time. "I am in the hospital," Ahmed Tajir said. "They are trying to kill me."[21]

Al Shabab gunmen had ambushed him and Hirabe as they walked in Bakara Market. Hirabe died, a bullet in his head. Tajir, shot in the hand and stomach, managed to stumble into a nearby building.

He was calling from the hospital. He needed money. He meant to flee to Uganda with his family. For him, the war was over.

Striking Back

On January 7, 2007, a Predator took off from an American base in Africa—all evidence suggests it was Camp Lemonnier in Djibouti. Command of the aircraft was then transferred to a two-person crew, most likely sitting in a trailer in Nevada.

The Predator cruised the roughly five hundred miles to the southern Somali town of Ras Kamboni. Following coordinates provided by Ethiopian intelligence, the Predator used its high-fidelity video camera to track a convoy of vehicles transporting Aden Hashi Farah, one of Somalia's top al Qaeda operatives. Farah had trained in Afghanistan and returned to Somalia, where he led the kidnapping and murder of aid workers.

The Predator was unarmed, possibly to save weight for its long-distance flight. So an AC-130 gunship opened fire, smashing the convoy. Farah was wounded but survived; he would be killed a year later in another U.S. air strike.[22]

While it failed to take out the primary target, the Ras Kamboni raid was the opening shot in a new phase of America's shadow war in Somalia, in which U.S. drones and commandos operated in concert with Washington's proxy armies—first the Ethiopians and later the Ugandan-led AU force.

There were some close calls early on.

While hunting terrorists in the town of Bargal in northern Somalia on June 1, 2007, a small team of U.S. Navy and Air Force commandos ran into stiff opposition from militant gunmen. The Americans were pinned down by gunfire. Fourteen years earlier, a similar situation had resulted in the deaths of eighteen U.S. servicemembers in Mogadishu, but the commandos in 2007 had a few high-tech advantages over their predecessors.

To escape Bargal, the commandos called in some surprising assistance: the U.S. Navy destroyer USS *Chafee* happened to be sailing just a few miles away off the Somali coast. High-explosive shells from *Chafee*'s 5-inch gun covered the commandos' retreat.

Blasting terrorists ashore was not *Chafee*'s only role. The 9,000-ton warship, of the same class as the ill-fated USS *Cole*, was in East African waters in part to fight an entirely different conflict—one that would, over time, fully merge with the land- and air-based shadow war in Somalia.[23]

Chafee was also hunting pirates.

Pirate Land

The hard-line ICU with its harsh sharia law had cracked down on sea bandits based in Somalia's coastal towns. But with Somalia again in turmoil, piracy boomed. In 2008 alone, Somali pirates captured more than forty large vessels in the Gulf of Aden, a shortcut between Asia and Europe via the Suez Canal that is vital to the global economy.[24] Ransoms paid to pirates in 2008 totaled between $18 million and $30 million, making sea banditry Somalia's biggest industry.[25]

While the forty captured ships represented just a fraction of the literally thousands of such vessels transiting the area every year, those few hijacked ships resulted in an economic cost far out of proportion to their number. The cost of insuring commercial cargoes against hijacking swelled by billions of dollars annually—an expense ultimately passed on to consumers. Some shipping lines abandoned the Suez Canal route altogether. The longer sea routes around Africa also meant higher costs for shippers and consumers.

The archipelago nation of the Seychelles reported that its tuna haul was down by a third due to the loss of fishing grounds to pirates.[26] In December 2008, Khalid Shapi, director of a tourism firm in Mombasa, warned that cruise ships were beginning to avoid East Africa owing to piracy, rendering jobless thousands of Kenyan tourism workers.

Jemma Lembere, a logistics manager for the UN World Food Program in Mombasa, said that ship owners were increasingly reluctant to take on UN contracts hauling the food aid that fed half of Somalia's 8 million people. It took the deployment of a European Union naval escort force in late 2008 to persuade the ship's crews to make the dangerous aid run into Mogadishu.

Aboard the small cargo vessel *Semlow*, an old veteran of the Somali humanitarian route that had been hijacked by pirates and held for 110 days back in 2005, workers installed a big red "panic button" in the radio room adjacent to the bridge.

Capt. Edward Kalendero, a mournful fifty-something veteran of the sea, would sail through pirate-infested waters only at night and with his lights extinguished. If he saw suspicious blips on his radar or glimpsed armed boats alongside, all he had to do was mash the panic button and a radio distress signal would go out to the ship's owners in Mombasa, who could then request assistance from the closest armed ship.[27]

By 2008, the number of warships on piracy patrols was on the rise. More than twenty navies sent vessels ranging from aircraft carriers to destroyers to submarines. The United States, the United Kingdom, France, Italy, the Netherlands, Germany, Denmark, Turkey, Greece, Canada, India, Russia, South Korea, Japan, China, Malaysia, Kenya, Iran, and others all sent ships or planes to support them. Some nations worked unilaterally: China, Russia, and Iran, to name a few. Others lumped their vessels under NATO, UN, EU, or U.S. command.[28]

The United States actually maintained several naval task force commands in the Indian Ocean. One, Combined Task Force 151, was solely dedicated to fighting pirates. Another, CTF-150, was a counterterrorism force whose activities were mentioned in the press far less often. Both organizations existed mostly on paper and in Pentagon organizational charts. With a simple declaration, a warship captain could swap one for the other, moving from the light into the shadows and back with a flip of a mental switch.

USS *Chafee*, the destroyer that bombarded Somali militants to cover for American commandos' retreat in 2007, battled pirates one day and terrorists the next, a blurring of missions that, at the time, were highly distinct.

Islamic militants were ideologically motivated. Pirates were in it for the money. In time and under great duress, they would merge. But for years they were very different groups with just two things in common: They were both based on land in Somalia.

And they just happened to find themselves hunted, captured, and killed by the same secretive U.S. forces.

Shooting Gallery

On April 8, 2009, four pirates armed with AK-47s clambered up the side of the U.S.-flagged container ship *Maersk Alabama*, sailing off the coast of Somalia. After a brief scuffle with some of the twenty crewmembers, the pirates abandoned the 508-foot-long ship, sailing off in one of its motorized lifeboats. They may not have captured the *Maersk Alabama*, nor looted its millions of dollars' worth of food and humanitarian aid bound for Kenya, but they didn't leave empty handed. The pirates had a captive: *Maersk Alabama*'s captain, Richard Phillips.

CTF-151's destroyer USS *Bainbridge* was the first to respond to the maydays from *Maersk Alabama*, which bobbed near the pirates in the stolen lifeboat, preventing it from escaping to land. The 9,200-ton-displacement *Bainbridge* had swapped its helicopters and pilots for a catapult-launched Scan Eagle drone plus the robot's operators. It also had a beefed-up intelligence team that included one of the navy's few Somali interpreters.

While technically part of CTF-151, *Bainbridge* had its own unique missions probably falling under CTF-150. "I'll go out on a limb here and guess that the mission had something to do with supporting U.S. Special Ops forces in Somalia," wrote Rear Adm. Terry McKnight, commander of CTF-151 in 2009.

Under the command of Cmdr. Frank Castellano, *Bainbridge* raced toward the *Maersk Alabama* at top speed. In the day it took the destroyer to reach the scene of the attempted hijacking, the crew began collating intelligence from the Scan Eagle and a navy patrol plane flying over the site of the hijacking as well as from reports radioed in by *Maersk Alabama*'s crew. The interpreter added local knowledge, including the fact that pirates often chew narcotic khat leaves to fight seasickness. In this case, "it turned out the pirates had run out of khat," McKnight wrote.

For that reason the bandits were already on edge when *Bainbridge* arrived on the night of April 9, freeing the *Maersk Alabama* to continue to Mombasa. The destroyer "lit up the place" with lights, sirens, and loudspeakers. "They were pissed," Castellano said of the pirates.

The bandits threatened to kill Phillips. In reality, they just wanted to reach shore and ransom the merchant captain, according to McKnight. But if they could not escape the U.S. Navy, the pirates seemed willing to die. Three more U.S. warships were on their way, but Castellano realized he needed more...*specialized* help. "I don't have sniper rifles on the ship," he recalled. According to McKnight, the *Bainbridge* skipper specifically requested Navy SEALs.

Perhaps Castellano was familiar with the naval commandos, having spent part of his deployment supporting them. Simultaneously, the White House determined that the SEAL Team Six, the same unit that would later kill Osama bin Laden, was the best force to handle Phillips's rescue. But those SEALs were located eight thousand miles away in Virginia. So in the meantime, another group of SEALs "working in the Horn of Africa" deployed to the warships. "This group would keep the situation at bay until the Team Six operators dispatched from the United States came in," McKnight recalled.

On April 10 six Team Six SEALs flew from Oceana, Virginia, direct to the Somalia coast. Their U.S. Air Force C-17 cargo plane refueled in the air at least three times during the sixteen-hour flight.

"SEALs are understandably concerned about stealth," McKnight wrote. "That tells me that the operation was planned so that they would parachute into the ocean under cover of darkness, probably a high-altitude low-opening jump so that the pirates weren't alerted."

The log book from the frigate USS *Halyburton*, recently arrived alongside *Bainbridge*, mentioned six SEALs embarking the ship at 2:30 in the morning on April 11, then transferring via a small boat to *Bainbridge*. McKnight says the SEALs brought their own sniper rifles.

At 4:45 that afternoon, President Obama, who had just been

in office for three months, authorized the use of lethal force in Phillips's rescue. Minutes later, the pirates radioed Castellano's interpreter, announcing they were going to start the lifeboat's engine and "make it to shore, no matter what."

On his interpreter's advice, Castellano informed the pirates that they had drifted eighty miles from their own clan's territory. The pirates would need to negotiate with the elders of a rival clan in order to even consider stepping on land. Castellano proposed that the meeting take place at sea and the pirates agreed. Later, they also agreed to let *Bainbridge* take the lifeboat under tow, ostensibly to keep the boat stable as the weather worsened. Sailors hooked a cable to the lifeboat and the destroyer slowly began winching the boat closer. The SEALs were apparently already lying prone on *Bainbridge*'s flight deck, scanning the lifeboat through their rifle scopes.

The tension ratcheted up the next morning, April 12. One of the pirates, only sixteen years old, had been injured scuffling with the *Maersk Alabama*'s crew. He asked to go aboard *Bainbridge* for medical help, effectively giving himself up.

At the same time, another pirate radioed that Phillips needed to see a doctor. A navy corpsman motored over with a change of clothes for the kidnapped captain: blue pants and a bright yellow shirt. "Capt. Phillips didn't figure it out right then, but there were people aboard *Bainbridge* who wanted to make sure that he more or less glowed in the dark," McKnight wrote.

Stressed near the breaking point, on the night of April 12 Phillips wrestled with his captors in a failed escape attempt. In the scuffle, a pirate fired his rifle into the sea. That was enough for the SEALs. The next time all three remaining pirates showed their heads, three SEAL snipers fired one shot each. The destroyer's log book was almost comically succinct. "BAINBRIDGE RETURNED FIRE."

"Each of the three pirates was struck in the head," McKnight wrote.[29]

It's not exactly fair to compare the *Maersk Alabama* incident to the Battle of Mogadishu sixteen years prior. One was a chaotic urban battle in which U.S. forces were outnumbered tens to one, the other a tightly controlled engagement at sea in which the Americans possessed nearly every advantage.

But there were similarities. Both operations took place in or near lawless Somalia, pitting U.S. Special Operations Forces against desperate Somali irregulars.

In that sense, the *Maersk Alabama* rescue represented a sort of redemption for a once-hapless Pentagon. On the Indian Ocean that day in April 2009, a new style of shadowy, high-tech warfare—born in the blood, confusion, and media exposure of Mogadishu more than a decade earlier—proved it could work. That it proved it could work in *Somalia* was no coincidence. The major land wars in Iraq and Afghanistan consumed the lion's share of U.S. military resources and more patience and willpower than most Americans could spare.

With nothing left over for a third large-scale land war, the expanding intervention on land, in the air, and at sea in Somalia could *only* be conducted cheaply, by specialist forces, by proxy, and preferably beyond the media glare.

Rise of the Robots

For nearly fifteen years drones had proven themselves in the Balkans, Afghanistan, the Philippines, Iraq, and, most recently, during the virtuoso rescue of *Maersk Alabama*'s Captain Phillips by U.S. Navy SEALs.

Development and production of new drones was ramping up—and fast. At a cost of $5 billion a year, the Pentagon and CIA were acquiring literally thousands of new UAVs, ranging from hand-thrown Ravens, forty-pound Scan Eagles launched by catapult, upgraded Predators, and new Reapers (enlarged Predator models), plus airliner-size Global Hawks. And that was just counting the unclassified drones. Secret 'bots accounted for billions of dollars more annually in research and acquisition funding.³⁰

Drone operators were getting better at using their high-tech new robots. In November 2009 I flew to Kandahar in southern Afghanistan to see up close the operations of the U.S. Air Force's 62nd Expeditionary Reconnaissance Squadron, the Pentagon's main drone unit for southern Afghanistan. I was greeted by Lt. Col. James Curry, a gregarious former tanker pilot now overseeing scores of contractors and British and American pilots controlling a force of potentially dozens of Predators, Reapers and—unknown to me at the time—top-secret Sentinels. (The exact number of UAVs at Kandahar was classified.)

The 62nd was tasked with launching and landing the drones as well as controlling the robotic aircraft on combat missions within sight of the airfield. As the 'bots flew beyond the horizon, their control passed to operators based in the United States.

Curry had something to show me: a new development in the then nearly fifteen-year history of frontline killer drones. The surprise was not, sadly, the Sentinel. Though repeatedly photographed and widely discussed in the media, the mysterious new drone had not yet been publicly acknowledged by the air force.

The 62nd lived on a remote corner of the NATO-run airfield in a nondescript row of trailers ringed by earthen barriers. Inside one of the trailers on a cool morning during my visit, two flight-suit-clad officers bent over keyboards, flat-screen displays, and control sticks. This was the standard ground control station for the U.S. Air Force's Predator and Reaper drones. The officers represented a typical flight crew of pilot and sensor operator.

What wasn't typical was the display mounted at the pilot's right shoulder. While the screen itself didn't look like much, it was the most visible aspect of an important change in the way the air force used its five-ton Reaper drones.

With the press of a few buttons, a series of images flashed on the screen: grainy, black-and-white snapshots of a road, seen from above. Each shot was slightly different from the one before, as the Reaper producing them flew a course following the road, snapping photos as it went.

Only they weren't really photos. The images were products of the Reaper's Synthetic Aperture Radar (SAR), a sensor that had long been standard equipment on the MQ-9 but until the summer of 2009 was virtually ignored by commanders who preferred sexier full-motion video.

Under Curry's leadership, the 62nd that summer had begun using the SAR to map key portions of Kandahar Province, taking veritable reams of high-resolution radar snapshots that could be dated and placed side by side. Comparing two snapshots from the same location on different days allowed an analyst to do what was called "change detection"—in other words, spotting the differences between two shots to see what changed during the span of time separating the images.[31]

Change detection allowed a high-flying drone to pinpoint even tiny alterations in the landscape. A buried roadside bomb would show up as a patch of disturbed earth. The presence of active insurgent cells could be marked by new gravestones popping up in special, walled-off portions of local cemeteries. A new TV dish on top of an otherwise vacant-seeming remote compound could indicate someone had just moved in . . . and was lying low.

This analytical method was not new, but before 2009 it was usually associated with satellite imagery. In 2004 CNN correspondent Barbara Starr explained how change detection might help the CIA and Pentagon locate Osama bin Laden.

"Satellites are scanning western Pakistan near the Afghan border looking for, perhaps, a newly paved road, cars at a mountain camp, initial tips—not that bin Laden is there, but clues that Al Qaeda may be gathering to plot," Starr said. "It's a trail of bread crumbs that bin Laden and his associates might leave behind."[32]

Five years late Curry was bringing change detection to America's fast-growing drone fleet, boosting the already impressive ability of the robots to spot insurgents and terrorists.

The drones were spreading. Once limited to just one or two conflict zones at a time, by 2009 they were flying over scores of countries on nearly every continent. The Pentagon and CIA stationed drones in Iraq, Afghanistan, Pakistan, Djibouti, the Philippines, Guam, the United Kingdom, and Italy, among other locations.

Many UAV bases were considered top secret, though their existence eventually came to light, sometimes years after they were established.[33] And more UAV detachments were coming on line all the time. In September 2009 the U.S. State Department approached the government of the Seychelles, an archipelago nation of more than a hundred islands a thousand miles off the East African coast, with a delicate proposal.

Chargé d'Affaires Virginia Blaser told Seychelles president James Michel the U.S. Navy would like to station Reaper drones and seventy-seven personnel at the country's main airport.

"The USG wanted to clarify our intent to conduct an array of intelligence, surveillance and reconnaissance activities with these airframes," Blaser stated in her official report, later leaked to the press. "Such activities, would include counter-piracy, counter-terrorism, counter-drug, force protection for African union missions and humanitarian assistance."[34]

Those missions were increasingly one and the same. Al Shabab had been known to run drug and wildlife smuggling operations for profit. Nevertheless, pirates and Islamists had been at odds. The Islamic Courts Union, Al Shabab's former master before its destruction by the Ethiopians, had even declared piracy un-Islamic and had cracked down on pirate safe havens on the Somali coast.

But around the time of Blaser's meeting there had been rumors of Al Shabab forging alliances with pirate groups. Al Shabab got a cut of pirates' ransoms, and, in exchange, the Islamists protected pirate land bases.[35] The rumors would be confirmed eighteen months later, when negotiations between Al Shabab and pirate leaders in the town of Haradhere broke down, and the militant group arrested the pirates. Miffed sea bandits promptly called news service Reuters to complain.[36]

Back in the Seychelles, Blaser told Michel the Reaper drones would be unarmed unless and until the Seychelles government allowed otherwise. "The UAVs originating from Seychelles and flying counter-terrorism mission will not conduct direct attacks," Blaser said she assured the president. She underscored the need for secrecy, especially acute in light of Washington's vow not to build new bases in Africa. "The [chargé d'affaires] stressed the sensitive nature of this counter-terrorism mission and that this not be released outside of the highest [government of Seychelles] channels."

Michel gave his consent to the unarmed deployment, with just one caveat. He wanted the navy to organize a ceremony for Seychelles residents to celebrate the first drone takeoff. "He thought this would go over very well locally," Blaser reported.

The Reapers arrived in late September.[37]

Going Global

In 2007, Landmine Clearance International, the security company started by young Princeton grad Michael Stock, got a new and fancier-sounding name—Bancroft Global Development—and new headquarters in a $4-million mansion on Embassy Row in Washington, D.C. In 2008 Bancroft scored a new client: AMISOM, the seven-thousand-strong African Union peacekeeping force staffed mostly by Ugandans and funded, to the tune of several hundred million dollars a year, by the United States, the UN, and the EU. AMISOM hired Bancroft to provide training for peacekeepers in close combat and bomb disposal. By 2010 Bancroft would be taking in $14 million a year.[38]

It took Bancroft four months and "a lot of lawyers and money" to set up facilities at the AU-controlled seaport-and-airport complex in Mogadishu, according to *SomaliaReport*, an online publication run by adventurer and war correspondent Robert Young Pelton. The new digs would expand to include rooms for rent for $155 a night plus a bar popular with military advisers, journalists, and visiting government officials.

Stock's approach was careful, deliberate. "You better know the rules," he said.[39] After seventeen years of war, those Somali bureaucrats who had survived were a hard and dangerous bunch. There were negotiations, mountains of paperwork, and not a few bribes to be proffered.

To staff its Somalia ops, Bancroft recruited two dozen veteran mercenaries—a mix of Europeans and South Africans. One of them was Richard Rouget, one of Bob Denard's protégés in the Comoros.

After a stint organizing safaris, Rouget had returned to the gun-for-hire business. In 2005, a South African court convicted him of illegally recruiting mercenaries to fight in the West African nation of Ivory Coast.

His fine was just shy of $9,000, but Rouget was evidently broke. He reportedly borrowed some money from a friend and raised some more leading a safari to Mozambique.[40] Clearly badly in need of cash, in 2007 or 2008, it seems, Rouget signed on with Bancroft and flew to Mogadishu.

He was assigned to teach Ugandan troops, long experienced in forest fighting, how to do battle door to door, building to building. Though unarmed, Rouget routinely accompanied his trainees into the dust and clamor of urban fighting.

He told the *New York Times* he relished his work. "Give me some technicals and some savages and I'm happy."[41] Rouget's glee belied the growing threat that the Somalia intervention posed to the U.S. homeland. America's shadow wars were coming home to roost.

III

Backlash

On October 29, 2008, Shirwa Ahmed drove a car full of explosives up to a government compound in Puntland, a region of northern Somalia, and blew himself up.

The blast, apparently orchestrated by Al Shabab, was part of a coordinated attack in two cities that killed more than twenty people. A BBC reporter described body parts flying through the air.

The attackers were "not from Puntland," said Mohamud "Adde" Muse Hersi, the regional leader. Muse couldn't have been more right. For most of his life, the Somali-born Ahmed had lived in Minnesota, where he was more accustomed to frigid winters than to the dry, yellow sands of East Africa.

The twenty-six-year-old former truck driver with the fluffy beard—"as American as apple pie," according to one acquaintance—was the very first American suicide bomber, and a harbinger of a looming crisis. Other American jihadists would return home to the United States after being radicalized overseas. They were blowback from America's shadow war in Somalia—and a major homegrown terror threat.

By all accounts, Ahmed hadn't gone to East Africa to die. His motive was apparently to help Al Shabab defend Somalia against the invading Ethiopian army. "We felt that if we didn't do any- thing, there wouldn't be any Somalia, just the Somali people," said a girl who gave only her first name, Najma. She was friends with Ahmed, she explained, and was scared to give her full name.

After Ahmed sneaked into Somalia in late 2007, potentially scores of other young Minnesotans followed him, many of them aided by al Qaeda and Al Shabab agents based in the United States.[1] The Somali-American community dubbed the recruits "travelers."

The travelers answered a call from Aden Hashi Ayro, one of Al Shabab's founders. "Gain self-respect and dignity by defend- ing your religion and people from non-believers and imperial- ists," Ayro reportedly told his recruits before he was killed in a 2008 U.S. air strike.

No one was sure exactly how many travelers there were. In late 2009 Special Agent E. K. Wilson of the Twin Cities FBI said that nationwide they numbered in the "tens." Omar Jamal, a civil rights advocate in Minneapolis, pegged the number in his city at seventeen or eighteen. Some trusted Somali sources said even the FBI's count was too low. "More than accounted for are there fighting," said one Somali resident of Minneapolis.

By early 2009, new recruits from the United States, Britain, Kenya, and Arab countries accounted for as much as a third of Al Shabab, but even these desperately needed reinforcements were neither fully trained nor fully integrated into the group. Instead, they were treated as cannon fodder, receiving "light training, after having freshly arrived from America, before going to the battlefield," according to Mohamed Omar Hussein, a reporter for SomaliWeyn in Mogadishu who investigated the American travelers. Hussein recalled seeing the bodies of some of the dead travelers on Somali TV.[2]

A few of the travelers sneaked back into the United States, bringing their terrorist training and indoctrination with them to their hometowns—and forcing the FBI and local law enforcement to mobilize an intensive surveillance and tracking effort that was largely unknown outside of the Somali-American community.

"We now must accept and plan for a new dimension: home-grown terrorism, where terrorists are recruited from our domestic population and trained and assisted in attacking Americans in a less organized and decentralized fashion, with dispersed and more frequent attempts to attack," wrote Richard Stanek, the sheriff of Minnesota's Hennepin County. "I write to emphasize this new reality," Stanek continued. "It can and does happen here."[3]

One twenty-two-year-old traveler returned to Minneapolis and went underground to avoid potential reprisal. "He simply didn't like what he saw over there," Jamal said, adding that at least one more traveler joined the man in hiding. Jamal said the FBI had questioned, but not arrested, at least one of the men in hiding.

Authorities nabbed two other returning travelers, however. Abdifatah Yusuf Isse and Salah Osman Ahmed returned to Minnesota in December 2008 and were quickly picked up by the FBI. In July a federal court indicted the two men for "conspiracy to kill, kidnap, maim or injure persons in a foreign country."[4]

Business Models

The flow of U.S. weapons, cash, and expertise into Somalia swelled. In early 2009, the bloodied Ethiopians mostly withdrew from Somalia, leaving AMISOM as the only U.S. proxy in the country and the major recipient of foreign backing. Bancroft's

Mogadishu operation grew in proportion to AMISOM's importance. The company's original two dozen mercenaries roughly doubled in number. Its sandbagged facilities in the embattled city expanded until they formed the main operating base for a host of advisers, journalists, and visiting officials.

Bancroft HQ even included a veterinary clinic for the company's bomb-sniffing dogs that doubled as a wildlife rescue. In the spring of 2011 Somali officials confiscated two rare Berbera lion cubs from animal smugglers and, lacking adequate facilities of their own, gave them to Bancroft to care for until the cubs could be placed in an institution overseas.[5]

The Bancroft buildings in Mogadishu were not far from the CIA's own base, adjacent to the international airport, where the agency trained Somali spies and from where U.S. agents helped oversee a windowless detention facility in the basement of the headquarters of the Somalia intelligence service.[6]

"We do not want an American footprint or boot on the ground," said Johnnie Carson, the State Department's top official for Africa. What he meant was that the administration didn't want an official, *acknowledged*, government presence. But American spooks and American mercenary companies were more than welcome—and indeed were vital to the escalating shadow war in Somalia.[7]

Washington never acknowledged its CIA base in Somalia, and it probably would have preferred to keep the mercenary forces under wraps, too. But Stock, the Bancroft boss, said he didn't like the CIA's "business model," presumably meaning its secrecy. Unusually for the head of a private army, Stock welcomed attention. He started by telling reporters that his men were not mercenaries, by his definition. "Mercenary activity is antithetical to the fundamental purposes for which Bancroft exists," Stock said. Bancroft "does not engage in covert, clandestine or otherwise secret activities," he added.[8]

Bancroft was focused on "capacity-building," Stock said, borrowing from the figurative nongovernmental organization (NGO)

handbook. But where most NGOs were strictly peaceful enti-
ties, Bancroft was a bastion of grizzled old warriors performing
a timeless military task: teaching young soldiers how to fight.

In another sense, Stock wasn't wrong. The knowledge and
experience of U.S.-paid mercenaries like Rouget was one of
AMISOM's most important advantages over Al Shabab, with its
unruly mix of clan militias, fiery jihadists, and impressed child
soldiers. Bancroft certainly did expand the peacekeepers' capacity . . . for warfare.

Working closely with the Ugandan and Burundian troops,
Rouget and the other Bancroft mentors helped "turn a bush army
into an urban fighting force," one adviser told Jeffrey Gettleman
of the *New York Times*. Bancroft's bomb disposal experts were
credited for the drastic reduction in African Union troops lost
to roadside explosives. The photos accompanying Gettleman's
reporting depicted the "husky" fifty-one-year-old Rouget accompanying Ugandan soldiers onto a Mogadishu rooftop to observe
a gunfight between peacekeepers and Al Shabab troops.

Rouget did not carry a weapon, but that didn't mean he wasn't
in the thick of the fighting. In 2010 he was wounded in the thigh by
shrapnel. Rouget's Bancroft colleagues faced similar dangers. In
the summer of 2011 Al Shabab fighters shot a Bancroft employee
in the stomach.

The very next day, Al Shabab gunmen wearing stolen government uniforms attacked a Ugandan bomb-disposal team while
a Bancroft adviser was instructing them. The gunmen shot and
killed six Ugandans and a demining contractor and wounded four
more Ugandans plus the Bancroft man. Weeks later, a reporter
saw bloodstains on the floor of a house where the injured Bancroft employee had dragged himself for cover.[9]

Accidents were another danger. In 2009, longtime dog of war
Duncan Rykaart, whose ties stetched all the way back to pioneer-
ing mercenary firm Executive Outcomes, died in a plane crash
while working for Bancroft.

The casualties did not deter Bancroft. By late 2011 the Bancroft-trained African Union peacekeeping force in Mogadishu was nine thousand strong and doubled as the heavy army of the U.S.-backed Somali Transitional Federal Government in its long war against Al Shabab. That fall, the AMISOM and Somali troops pushed Al Shabab out of Mogadishu, apparently for good. The company did all of this on the U.S. taxpayers' dime. Among other U.S. funding, Washington agreed to reimburse Uganda and Burundi for the $7 million the two countries paid Bancroft for counterinsurgency training in 2010 and 2011.[10]

The circuitous funding lent U.S officials a measure of cover. The United States were at war in Somalia, but every battle was waged through a proxy, and every relationship could be denied or explained away.

Proxy Problems

There was other blowback. Besides inspiring potentially scores of Americans to join a terrorist group, the U.S. proxy war in Somalia was self-defeating in other ways. For one, the very people Washington paid to fight its war in East Africa were largely responsible for arming America's enemies in the region, potentially prolonging the conflict.

An internal UN report obtained by Robert Young Pelton's *SomaliaReport* revealed that as much as a third of the Al Shabab weaponry captured by AMISOM was originally provided to AMISOM by the United States and other donors. It wasn't hard to see why. A Ugandan or Burundian peacekeeper in Somalia was paid only $550 a month by the AU for risking death on a daily basis. Poor accounting procedures meant a soldier could go months at a time between paychecks, exacerbating conditions that were already austere.

"AMISOM soldiers put up a brave face but their daily rations and grim existence is brightened only by the occasional soda, snack or comfort sold to the Ugandans and Burundians by enterprising Somali women," Pelton wrote. "That money comes from the sale of ammunition to intermediaries who then sell it to Al Shabab."[11]

The sale of U.S.-supplied arms to Al Shabab was not decisive: even with the American weaponry, Al Shabab was outgunned by the U.S. proxy forces in Somalia. But the hijacking of U.S. logistical support by America's own clients was indicative of the risks inherent in paying another country to fight your war.

Proxies can have their own agendas.

The Peacekeeping Age

The stand-up of the UN-sponsored AMISOM was part of a massive expansion of peace operations worldwide. The explosive growth of peacekeeping that began in 2000 continued essentially unabated for more than a decade. The UN deployed 50,000 peacekeepers in 2001, 70,000 in 2005, and crossed the 100,000 threshold in 2009. Among others, AU and EU missions in Somalia and Chad, respectively, added tens of thousands to the total.

The peacekeepers were better funded (to the tune of $9 billion annually), more heavily armed, and operated under looser rules of engagement than ever before—a conscious reaction to the experiences of the previous decade. "Many lessons were learnt from the serious failures of the mid-1990s in Somalia, Rwanda and Bosnia," UN peacekeeping chief Alain Le Roy said in 2009.[12]

The new generation of blue helmets fought and died: more than a hundred were killed in 2009. Their greater numbers and new assertiveness contributed to the continuing reduction in world battle deaths. That's no mere conjecture. According to Simon Fraser University's Human Security Report Project, conflicts that ended in peace agreement, which often meant a post-war peacekeeping presence, resulted in the fewest number of post-peace deaths compared to other means of resolving conflict, such as a cease-fire or a battlefield victory.

In 2009, battle deaths from state-based fighting in which at least one warring party was a government remained at its historic low of fewer than 40,000 people.[13]

Fatalities in irregular warfare pitting only nonstate groups against each other—that is, civil wars with no outside intervention—totaled around 3,500 for the year, a slight increase over 2008 but half the death toll in 2002 and a third of that in 1993.[14] Civil wars with foreign intervention claimed just over 2,000 people that year—again, a small increase over the years immediately before, but a massive drop compared to the 1997 peak, which saw 8,000 killed.[15] Slowly and erratically, the world was becoming more peaceful.

And the coming end of the era of U.S.-led wars would only accelerate the overall move toward peace. For as Simon Fraser University's study group found, conflicts featuring outside intervention other than peacekeeping tended to be twice as bloody as those civil wars that were left alone.

American-led *military* interventions, whether direct or through a proxy, tended to boost the death toll, whereas UN-approved international *peacekeeping* operations usually had the effect of decreasing the bloodshed. In other words, if it was a more peaceful world Washington wanted, it was better to back peacekeepers than to prop up some regional power in an invasion of a troubled neighboring state.

Warts and all, peacekeeping was, in the balance, working. It should come as no surprise, then, that the United States was becoming more likely to intervene in a conflict through, or at least alongside, the UN or another world body.

A Reaper drone and one of the contractors who helps maintain it in Kandahar, Afghanistan, in 2009.

A drone sensor operator from the 62nd Expeditionary Reconnaissance Squadron, in Kandahar, Afghanistan, in 2009.

Capt. Edward Kalendero of the merchant ship *Semlow* in Mombasa, Kenya, in 2008. *Semlow* had been hijacked by pirates and released.

Irish peacekeepers in a sandstorm near Iriba, Chad, in 2008.

Congolese soldiers learning combat techniques in a class taught
by American troops in Kinshasa, Congo, in 2010.

U.S. and Romanian Special Forces training Afghan police in Laghman
Province, Afghanistan, in 2012.

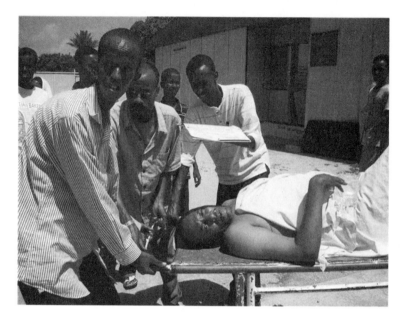

Ahmed Tajir is rushed to Medina hospital in Mogadishu following his
shooting by Al Shabab gunmen in 2009.

The author, at right, embedded with British troops in southern Iraq in 2006.

More Harm Than Good?

But the UN, EU, AU, and other peacekeeping organizations walked a fine line between making peace and prolonging conflict. In June 2008 I went to Chad to find out if the new 1,200-strong EU peacekeeping force really was helping suppress the decades-long proxy war between Chad and Sudan, a conflict that encompassed the Darfur genocide. That's where I spent one hot night dodging bullets during a chaotic street battle with no clear cause or sides.

With my photographer Anne, I also traveled to the Iridimi refugee camp in eastern Chad near the border with Sudan. With some 18,000 refugees, Iridimi was one of a dozen large UN-administered camps that had housed around 250,000 Darfuri refugees since 2004. I sat with refugee Hawa Mamhat Dijme in her earthen hut and, through my interpreter, posed a question: "Where is your husband?"

On the day of my visit, Dijme's clan was all in attendance, her three children and her grown niece and sister and their own children—around a dozen in all—but no men. So where was her husband—or for that matter, any of the women's husbands? It might have seemed an impertinent question for a Western journalist visiting remote, conservative Central Africa, but it was also an important one.

The United States had sent $600 million to feed, clothe, and protect Darfuri refugees fleeing the civil war in their native Sudan, and many millions more to prop up the breakaway region of South Sudan, America's proxy in the conflict. European agencies and donors also had ponied up hundreds of millions of dollars. Food aid alone for Darfuri refugees totaled $240 million in 2007.

The UN was saying that the war showed no signs of ending and more aid would be needed.

Never mind America's risky support for South Sudan. Based on my conversations with sources at Iridimi and elsewhere in Chad, it also seemed possible that the largely Western-funded peacekeeping and humanitarian effort meant to "save Darfur" might actually be prolonging the conflict by providing a safe haven in Chad for the rebel groups fighting Khartoum and its Janjaweed militia proxies.

I asked Dijme about her husband because I'd been told that many Darfuri men living in the UN's refugee camps actually spent most of their in time Sudan. Some were just working or tending their herds, but others returned frequently to Darfur to fight. For the latter, the refugee camps and the growing international force whose job it is to protect the camps—the EU peacekeepers in Chad and a UN force across the border in Sudan—were a godsend.

Rebel fighters could charge into battle knowing their families were safe, well-fed, looked after by Western doctors, and guarded by a mixed brigade of French, Swedish, Polish, and Irish troops called EUFOR. And the surviving combatants could return to these safe havens to rest and reinforce their ranks through the forced enlistment of other refugees, including young boys.

"He's in Sudan working," Dijme told me. Just minutes later, she changed her mind. "He's here in the camp," she said. I never got a straight answer. But then, I never expected one from a woman whose family may have been directly involved in the Chad-Sudan conflict.

Next I visited Serge Malé, the Chad-based representative of the UN High Commissioner for Refugees (UNHCR), in his air-conditioned office in the capital of N'Djamena, in western Chad. Malé smoked a cigarette, then sat on a soft leather sofa to discuss the camps. "I don't say there are not any problems," he said. "There are some problems. But there are not very many problems.

"About the non-respect of civilian and nonmilitary nature of the camps," he continued, using UN code for rebel activity, "especially as this is linked to the recruitment of people [either] enforced or even voluntary—it is completely unacceptable to UNHCR. [But] it has happened, it continues to happen, and it will continue to happen." U.N efforts to "educate" the camp population against recruitment "proved to be insufficient," he said.

One of the roots of the problem was also the solution, Malé said. EUFOR, the very force that possibly facilitated the rebel presence inside the refugee camps, could also help the UN to reform the camp. "Our expectation and hope now is that with the deployment of EUFOR ... we will have more capacity to give more sustainable, more reliable solutions to this kind of problem."

In other words, the security that EUFOR provided would hopefully allow the UN to redouble its efforts to break the rebels' hold on the camps. "But we know," Malé said, "we can do more harm than good."[16]

Army of God

Some conflicts threatened to overwhelm even the largest, most lavishly funded peacekeeping forces, and none more so than the overlapping rebellions, proxy wars, and terror campaigns in the Democratic Republic of Congo.

In February 2006, rebels from the Lord's Resistance Army (LRA) descended on Duru, a farming community of five thousand in eastern Congo. The LRA had its roots in a bloody civil war in Uganda in the 1980s and 1990s. Chased out of their home country, the pseudoreligious LRA spent a few years as a proxy of Sudanese president Omar al-Bashir before international pressure ended that arrangement and the LRA fled south into the thick, roadless forests of northeastern Congo and southern Central African Republic.

In Duru the LRA, commanded by charismatic madman Joseph Kony, raided a few outlying farms, taking what they could carry and leaving behind several traumatized women.

A month later, the Forces Armées de la République Démocratique du Congo, or FARDC—the Congolese army—arrived to "protect" the town from LRA attacks. That's when the real trouble started. As they often do when they garrison in a new town, the Congolese soldiers began raping Duru's women and girls.

The Congolese army arrived ostensibly to defend the parish against the LRA but, in fact, ended up out-pillaging and out-raping the rebels, without even making an effort to protect the town from other threats. "The LRA was only a danger when they passed through, but with the FARDC, it was the same story every day," local priest Ferruccio Gobbi recalled. "They raped, they stole, and when they saw the LRA, they ran away."

After they'd taken all they wanted, the FARDC moved on, leaving Duru wide open to rebel attack. The LRA returned in September 2008, burning, killing, and kidnapping across a wide swath of Duru. Most of the town's residents grabbed what they could carry and fled. Hundreds died. Hundreds more were taken. Thousands stumbled into neighboring towns penniless, exhausted, and traumatized.

Fidel Mboligikpele, a teacher in Duru, lost his entire school that day: seventy students, kidnapped by the LRA. Along with hundreds of his neighbors, he headed toward Dungu, a town forty miles away. "On the road, we saw the bodies of our friends, our parents, our kids," he says. In a Dungu refugee camp, Mboligikpele organized a makeshift school for Duru survivors. He managed to enroll 103 boys, but only 68 girls. I flew to Dungu in October 2010 to interview Mboligikpele and other attack survivors. The teacher grimaced when I asked him why there are so few girls. Most were still enslaved by the LRA, he said.

It was just another episode in Congo's long history of mass sexual violence. The army and police, rebel groups such as the LRA, and, increasingly, private citizens, committed tens of thousands of violent rapes every year—though in fact, no one knew the exact number, as most victims could not or would not seek treatment or justice from Congo's dilapidated hospitals and corrupt courts.

Congo was the "rape capital of the world," according to the United Nations. The problem had gotten so bad that it could result in the ground-up "reversal of a society's norms and values," according to a report from Harvard University and the aid group Oxfam International.[17] Infuriatingly, this mass sexual violence took place under the noses of twenty thousand UN peacekeepers, together amounting to the world body's largest troop deployment. For all its size relative to other peacekeeping contingents, the Mission de l'Organisation de Nations Unies en République Démocratique du Congo, or MONUC, was still too small.

Roughly the size of Western Europe, with an exploding population of no fewer than 70 million people and a battleground for dozens of rebel groups, Congo practicaly swallowed MONUC. And when the LRA went on its bloody rampage in 2008, "MONUC peacekeepers were too few and too ill-equipped to assist civilians who came under attack," according to Human Rights Watch.[18]

It wasn't until mid-January 2009—four months after the LRA assault—that peacekeepers and UN relief workers were able to organize a mission to Duru, traveling ten days by road from Goma, the regional administrative center. The UN high commissioner for refugees reported finding Duru "deserted and overgrown with vegetation." Surviving residents were "traumatized and in urgent need of assistance." In the following months, the UN built an outpost in Duru, supplied by helicopter. As a sense of security returned to Duru, so did many displaced residents.[19]

Congo isn't just some jungle backwater. It shares borders with ten other countries. And underneath its tropical forests lie substantial reserves of uranium, tungsten, tin, tantalum, gold, and other valuable minerals. Even to the most cynical of world leaders, Congo mattered. It mattered to the United States despite the distraction of America's wars in Iraq, Afghanistan, Somalia, the Philippines, and other, lesser known places.

U.S. Secretary of State Hillary Clinton first visited Congo in an official capacity in August 2009, as part of a seven-nation African tour. Her goal in Congo, she said on arrival in Kinshasa, was to pressure President Joseph Kabila to prosecute those responsible for the country's epidemic of sexual violence. "It is no longer acceptable for there to be violence against women in the home, in the community," Clinton said.

The day after her sit-down with Kabila, Clinton flew to Goma, where she spoke with a woman who had been gang-raped while eight months pregnant. The fetus died. The woman only survived because someone stuffed grass into her wounds to staunch the bleeding. Leaving Goma, Clinton was visibly shaken. "I was just overwhelmed by what I saw," she said. "It is almost impossible to describe the level of suffering."

Clinton left Congo determined to do something to help. During the trip she had unveiled a $17-million plan to build health clinics. The clinics plan was a cover for a far more serious *military* effort. Clinton quietly arranged to send American soldiers to work alongside the Congolese military. "We feel that assistance in security-sector development will help support our foreign-policy goals," said Marc Dillard, a State Department spokesperson in Kinshasa.[20]

Congo was about to become the latest front in America's shadow wars, and the Congolese army and the weak MONUC its latest, and possibly most difficult, proxies.

8

The American Way of War

The U.S.-led training began in Kinshasa in December 2009 with a small contingent of FARDC officers. The idea was to create a new battalion around a core of officers steeped in human rights and international law, without disbanding the entire army—a major flaw in American security-reform efforts in Iraq.

In February, the training shifted to a base in Kisangani, in central Congo. There, the American instructors focused their attention on the new battalion's rank and file. Much of the training was in such traditional military tasks as shooting, patrolling, and communications.

The soldiers also got agricultural training and a lot of the same human rights instruction as the officers. Lessons in farming and fishing were supposed to ensure that the model battalion would never need to pillage civilian farms for its own survival.

The human rights curriculum was oriented toward preventing sexual violence.

Rape prevention was a tricky subject for the American instructors. "That's something that we didn't know how to do. We don't have those textbooks," one officer told *Stars and Stripes*. Indeed, the American military itself has long been marred by a rate of sexual assault twice that of the civilian population. But as a curriculum for foreign students, rape prevention was new to the American trainers.[1]

The command, based in Germany, was taking the sexual violence in Congo seriously. Using information gathered on the ground, U.S. Command Africa developed an anti-sexual violence program to integrate into the training of forces in the Congo. A third of the battalion also received training in how to be an instructor—"training the trainer," the U.S. Army called it.

While the model battalion would ideally set an example of how the rest of the FARDC should behave, the instructors were meant to fan out across the Congolese military to deliberately seed other units. "Hopefully, that's a platform from which additional training of Congolese troops can be done by very well-trained Congolese troops," U.S. ambassador to the DRC William Garvelink said.[2]

As the commandos in Kisangani were wrapping up their courses, a fresh contingent of American troops flew into Kinshasa. I went to Congo to observe them.

The roughly one hundred medics and doctors from the North Dakota National Guard spent two weeks working to improve a FARDC medical unit. The "final exam" was a free health clinic, supervised by the Americans, where Congolese medics, doctors, and dentists conducted physicals, pulled rotten teeth, and handed out medicine to some two thousand Kinshasa residents.[3]

The U.S. presence in Congo, utterly unknown to all but a handful of Americans, was rapidly expanding. But the biggest developments were yet to come.

Get Kony

Years of determined lobbying by international aid groups led to the passage, in May 2010, of a law requiring the United States to formulate a comprehensive strategy for beating the LRA. The U.S. approach so far had been too scattered, too soft. Unsurprisingly, the new strategy borrowed pages from the shadow war playbook presently seeing heavy use in Somalia, the Philippines, and other conflict zones.

In October 2010 the White House announced the deployment of a hundred Army Special Forces to Congo. "These forces will act as advisers to partner forces that have the goal of removing from the battlefield Joseph Kony and other senior leadership of the LRA," President Barack Obama said.

These "partner forces" would include the UN peacekeepers, the Congolese FARDC, plus the armies of Uganda, Central African Republic, and South Sudan—the latter a major beneficiary of covert U.S. military support as it continued the uneasy process of breaking away from genocidal Sudan.

The U.S. advisers began deploying the same week as the announcement. "Although the U.S. forces are combat-equipped, they will only be providing information, advice and assistance to partner nation forces," Obama said. "They will not themselves engage LRA forces unless necessary for self-defense."[4]

Still, any effort against the LRA posed serious risks. Previous operations targeting Kony had all ended badly. In 2006, Guatemalan commandos trained by the United States trekked deep into the Congolese forest to attack an LRA encampment. Kony was away, but his fighters were there in strength. In the ensuing firefight, LRA troops wiped out the entire eight-man commando force and beheaded the commander.

Three years later, a small team of advisers from U.S. Africa Command helped the Ugandan army plan a complex raid on LRA camps, codenamed Operation Lightning Thunder. But the

Ugandan air and ground forces failed to coordinate their attacks. Aircraft arrived overhead before the ground troops, giving the rebels advance notice of the coming assault. The enraged LRA fighters fanned out, killing more than six hundred civilians in nearby villages as they fled deeper into the forest.[5]

This time promised to be different. With U.S. Special Forces permanently assigned to military camps in Congo and neighboring South Sudan, Central African Republic, and Uganda, American assistance would be sustained and widespread.

Plus, they would be bringing drones.

Proliferation

In late 2010 or early 2011 at Arba Minch, Ethiopia, a fruit-growing community of 93,000 on the western side of the Great Rift Valley, U.S. contractors began laying concrete and erecting hangars on a lot adjacent to the town's modest airport. Civilians flying into and out of the airport on the occasional commercial flight knew early on what it took another year or so for the rest of the world to discover: America was building a drone base in Ethiopia, putting military and CIA drones within range of a host of new battlegrounds, including Congo.

Work was still underway when, in early 2011, U.S. Air Force personnel arrived with a detachment of Reaper drones.[6] The Reapers immediately began flying missions over Somalia. But they were also "well placed" for patrols over Congo, according to Bill Roggio of *Long War Journal*.[7]

The Arba Minch drone base was part of a second batch of new overseas facilities for American UAVs, coming behind older bases—some now shuttered—in Albania, Uzbekistan, Afghanistan, Pakistan, the Philippines, Qatar, Iraq, Djibouti, the Seychelles, the United Kingdom, and Italy.

Sometime after November 2010, the United States initiated

construction on one of its most impressive new drone bases. The three-airstrip facility in the desert of southern Saudi Arabia was remarkable not for its size, but for its sheer remoteness.

"It's way, way out in the Rub al Khali, otherwise known as Hell, and must have been built, at least initially, with stuff flown into Sharorah and then trucked more than 400 kilometers up the existing highway and newly-built road," a former intelligence official told Noah Shachtman of *Wired*. "It's a really major logistics feat. The way it fits inconspicuously into the terrain is also admirable."[8]

While drones based in Djibouti were capable of striking Yemen, and had done so on many occasions, flying them from Saudi Arabia put the 'bots much closer to their targets, reducing the time between tips from informants or electronic eavesdroppers and the moment a missile-armed UAV arrived overhead. There were more than enough robots to go around: a stark improvement over the shortage of drones that had plagued military and CIA efforts from the 1990s all the way through the Iraq War.

In late 2009 the air force maintained 37 round-the-clock Predator and Reaper "orbits," each orbit populated by 3 or 4 drones. Two years later the U.S. military alone—never mind the CIA—possessed 678 medium or large drones of 18 different types, plus literally *thousands* of small, hand-thrown models.[9]

Drones came and went at Camp Lemonnier on a temporary basis between 2002 and 2010. In 2010, the Pentagon made the drone presence at Lemonnier full-time, with eight Predators permanently assigned. In September 2011, a Djibouti-based Predator took out Anwar al-Awlaki, an American-born cleric and top al Qaeda member. Al-Awlaki's killing would eventually spark a minor crisis in the United States as Washington sought to further expand its global drone campaign.[10]

Alongside the drones, fighters, and other warplanes, Camp Lemonnier hosted three hundred commandos and Special Operations Command support staff, including a man known as Frog, whose job it was to tell air force crews to launch drones on commando-support missions.

"Who is Frog?" an air force official asked while investigating a drone crash at Camp Lemonnier.

"He's a Pred guy," an airman responded. "I actually don't know his last name."

SOCOM wanted to boost its force in Djibouti to 1,100, making it one of America's biggest concentrations of Special Operations Forces, but Camp Lemonnier was already too crowded. The base shared its sole runway with Djibouti's only international airport. Every day the military and CIA launched sixteen drones and four fighters, according to an August 2012 memo from Deputy Defense Secretary Ashton Carter to Congress that was obtained by the *Washington Post*.

The base also launched an unspecified number of fighter-bombers, transports, patrol planes, and manned surveillance aircraft, for a total of 1,666 military takeoffs in July 2012, compared to 768 in one month two years earlier. Carter warned that the pace of activity would only increase.

In September 2012 the Pentagon spent $62 million on a taxiway expansion at Camp Lemonnier, $7 million to improve air traffic control, and an undisclosed quantity to build an emergency landing strip out in the desert.

But even that wasn't enough. In August 2012 the Pentagon presented Congress with a $1.4-billion plan to massively expand the base's aircraft parking and living facilities.

"This is not an outpost in the middle of nowhere that is of marginal interest," Amanda J. Dory, the Pentagon's deputy assistant secretary for Africa, told the *Post*. "This is a very important location in terms of U.S. interests, in terms of freedom of navigation, when it comes to power projection."[11]

American agents, commandos, or contractors in Mogadishu—it's not clear who, exactly—received an unknown number of five-pound, hand-launched Ravens from manufacturer Aero-

Vironment. The simple, camera-equipped Ravens were ideal for short-range surveillance flights during the urban battles aimed at liberating Mogadishu from militants. In 2011 Washington approved a $45-million package of arms and training to Ugandan peacekeepers in the city that included another four Ravens.[12]

Navy ships sailing off the Somali coast began carrying catapult-launched Scan Eagles as well as vertical-takeoff Fire Scout robo-copters. The Fire Scouts initially helped in navy counterpiracy efforts but by 2011 had shifted to "overland intelligence, surveillance, reconnaissance . . . for Special Operations Forces," according to the navy.[13]

The sailing branch also deployed one of its five RQ-4 Global Hawks—Northrop-built spy drones with the wingspan of a 737 airliner—to an unspecified Indian Ocean base to, among other duties, provide air cover for the 5th Fleet off the Somali coast. And although unmentioned in press reports, air force Global Hawks were also theoretically available for Somalia patrols from their forward base in the United Arab Emirates.

There were so many American UAVs buzzing over so many battlefields that they actually posed a significant danger to airliners and other manned planes, plus people and infrastructure below in the event they crashed. The UN Monitoring Group on Somalia and Eritrea warned about the danger drones posed to "AMISOM air operations and to aviation safety in general."[14]

The group said it tracked sixty-four unidentified military aircraft over Somalia, including drones, in just the eleven months between June 2011 and April 2012. There were many more flights before those dates—and others during that time period that UN observers did not see.[15]

As in the Philippines, UAV crashes in Somalia offered some clues as to the intensity of robot operations. In March 2008, what appeared to be a ship-launched UAV tumbled into the sea near Merka, then a contested town in militant-controlled southern Somalia.

"It's small and can be carried by three people," local government official Mohamed Mohamoud Helmi said of the winged object his people dragged from the water. The description roughly matched that of the navy's forty-pound Scan Eagle.[16]

On May 13, 2009, a Predator was destroyed following an incident at what air force investigators described as a "forward operating location." It probably wasn't Iraq or Afghanistan, as those countries were usually named in crash reports. Nor was the location likely to be Pakistan, as drones there generally belonged to the CIA and were rarely mentioned, even in official reports. By process of elimination, the 2009 crash was probably in East Africa.[17]

In 2011, Predators crashed near Djibouti's Camp Lemonnier on January 14, March 15, May 7, and May 17.[18] A Reaper struck the ground in the Seychelles on December 13, 2011, and another crash-landed on the archipelago nation on April 4, 2012.[19] Unidentified drones, possibly hand-launched Ravens, crashed in Mogadishu on August 19, 2011,[20] and February 3, 2012.[21]

Twice drones nearly caused serious accidents in Mogadishu. On November 13, 2011, a Raven flew over a UN fuel depot, alarming personnel on the ground who feared a crash might spark a devastating fire. And on January 9 a chartered airliner carrying Ugandan peacekeepers "almost collided with a UAV" on takeoff from Mogadishu's international airport.[22]

While most of the flying robots were not armed, those that were inflicted a shocking death toll on suspected militants. Covert U.S. strikes in Pakistan, Yemen, and Somalia between 2002 and 2013—most of them drone attacks—killed as many as 3,200 people, including known and suspected insurgents and terrorists and potentially hundreds of innocent bystanders.[23] UAV strikes in Iraq, Afghanistan, the Philippines, and other conflict zones resulted in thousands more deaths.[24]

"Very frankly, it's the only game in town in terms of confronting or trying to disrupt the Al Qaeda leadership," CIA Director Leon Panetta said in 2009, referring to drone attacks.[25]

But the drone wars were only beginning. New models, methods, and policies—and America's shriveling appetite for manpower-intensive warfare after years of costly occupations in Iraq and Afghanistan—combined to escalate robotic warfare even further.

Into the Light

With the flurry of surreptitiously snapped photos and the air force's subsequent confirmation, in mid-December 2009 the stealthy Sentinel drone, derived from the ill-fated Dark Star prototype, was now out of the bag.

The implications were enormous. When the Pentagon oversaw the initial development of the Predator, the larger Global Hawk, and the Dark Star, it ranked the three vehicles by order of vulnerability. Owing to its slow speed, low altitude ceiling, and lack of defensive systems, "the Predator is the most vulnerable of the three platforms to hostile threats," the Defense Department concluded.[26] Sure enough, the Serbs and Iraqis between them had shot down several Predators, even shooting one up with a machine gun fired through the open window of a helicopter cruising alongside the drone.

The high-flying Global Hawk was considered better protected than the Predator but still vulnerable to the best surface-to-air missiles. Only the Dark Star, with its high ceiling, jet power, and radar-evading qualities, would be able to "accomplish a penetration surveillance and reconnaissance mission in an integrated air defense system environment," the Pentagon asserted.[27]

Prior to December 2009 only the Predator and Global Hawk were known to be in service, meaning the acknowledged extent of U.S. military and, by extension, CIA drone ops was necessarily limited. The Americans' robots could only probe the least-defended airspace. Countries like Iran and North Korea were most likely off limits. A Global Hawk or Predator could only surveil around those countries, not directly over them.

In one fell swoop, the Sentinel's debut altered this understanding of the U.S. government's reach. Where once large swaths of the world appeared to be off limits to the Pentagon and CIA's probing eyes and deadly missiles, with the Sentinel's appearance it was clear no country was truly and completely drone-proof. At the moment the Sentinel entered service, sometime before 2003, the Americans possessed the ability to spy on, and in theory strike, targets anywhere in the world.

Within days of the air force confirming the Sentinel's existence, a South Korean newspaper reported that the stealthy 'bot was being deployed to the Korean peninsula to spy on the North.[28] And in the hours after Osama bin Laden was killed by U.S. Navy SEALs in his compound in Abbottabad, Pakistan, the *National Journal*'s Marc Ambinder got a tip on the Sentinel's involvement in that mission. "RQ-170 drone overhead," Ambinder wrote on his Twitter microblog.[29]

Seven months later, on December 4, Iranian state media reported that the country's army had forced down an American drone inside its airspace. The accompanying photos and video left no doubt: the Iranians had captured a partially wrecked Sentinel that had somehow malfunctioned, probably while overflying Iranian airspace that was defended by overlapping radars, surface-to-air missiles, and jet fighters.

The capture belied a chilling reality for America's enemies. U.S. drones—one model, at least—could now be anywhere and everywhere Washington wanted to watch and listen.

With caveats.

Hacked

Iran's "acquisition" of the high-tech Sentinel reflected worrying vulnerabilities in America's drone fleet. In the rush to develop and deploy Predators and other drones, the Pentagon had knowingly skimped on certain protections for the 'bots' control and data links.

"Depending on the theater of operation and hostile electronic combat systems present, the threat to the UAVs could range from negligible with only a potential of signal intercept for detection purpose, to an active jamming effort made against an operating, unencrypted UAV," the air force admitted in a 1996 report. "The link characteristics of the baseline Predator system could be vulnerable to corruption of down links data or hostile data insertions."[30]

For many years the air force's Predators and Reapers lacked any encryption, meaning a determined foe could potentially hijack a drone's sensor feed and GPS link. In 2002, a British engineer using commercial hardware and software had been able to intercept the video feeds from U.S. drones patrolling Kosovo.[31] In 2008 U.S. troops in Iraq confiscated from a Shi'ite extremist a laptop computer containing videos apparently intercepted from Predator drones.

Some encryption was added piecemeal, but comprehensive data protection had to wait for an upgraded robot with adequate capacity and electrical generation to handle the code-applying crypto boxes.[32]

Loose sensor data was bad. Hackable drones were worse. During an exercise with the U.S. Department of Homeland Security in the summer 2012, University of Texas–Austin professor Todd Humphreys and a team of graduate students were able to alter the GPS signal to a civilian drone and change the robot's course—even ordering it to land. "You can think of this as hijacking a plane from a distance," Humphreys said.[33]

During the crashed stealth drone fiasco the previous December, Iranian officials claimed they performed a similar trick with the air force Sentinel spy drone that had been lost over the Afghanistan-Iran border and captured by Tehran. The officials said they interfered with the Sentinel's navigational link and ordered it to crash land. U.S. sources disputed the claim, saying the Sentinel had redundant GPS systems that were not easily hacked.

In any event, the GPS was a separate system from the video feed: hijacking one did not imply control of the other. Still, apparent vulnerabilities with both systems helped explain the air force's lingering reservations about the bulk of its unmanned aircraft fleet. "At least for the near term, the remotely piloted aircraft capability is not for contested air space," former U.S. Air Force chief of staff Gen. Norton Schwartz said. "It is a benign airspace capability."[34]

Fortunately, the large majority of America's shadow battle-grounds were fairly benign, as far as drones were concerned. The United States could safely use its Predators and Reapers in most places. Al Shabab, for one, did not possess sophisticated air defenses. It did not need them to fight its main foe, the Ethiopians, who by the start of 2009 were in full retreat from Somalia.

Afraid

The Ethiopians were pulling back to the border. The African Union troops were bottled up in Mogadishu at the airport, seaport, the strategic Kilometer Four roundabout, and the former presidential palace. In early 2009, Khalif Ibrahim Noor decided God was on the side of Al Shabab. "I thought that it is a religious group," he said. He commanded a group of thirty fighters. "We have carried out attacks against Somali government soldiers and their African Union ally in several regions, for instance in Bana-dir, Hiran and Gedo region."

Through 2010 Noor rated Al Shabab as being "very strong" and "unshakable," but by early 2011 things began to change. International efforts to cut off the group's funding began to have an effect on the ground in Somalia. And Al Shabab's excesses—for example, "torturing innocent people," according to Noor—turned everyday Somalis against the group.

In the spring of 2011, the CIA and other U.S. intelligence agencies tracked Osama bin Laden to a hideout in Abbottabad, Pakistan. Early on the morning of May 2, 2011, U.S. Navy SEALs riding in secret, stealthy U.S. Army helicopters dropped in on the compound, having evaded Pakistani air defenses. Bin Laden and four others died in a hail of bullets. Militant websites confirmed the killing four days later.

"The well-organized killing of Osama Bin Laden has, as well, caused heartbreak to [Al Shabab]," Noor said. In June Noor claimed to have seen the light. He abandoned Al Shabab and offered his services to the U.S.-sponsored Transitional Federal Government. "They won't frankly say verbally that they are frightened by the actions of the American commandos," Noor said of his former Al Shabab comrades, "but I am sure they [are]."

The same could be said for himself. Noor had rehearsed his explanation for switching sides. "Previously, I had a good relationship with Al Shabab and believed none other than them, but now I have repented and realized what they really are," he said. "At the end of the day I realized that the group is a political group which is disguising itself in the name of religion."

In reality, Noor's allegiance belonged to the side that appeared to be winning. By mid-2011, the TFG and the African Union, backed by the UN, EU, and the United States, were clearly the major power in Somalia. "Al Shabab is no longer strong, but weak," Noor admitted.

Most important, from Noor's point of view, was the TFG's payroll. "The current Transitional Federal Government of Somalia, whose PM is Mohamed Abdullah Farmajo, has come up with effective [ideas], unlike the previous government, whose PM was Sharmarke," Noor explained.

"During Sharmarke's era, Somali government soldiers and the other government staffs were never paid and the soldiers never defeated Al Shabab, but remained in defense," he added. "Farmajo's government has succeeded in paying the salaries of the Somali government soldiers and the other government staffs.

Paying the military has resulted in Al Shabab being beaten in several attacks."

What Noor did not mention, and may not have even known, was that the TFG's funding came almost entirely from the United States. In effect, it was Washington paying Noor and the other Somali fighters, in addition to financially backing the AU peacekeepers.

America was winning its first proxy war of the twenty-first century.

"The future of Al Shabab is depressing and soon the will of the population will overwhelm that of Al Shabab, and they will have no other place to escape or hide," Noor said.[35]

One by one, the United States and its allies in Somalia convinced, coerced, bribed, or frightened top militants to switch sides away from Al Shabab. The ones who could not be flipped were hunted down and killed.

Fazul Abdullah Mohammed, a Comoros native and one of the masterminds of al Qaeda's bloody attacks on U.S. embassies in Kenya and Tanzania in 1998, spent nearly a decade hiding in plain sight with Al Shabab in Somalia. Around midnight on June 7, 2011, Mohammed was traveling somewhere in the vicinity of Mogadishu's Bakara Market when his driver took a wrong turn.

Thinking he was approaching an Al Shabab checkpoint, instead the driver pulled right up to a government position manned by an illiterate twenty-two-year-old soldier named Abdi Hassan who was being paid with U.S. funds. When Hassan saw Mohammed's AK-47, he opened fire, killing the driver and the man who had evaded the United States for more than a decade. "I'm happy that I killed the troublemaker," Hassan told the Associated Press.[36]

Washington was equally elated.

With Friends Like These . . .

Yusuf Mohamed Siad, a.k.a. "Indha Adde," a.k.a. "The Butcher," also switched sides.

Siad once ruled an entire region of southern Somalia with a bloody fist. "There are allegations that he ran drug and weapons trafficking operations from the Merca port," *The Nation*'s Jeremy Scahill wrote about Siad. The warlord also readily admitted providing protection to al Qaeda operatives and spoke fondly of Osama bin Laden. But by 2011, Siad was one of the top generals in the army of Washington's closest allies in Somalia.

For years, Siad resisted CIA efforts to lure him and his hundreds of militiamen to the American side. It took a lot of sweet-talking plus seismic shifts in Somali politics and U.S. strategy to draw in Siad. The first shift came in 2008, when the Ethiopians were just beginning their retreat and, to help take their place, Washington backed Sharif Sheikh Ahmed, the moderate Islamist, former ICU chairman, and onetime ally of Siad's, for Somali president.

Ahmed and Siad both changed sides as Al Shabab grew more extreme and foreign governments organized to destroy it. For the moment, the United States and its shady Somali partners shared a common enemy.

It was unclear how long the alliance would last. "Ahmed claims that Indha Adde and other warlords have sworn allegiance to the government," Scahill wrote, "but it is abundantly clear from traveling extensively through Mogadishu with Indha Adde that his men are loyal to him above all else."

"The warlords being backed by you [America] have only a conflict of interest with the Shabab, not of ideology," another former warlord told Scahill. "That's why [arming and supporting them] is a dangerous game."[37]

But in the short term, flipping Islamist chieftains was a winning maneuver. It was proxy warfare at its most immediate and urgent.

The proxy strategy in Somalia reached its zenith a full twenty years after the fall of Siad Barre and the beginning of Somalia's civil war. In late 2011, East Africa's major regional power abruptly joined the U.S. shadow war, setting the stage for the conflict's final major battle.

On the Heels

Much like the Ethiopians before them, the Kenyans saw an opportunity in Somalia. It was January 2011, and the tide of war was beginning to turn in the ravaged East African nation. The Ugandans and their AU allies, with strong U.S. backing, were on the offensive in Mogadishu, steadily liberating neighborhoods long held by Al Shabab.

The African Union was holding its annual summit in Addis Ababa. After the conference had ended for the day on January 30, a delegation led by Kenyan foreign minister Moses Wetangula met with their American counterparts, headed by Johnnie Carson, the new U.S. assistant secretary of state for African affairs.

At the meeting, Wetangula showed Carson his country's plan to invade southern Somalia, with the ultimate goal of liberating Kismayo, the region's biggest port and economic engine. Nairobi wanted Washington's help, Wetangula said. The kicker: the invasion force would be composed of Somali fighters recruited from the massive refugee camps in northern Kenya and trained by the Kenyan army. Wetangula was proposing a Kenyan-led shadow war modeled on the U.S. proxy campaigns in Somalia. If the Americans were to back the Kenyans in the effort, then Washington would find itself waging a shadow war within a shadow war.

Still, the arguments for the Kenyan-backed attack were compelling. With the U.S.-supplied and -trained AU forces on the offensive in Mogadishu and U.S.-supported Ethiopian troops quietly clearing militants from a chain of Somali border towns, an assault from the south would open up a third front in the conflict and spread Al Shabab forces thin.

But Carson saw the downsides. The Kenyans lacked experience training and leading a proxy army. They had never fought a war outside their own borders, to say nothing of a secret shadow war. An invasion would be more costly than Narobi seemed to believe. And it appeared the Kenyan government was downplaying the possible political repercussions in Somalia and in Kenya if the attackers' true backers were found out.

Carson turned down Wetangula's request. He had a counterproposal. Surely there was a more "conventional and convenient" way Kenya could contribute to the Somalia campaign, Carson said. Maybe the Kenyan army could be directly involved alongside Kenyan-trained Somali troops.

"I may not have been as convincing as I should have been," Wetangula lamented as the meeting ended. But he took Carson's advice to heart. The Americans were proving they knew how to wage war by proxy. If they said it couldn't be done, then it probably couldn't be done.[38]

Nairobi rewrote its attack plan to include five thousand Kenyan army troops plus a single unit of Somali militia, the Ras Kamboni Brigade under the command of Sheikh Ahmed Madobe, an avuncular, red-bearded warlord described by the Kenyan press as "the smiling warlord." A former Al Shabab gunman, Madobe had split from the militants as the tide of war turned against them.[39]

The thirty-nine-year-old Madobe seemed to relish his new role as the Kenyans' dog of war. "We will deal with them robustly, I assure you," he said of his former Islamist colleagues. That fall, the combined Kenyan-militia force attacked.[40]

On October 17, 2011, five thousand Kenyan troops surged across the border into southern Somalia. At the same time, the Ras Kamboni brigade launched its own attack on militant strongholds. Attack helicopters and F-5 fighter jets flew top cover, firing rockets and bombs at the lightly armed Al Shabab infantry.

Kenyan patrol vessels fired guns at targets ashore. Kenyan losses were light, although two F-5s crashed. Nairobi claimed seven hundred insurgents killed.[41]

Officially, the invasion was a response to the abductions of Western tourists and aid workers by Al Shabab agents.[42] Pirates working for the extremist group had grabbed Westerners in Kenyan towns on September 11, October 1, and October 13. One British and one French tourist had died in the kidnappings, the latter after being deprived of her medicine. "This was an act of unqualified barbarism, violence and brutality," Alain Juppé, the French foreign minister, had said of the French tourist's death.[43]

But the abductions were a fig leaf. Kenya had long planned the assault—and for good reason. Nairobi had claims on offshore oil and gas resources near the Somali border worth hundreds of millions of dollars, which it could not safely exploit while Al Shabab thrived.[44]

An American official claimed the Kenyan invasion of Somalia caught Washington "on its heels," but that was a lie.[45] The State Department had reviewed Nairobi's attack plan nine months earlier and had advised major changes, which the Kenyans implemented. The department knew the Kenyans mostly just wanted the oil and gas, but Nairobi's aims dovetailed with America's desire for a stable, terrorist-free Somalia. As in the Philippines, Congo, and elsewhere in Somalia, Washington sought to downplay if not totally obscure its own role in the fighting.

Straying from the script, Kenyan military spokesman Maj. Emmanuel Chirchir implied that the United States was actively aiding the invasion. There were "certainly other actors in this theater," Chirchir said. Assistant Secretary of State for African Affairs Johnnie Carson denied the allegation, but in the most careful language possible. The United States hadn't "provided Kenya with any cross-border assistance," Carson said.[46]

Technically that was true. American support for Kenya's Somalia campaign occurred strictly within Kenya. It was extensive, involving potentially hundreds of advisers delivering tens of millions of dollars in military assistance over more than a decade.

Despite a brief kerfuffle over U.S. aid in 2006 (Nairobi was reluctant to extend diplomatic immunity to American contractors), since the 1998 embassy bombings Kenya had enjoyed steadily rising foreign military financing, foreign military sales, and other military aid from Washington, totaling several million dollars a year.[47] Evoking the U.S. revamp of the Philippines' OV-10 attack planes, some of the money was spent on maintaining and upgrading the Kenyan air force's dozen or so F-5s.

For years the Pentagon had periodically sent military and civilian maintainers to help the Kenyans take care of the aged jets. Scott Gration, the U.S. ambassador to Kenya in 2011 and 2012, was a former air force officer whose duties had included training the Kenyans to fly the F-5.[48]

In 2007 an eight-man U.S. team from the 9th Air Force headquartered in South Carolina spent a week at two Kenyan air bases training more native maintainers on the 1970s-vintage Northrop warplane.[49] "We owe our expertise in operating this aircraft to the training we received in the U.S.," Col. Francis Agolla said.[50]

The F-5s had an effect far out of proportion to their small number. And the Kenyan military quickly learned to leverage the air attacks for maximum psychological effect, using the microblogging service Twitter to warn of impending air raids. "BAIDOA, BAADHEERE, BAYDHABO, DINSUR, AFGOOYE, BWALE, BARAWE, JILIB, KISMAYO and AFMADHOW will be under attack continuously," tweeted Major Chirchir.[51]

Nairobi petitioned for its troops in Somalia to join the UN-backed AMISOM peacekeeping force, and the world body approved the addition in February. The move relieved Kenya of the burden of fully funding its assault in southern Somalia, instead passing most of the estimated $3 million cost to UN donors, most notably the United States.[52]

Amid the bureaucratic reorganization, the Gu rains came in

April and bogged down the Kenyan forces. In anticipation of the rains lifting, the Kenyan navy—likewise heavily supported by the Americans—massed off the coast. As the weather improved in August, Kenyan and militia forces retook the port town of Merka, then began a buildup outside Kismayo, a major southern port city and the last remaining stronghold of Al Shabab.

The final assault was codenamed Operation Sledgehammer. The Ras Kamboni Brigade raced ahead in its technicals, securing towns surrounding the port and closing land escape routes.[53] F-5s flew low passes to spot militant positions.[54] Special Operations Forces—American, apparently—infiltrated ahead of the invasion force.[55] Drones, also apparently American, gathered intelligence.[56]

Kenyan helicopters fired rockets at Al Shabab positions. Navy ships converged on the port and fired at targets on land and at sea, accidentally killing several fishermen and civilians on shore. And at 10:00 at night local time on October 28, 2012, seven Kenyan navy ships began landing "terrified" army troops north of the city, according to *SomaliaReport*. The flotilla included the gun-armed offshore patrol vessels *Jasiri* and *Nyayo II*.[57]

As the Kenyans and their militia allies closed in, Al Shabab's remaining fighters in Kismayo fled by *dhow*, a type of small fishing boat, bound for parts unknown. Al Shabab spokesman Sheik Ali Mohamed Rage said the militants were in "tactical retreat." In reality, they had nowhere left to go. Somalia's cities and towns were under control of America's proxies.[58]

The taking of Kismayo was a triumph for the Kenyan military and for the Americans backing them. For the first time in twenty years, Somalia was free of the Islamists, and the Transitional Federal Government, though still weak and disorganized, was the *only* government with a claim to the ravaged country.

America's first and longest shadow war was won. Somalis took to the streets and beaches to celebrate.

Lucky

The war against pirates was being won in parallel. The Special Operations Forces rescue of *Maersk Alabama*'s Captain Phillips in April 2009 had showed the way. Rather than relying on high-tech warships to combat pirates on the open seas, a new strategy emerged, relying heavily on commando-style forces to hit the pirates at the point of contact between the bandits and their targets.

Since 2008 the world's leading navies had maintained a rotating force of no fewer than three dozen major warships in Somali waters, hoping to deter and intercept pirates before they could attack civilian ships. Problem was, until they brandished weapons, pirates were indistinguishable from legitimate fishermen. Naval crews had to stop and interrogate a lot of innocent seafarers in order to have any hope of disarming pirates before they attacked.

With tens of thousands of fishing boats plying the Indian Ocean alongside just thirty or forty warships, lots of pirates were sure to slip through. "We've just got to be incredibly lucky," Cmdr. Derek Granger, captain of the destroyer USS *Donald Cook*, told me when I boarded his ship for a fruitless pirate hunt in late 2009.[59]

That meant the warships could only *react* to attempted hijackings, racing to intervene after the sea bandits attacked. It wasn't enough. Harmless-seeming vessels could turn hostile in mere minutes. With more than 2 million square miles of ocean to patrol and 25,000 commercial ships a year to protect, the warships were spread thin—and usually too far away to respond in time.

No wonder successful hijackings of large vessels held steady at around fifty per year for three years, despite the escalating naval patrols. "These guys [pirates] are making more money, we're spending more money," lamented piracy expert Martin Murphy.[60]

In addition to pursuing a doomed military strategy, the world's governments dragged their heels on what seemed like the common-sense approach to beating pirates. A few armed guards should have been sufficient to defeat a pirate attack, but allowing weapons on board civilian ships required new regulations, which governments were slow to write.

Far from any military assistance and lacking weapons of their own, some ships' crews resorted to desperate measures. One Chinese fishing crew fought back against a pirate boarding party using Molotov cocktails and fire hoses.[61] Such heroics made good headlines but also risked getting ships' crews killed in lopsided battles. The unworkable military solution and the legal limits on ship self-defense combined to tilt the advantage toward the sea bandits. "The pirates are winning," Murphy said in 2009.[62]

Change came slowly, as governments and shippers gradually realized their existing approach wasn't working. With strong encouragement from the U.S. Coast Guard, some shipping lines began installing "passive defenses," including engine kill-switches, safe rooms lockable from the inside, and emergency alarms—literally big, red buttons, in some cases. Meanwhile, regulators mulled allowing civilian armed guards to at-risk ships, or having the guards sail alongside the commercial ships in privately owned patrol boats.

Spain was one of the first countries to enact a law allowing guards on its commercial ships. Early on, some of these guards were unarmed, relying on sonic weapons and water hoses for defense. In 2008, one unarmed guard team found itself "overwhelmed" by gun-firing pirates and abandoned ship.

"They were ex-supermarket security guards," John Dalby, founder of Spanish maritime-security company Marine Risk, said of the retreating team. "One had been on a one-week training course in a swimming pool. That was the extent of it."[63]

Around the same time, notorious U.S. mercenary firm Blackwater, later known as Xe, equipped a patrol boat for escort duties and offered its guard services on the Indian Ocean shipping route. But Blackwater's involvement in the Nisoor Square shooting in Iraq in 2007 scared off potential customers, and the company soon shuttered its pirate-fighting division.[64]

Poorly trained guards and shady mercenary firms gave the first generation of private ship protectors a bad reputation. But in time, better training facilitated by expanding regulation ushered in a new era for ship's guards.

In March 2010, guards shot and killed a pirate attacking a Panamanian vessel—a first for private pirate-fighters. "I think we're on the cusp of the next threshold, in which privately owned escort vessels are more acceptable," Claude Berube, a professor at the U.S. Naval Academy, said in January 2010.[65]

"Every ship transiting the area should have four [security] professionals on board," Dalby proposed.

By 2011, many shippers and governments agreed. New maritime-security companies, including British firm Protected Vessels International (PVI), sprouted all over the world as ship's guards became more popular. Most of these new companies sought out former military personnel, many of whom had participated in naval piracy patrols during their government service.

Maersk, one of the world's leading shippers, opted to use only former U.S. Navy SEALs. "The result is we, a responsible operator, have the best trained, but very expensive, operators in the world," vice president Stephen Carmel explained. He said Maersk paid around $5,000 a day, per ship, for protection. A typical transit could net a security firm $100,000 or more.[66]

PVI recruited its roughly two hundred guards from the ranks of former Royal Marines and British soldiers. "PVI has witnessed a huge increase in demand for its services recently," company spokesman Paul Gibbins said.

By 2010 the British company had completed more than a thousand escort missions and defeated thirty pirate attacks, all with "no use of lethal force, no loss of vessel, master and crew."[67]

Motherships

In April 2010, "Dave," a forty-four-year-old from Wiltshire in southwest England, was standing watch on the upper deck of a commercial car carrier bound from Mumbai to Mombasa.

Scanning the horizon with a pair of high-powered binoculars, the former British Royal Marine with twenty-four years' experience spotted something suspicious ahead of the carrier: a small freighter matching the profile of a pirate "mothership," a sort of floating base for heavily armed sea bandits and their small boats.

Dave and his three teammates from Protection Vessels International, a then three-year-old English firm offering "safe passage for vessels, master and crew through high-risk environments," watched as the suspected pirate mothership silently approached the car carrier. Seven miles from the carrier, the mothership launched a boat crewed by four men armed with AK-47s.

That's when the PVI guards, all former Royal Marines, knew for sure that the carrier was under attack. "We immediately increased speed to 19 knots, altered course, activated the piracy alarm and informed [the authorities]," Dave said.

They prepared for battle, "kitting up" with body armor, helmets, warning flares, and rifles. As the pirates closed in on Dave's ship, the former Royal Marine hurried to assemble and deploy his team. "In consultation with the master, I requested permission to fire a red flare to warn off the incoming craft. The flare was fired to no response; they continued to close."

It was time to make it clear to the pirates that the car carrier was not the usual defenseless prey—that this vessel was on the cutting edge of pirate-fighting tactics and could shoot back. "At approximately a half nautical mile [distance], permission was given to fire a warning shot above the incoming craft, in order to give clear indication there was an armed security team on board," Dave said. "The shot was fired and it continued on its course."

Maybe the pirates had failed to notice the shot, because of all the wind and spray. Maybe they saw it but just didn't care.

The guards fired again, this time into the water in front of the pirate boat. The skiff jinked to the side . . . and kept coming. Soon it was within five hundred meters of the car carrier—close enough to hit the ship with rockets and rifles. There was time for just one more warning shot before Dave and his team would be forced to kill the attackers.

"The final shot worked and the skiff slowed and stopped in the water. They had gotten to within 400 meters of the vessel and realized that an armed team was on board." That realization was enough to end the attack.[68]

No one pretended ship's guards could end the practice of piracy. They could defeat individial attacks—even most individual attacks, at the point of contact. According to piracy expert Martin Murphy, suppressing the phenomenon of Somali sea banditry required "something happening on land" where the pirates and their sponsors enjoyed safe haven.[69]

By late 2012, with AMISOM having liberated all but a few remote towns in Somalia, that something was happening. The International Maritime Board reported just 70 attacks by Somali pirates between January and September 2012, down from 199 assaults in the same period a year prior. In the summer of 2012, only 1 ship in Somali waters was attacked, compared to 36 the year before.

Squeezed on land by America's proxies, tracked by U.S. drones, and defeated at sea by commandos and mercenaries from the United States and its allies, pirates were giving up. In January 2013, Mohamed Abdi Hassan, a pirate boss with several major hijackings to his credit, called a press conference to announce his retirement.

"After being in piracy for eight years," Hassan said, "I have decided to renounce and quit, and from today on I will not be involved in this gang activity."[70]

Jackals

But the very proxy strategy that was winning the war on piracy was also responsible for some of its greatest setbacks. With inadequate controls, proxies could shrug off their former sponsors and run rampant, essentially waging war on their own terms and with frightening effect.

In mid-2010 the government of Puntland, a semi-autonomous region of northern Somalia that was home to many pirates, determined to stand up a new land-based counterpiracy force that would patrol coastal towns, hopefully restoring law and order and preventing sea bandits from ever casting off. Puntland's strategy reflected piracy expert Martin Murphy's assessment that pirates could only truly be defeated on dry land.

"The government of Puntland is of the firm belief that Saracen International will make a significant contribution to establish, train and mentor the Puntland Marine Force according to the strict rules, guidelines and restrictions that are issued by the highest office of the Puntland government," the regional administration announced.[71]

But Puntland was as impoverished as the rest of Somalia and could not afford to pay for the pirate-fighters and the tens of millions of dollars it would cost to raise, train, equip, and sustain them. And that's how the United Arab Emirates and Erik Prince, the founder and former head of mercenary firm Blackwater, got involved.

Prince had stepped down as Blackwater CEO in 2009 when controversy swirled around the billion-dollar firm for its role in the 2007 Nisoor Square shootings in Iraq plus a long list of other allegations, ranging from gun and drug smuggling to wrongful death.

Prince told Robert Young Pelton he and other current and former Blackwater managers were being regularly deposed by a host of federal agencies. The company had been levied tens of million of dollars in fines. Prince was being audited by the IRS.

Prince had had it. He sold his roughly thirty companies, most of them set up to facilitate government contracts, and plotted a move to the autocratic, oil-rich United Arab Emirates (UAE), which does not have an extradition treaty with the United States. "I'm done. It's all sold or shut down. I'm getting out of the government contracting business," he said. Relocating in the UAE would "make it harder for the jackals to get my money," he told Pelton.[72]

But Prince was not really quitting government contracting—far from it. He simply switched customers. In the Emirates he became a trusted adviser to Abu Dhabi crown prince Sheikh Mohammed bin Zayed Al Nahyan, who was close to U.S. military officials and had earlier congratulated the Pentagon on its "fantastic" proxy war in Somalia. The prince, not trusting his own security forces, wanted to form a new commando unit. He hired Prince to create and run it, with $529 million provided by the UAE.

Separately, the UAE, which utterly depends on seaborne trade for its national wealth, offered to pay for Puntland's counterpiracy force. It's not clear if the idea was originally Prince's, but in any event the former Blackwater chief "was involved in the creation of the antipiracy force," according to the *New York Times*.[73]

The UAE contracted with Saracen, a private military company staffed in large part by the same pool of South African ex-soldiers that was the backbone of other mercenary outfits stretching back to Bob Denard's presidential guard in the Comoros. At the time, Saracen was headed by Lafras Luitingh, one of the founders of the trailblazing Executive Outcomes PMC in the mid-1990s.[74]

When the UN and press began poking around Saracen's operations, many of its officers moved to a new firm, Sterling, which took over Saracen's operations in Puntland. It was an obvious attempt at dodging the authorities.[75] The UAE arranged millions of dollars in secret payments to Sterling, né Saracen, in possible violation of a UN arms embargo on Somalia. Saracen built a camp in the middle of Puntland desert and recruited hundreds of trainees.

The camp environment was, by all accounts, brutal. The UN, possibly tipped off by the comings and goings of supply planes, among other clues, investigated and found evidence of violence against the trainees.[76] The UN circulated a photo depicting the corpse of one alleged trainee, left to bake in the sun after being hogtied and beaten to death by the mercenaries. Luitingh insisted the man died of "Somali-on-Somali violence."

The Transitional Federal Government canceled the contract, and Sterling abandoned the camp, apparently in mid-2012. AMISOM sent its most trusted mercenary boss, Bancroft's Michael Stock, to assess the Puntland facility, with an eye toward Bancroft continuing the training, but Stock compared conditions to the American "Wild West," with some five hundred trainees, unpaid for weeks, wandering a compound stocked with weapons amassed over two years of Sterling operations.

"Sterling is leaving behind an unpaid but well-armed security force in Puntland," Andre Le Sage, a research fellow at the National Defense University in Washington, D.C., told the *New York Times*. "It's important to find a way to make them part of a regular force or to disarm them and take control of them. If that's not done, it could make things worse."

But Stock, perhaps wisely, refused to have anything to do with it. And five hundred armed, partially trained men were left to fend for themselves—perhaps, as the *Times* pointed out, to join the very pirates they were supposed to help eradicate.[77]

It was delicate work, these shadow wars. They had a nasty habit of backfiring just as they were beginning to work.

Smart Bombs

Progress was less ambiguous in the Philippines.

In mid-2010 the U.S. Congress approved a $19-million package to further upgrade the Philippines' small force of OV-10 Bronco bombers. The arms transfer, handled by Raytheon, included at least twenty-two 500-pound satellite-guided bombs plus the training and technical assistance to use them. The first bombs arrived in the Philippines in November. The following month, Bronco pilots sat down with an American expert in precision munitions. Training ramped up in January, and in March technicians began modifying the Broncos to carry the new bombs. The first test drops occurred in May. In June another batch of bombs arrived.[78]

In early 2012 the U.S. shadow war on Islamists in the Philippines was a decade old. U.S. Special Operations Forces—some seven hundred at their peak—trained and equipped Philippine forces, fed them intelligence from drones and satellites, and accompanied them into battle.

Seventeen Americans had died.[79] So had some six hundred Philippine soldiers.[80] But the militants suffered proportionally greater losses. In 2002 the U.S. and Philippine governments printed wanted posters depicting the twenty-four most wanted terrorists from Abu Sayyaf, Jemaah Islamiyah, the Moro Islamic Liberation Front, and other groups. Ten years later, nineteen of the terrorists were dead or in custody.[81]

Before dawn on February 2, an informant texted U.S. and Philippine commanders to say he was with three of the remaining five wanted men—Zulkifli bin Hir and Muhamda Ali from the Indonesian Jemaah Islamiyah group and Abu Sayyaf's Gumbahali Umbra Jumdail—at a remote Abu Sayyaf camp on Jolo Island. U.S. troops launched a Scan Eagle drone that silently orbited over the rebel base, matching observable details with the informant's texts.

American and Philippine commanders confirmed the targets' identities. They sent requests up their respective chains of command, seeking approval for an air strike. The replies came back promptly.

Approved.

Two Broncos, each carrying two of the precision bombs,

launched—most likely from Edwin Andrews Air Base, the Philippine air force's main southern outpost in Zamboanga.

The informant walked away from the encampment, observed the whole time by the overhead drone. Between 2 and 3 a.m., the Broncos dropped their four bombs, pulverizing the rebel base. Survivors stumbled away under the Scan Eagle's watchful gaze. Philippine troops were on their way.

The informant strolled back into the blast zone to count the dead. Jumdail had been "obliterated," bin Hir was "cut in half," and Ali was heavily bleeding and barely breathing, according to the informant's texts.

Later there would be official doubt over bin Hir and Ali's deaths, but the blow against the Philippines' terrorists was a decisive one nonetheless.

Sensing an opening, in late 2012 Philippine president Benigno Aquino extended an olive branch to MILF, by far the largest of the Philippine insurgent groups. In exchange for laying down their arms, the Islamists would gain political autonomy within a new southern Philippine state.[82]

MILF, perhaps sensing doom in a continued struggle, pounced on the offer. The rebel group renounced its ties to Abu Sayyaf and Jemaah Islamiyah, sparking at least one gun battle between MILF and its former allies. In February 2013 Aquino visited the rebel stronghold in Mindanao to finalize a peace deal. The treaty promised to finally deprive terrorists of their safe haven in the Philippines.[83]

With the signing of the peace deal, America could tentatively claim victory in two shadow wars. But what could be the most difficult shadow war had barely begun.

The Iraq War, which had never really been about terrorism at all, ended fairly neatly for the United States with the final withdrawal of American ground forces in December 2011. Nearly 4,500 Americans had died in more than eight years of fighting, with no discernible gain for U.S. national security.

Weary of full-blown war, the Obama administration struggled to transition the Afghanistan conflict, which *was* in part about terrorism, from a large-scale occupation and ground war back into a smaller-scale—and hopefully more effective—intervention built around drones and Special Operations Forces. As it had been in 2001.

The transformation wasn't going well.

9

Full Circle

It was hot. And after three days spent searching the village of Andar in eastern Afghanistan for insurgent bombers and bomb-making materials, the U.S. and Afghan troops were tired and hungry. With a few soldiers keeping guard on the perimeter, the others removed their body armor and sat down to eat lunch in the courtyard of an abandoned mud home.

It was the afternoon of October 2, 2009. Twenty-six-year-old Capt. Tyler Kurth was chatting with one of his soldiers when he heard gunfire and screaming. "As I turned to look, I see this particular Afghan police officer with his AK-47 at his hip, and he's firing away in a sweeping motion," he told reporter Jessica Stone a year later. "And it dawns on me very quickly that he's not shooting past them. He's shooting at them."

Kurth stood and reached for his sidearm. He stepped through

a doorway and came face-to-face with the attacker—a cop the Americans had nicknamed "Crazy Joe," a tall man in his thirties who always wore black goggles. "He was shooting me," Kurth recalled, "and [I saw] his little smirk on his face when he was doing it." The young captain was hit in the chest and leg, the impacts spraying blood in a fine mist. Behind him, Sgt. Christian Hughes was still climbing to his feet. Crazy Joe shifted aim and shot Hughes in the legs. "I could see white, blood, and muscle," the sergeant remembered later.

Spec. Sean Beaver, Sgt. Aaron Smith, and Pvt. Brandon Owens were hit, too. Owens died quickly. Kurth managed to radio for a medical evacuation before slipping into shock. Sprawled in the dirt in shock, he watched Smith stop breathing. U.S. and Afghan soldiers raced to provide first aid to the survivors.

Crazy Joe slipped away. Kurth and Hughes believed he had been paid by the Taliban to attack his comrades, but there was no way to be sure. Asked if he would ever voluntarily fight along-side Afghan forces again, Kurth was unequivocal. "Nope. Never again."[1]

His sentiment would be shared by many U.S. and coalition troops in coming years—and by Afghan soldiers equally wary of their erstwhile partners from foreign armies. There would be far-reaching consequences of the mutual suspicion.

Insiders

Barack Obama swept into the White House in 2008 in part on his promise to end the Iraq War. In contrast, Obama actually vowed to *escalate* the war in Afghanistan. "I think one of the biggest mistakes we've made strategically after 9/11 was to fail to finish the job here, focus our attention here," he said of Afghanistan. "We got distracted by Iraq."

"The situation is precarious and urgent here in Afghanistan,"

Obama said. "And I believe this has to be our central focus, the central front, on our battle against terrorism."[2]

In 2007 on the recommendation of his top advisers, including Gen. David Petraeus, then-president George W. Bush had "surged" an extra twenty thousand troops to Iraq—a move that at the time was widely seen as helping tamp down on the sectarian violence unleashed by the U.S. invasion.[3] Later, many observers would attribute the waning bloodshed to the self-segregation of the once mixed Iraqi population as well as to the spontaneous rise of the Sons of Iraq militias that patrolled vulnerable communities, rather than to a modest and fleeting boost in U.S. force levels.

Once in office Obama essentially copied the surge strategy in Afghanistan even as he accelerated the reduction of U.S. forces in Iraq. In 2009 an additional thirty thousand U.S. troops deployed to Afghanistan, boosting the American force there by half for a period of just over two years. But the Afghan surge, like that in Iraq, failed to meaningfully alter the course of the war. In September 2012 the U.S.-led International Security Assistance Force issued a report charting armed violence in the country month by month . . . and found no decrease correlating with the thirty thousand U.S. reinforcements.

In August 2009 there were some twenty-seven hundred insurgent attacks, including six hundred bombings. In August 2012, there were three thousand attacks, including six hundred bombings. "The same trend holds for every other month in 2009 compared to every month in 2012 for which there is data," *Wired* war reporter Spencer Ackerman noted.[4]

Most chilling was the increase in so-called insider attacks, such as that in Andar in October 2009. In 2010 insider attacks accounted for 3 percent of U.S. dead in Afghanistan. The rate doubled in 2011 and doubled *again* in 2012, for a total of seventy coalition troops killed by their trainees between 2001 and early 2012.[5] With disturbing frequency, Afghan army and police recruits were turning their weapons on their American and coalition trainers—whether out of frustration, resentment, or insurgent infiltration, no one knew for sure.

In 2011 then-secretary of defense Robert Gates said any future Pentagon head who advocated sending "a big American land army into Asia or into the Middle East or Africa" should "have his head examined."[6]

Obama took Gates's words to heart. "This president has learned the lessons the hard way in many ways of large land deployments and the backlash that can cause in Muslim countries," New York Times journalist Eric Schmitt said in late 2012. "It becomes a very attractive political option to deploy small numbers of forces that can do a . . . range of tasks."[7]

In other words, to wind back the clock in Afghanistan and try to end the U.S. intervention the way it started: with drones and Special Operations Forces, which under Obama had enjoyed such a massive expansion.

There were other arguments—political arguments—in favor of bringing shadow warfare back to Afghanistan. Oversight, or the lack thereof. "The reporting requirements aren't quite as clear when it comes to Special Operations Forces, particularly if they're operating [on] a covert-type basis," Schmitt explained.

The more Obama relied on drones and commandos, the less accountable he was to Congress and, by extension, the media and the public. A covert U.S. war could go superbly, or terribly, without anyone outside of certain privileged corridors knowing much of anything about it.

On that basis, in 2012 the Obama administration began converting the then-eleven-year-old major ground war in Afghanistan to a shadow war waged mostly by Special Operations Forces and armed, robotic aircraft.

It was a rocky transition.

Bad Days

Tom, the U.S. Army Special Forces officer, was having one of the worst days of his war tour. And that was *before* the Soviet-made anti-personnel mine packed with seven hundred ball bearings exploded at his feet.

At thirty-seven, he was older than most Special Forces team leaders. He owed his relatively advanced age to an unusual and circuitous entry into the Green Berets.

He'd enlisted in the army as a teenager and joined Special Forces, for the first time, as a junior team member. That had meant passing the grueling Qualification Course, or "Q Course," a more-than-yearlong chain of physical-fitness tests, combat exercises, and foreign-language training: Russian and French, in Tom's case. Feeling unfulfilled, Tom decided to get his officer's commission and transferred to the air force to be a navigator on cargo planes.

But that didn't quite satisfy him, either. So Tom transferred back to the army, went through the Q Course *again*, and rejoined the Green Berets as an officer. He spent some time as a Special Forces diver and nearly drowned after getting caught in an undertow off the coast of Florida.

He was awoken by his panicked girlfriend on the morning of September 11, 2001. He spent most of the following decade at war and, in late 2011, deployed to Laghman Province in mountainous eastern Afghanistan to train Afghan police as part of the accelerating conversion of the American ground war into a shadow war.

In late September 2011, after several weeks of daily training, Tom and his team of roughly a half-dozen U.S. commandos took their first batch of Afghan police trainees out on their inaugural operational patrol. The Americans and approximately twenty Afghan police walked north from Mehtar Lam. Returning to town the same day, the force "came under fire from twenty to twenty-five insurgents," Tom told me three months later, during my visit to his walled, gated compound adjacent to a regular army outpost in Mehtar Lam, the capital of Laghman.

It was a moment of truth for the cops and for the Green Berets training them. Tom admitted that unseasoned Afghan troops had a habit of fleeing when under fire. Expecting a route, the thirty-seven-year-old team leader said he was pleasantly surprised that *some* of his Afghans stood and fought. "They held the line and, in fact, some of them bounded forward."

Tom said one police trainee fearlessly advanced on the Taliban ambushers, spraying rounds one-handed from his PKM machine gun. "He must have watched *Rambo* the night before," joked "Red," Tom's weapons sergeant and right-hand man.

Tom said he was impressed at first but grew alarmed when the machine gunner started shooting wide of the Taliban. He decided to cut short the cop's little show. "Somebody tackle his ass before he shoots us all," Tom recalled ordering. It was a violation of his personal rule against rough handling of his trainees, but justified with everyone's life at stake.

The Taliban retreated. The Green Berets and their trainees, having suffered no casualties, regrouped. Tom says he delivered an impromptu "Braveheart speech" and together they headed back to Mehtar Lam. That's when Tom glimpsed a mound of disturbed earth and, without thinking, approached it. He realized too late it was a buried Taliban mine. A weapon like that could turn a man into "pink mist," Tom told me.

Luckily the mine was a dud, its main charge decayed by time. Only a precursor charge went off, resulting in an underwhelming "pop" sound. Tom flashed a hand signal that sent his troops scurrying for cover, in case the malfunctioned mine was just the first blow in larger ambush. "God, please don't let me fuck up," he recalled thinking.

But nothing else exploded. No Taliban fighters opened up with machine guns. "My first reaction was anger," Tom told me over cups of green tea he brewed in his plywood living quarters. He was angry not only at his would-be attackers but also at himself. Walking up to the mine "was a JV move," he admitted. Tom's frustration deepened as he tried to get his Afghan police trainees to learn from the mistake. He showed the now-harmless explosive device to one of his best Afghan cops. The American's aim was to teach the Afghan to fear explosives and keep a close watch for them in the future.

"But he didn't get it," Tom said. To the Afghan, avoiding a bomb blast wasn't a function of superior tactics or even luck. No, the troops' escape from the fizzling mine "was a direct representation of the intervention of God," Tom said.

For six months, Tom and the approximately eighteen U.S. and Romanian commandos he led had struggled to prepare their Afghan police unit to begin enforcing some real law and order in Laghman, a violent province of some 400,000 people. It was all part of the coalition's evolving plan to turn over more responsibility to Afghan security forces, steadily withdrawing conventional combat troops through 2014. Special Operations Forces would stay behind to continue mentoring the Afghans.

But the shadow war approach was no panacea. Understanding rugged, landlocked Afghanistan could be hard even for highly trained warriors like Tom. A decade into the U.S.-led intervention, the coalition was still learning this important truth.

"Look at the magnitude of the problem," Tom told me. "I am not cynical about this, but I recognize the magnitude. Lots of people frame the problem in simplistic terms that are not realistic."

Tom told me he quickly began to appreciate the extent to which Afghanistan is a "man-culture," big on pride, physical bravado, and reputation. Offending that sense of masculinity can be counterproductive—even deadly in light of the increasing number of attacks by Afghan troops on their foreign trainers.

"I've seen too many guys disrespecting their Afghans," Red, Tom's weapons sergeant, chimed in. With that in mind, Tom and his teammates drew up a list of guidelines for dealing with police recruits: no aggressive touching, no cussing out the trainees, congratulate them frequently and individually, and reward them with symbols of their progress such as patches or new uniforms.

But for all their success in shaping their training program to match Afghan mores, the Green Berets hadn't figured out how to get the cops to start thinking tactically, operationally, and strategically. "They're not there yet," Col. Isaac Peltier, Tom's commander, said of the Afghans.

"It's a long-term thing," Tom added. Washington clearly agreed, which is why men like Tom would be staying in Afghanistan even after most U.S. forces will have departed in 2014.[8]

Affront

In late February 2012 American troops guarding a U.S.-run prison at Bagram Air Field in central Afghanistan accidentally sent at least ten Korans and a stack of other Islamic literature to a garbage burn pit. Horrified Afghan workers at the base pulled the holy books from the flames and sent them to religious officials in Kabul. "These people must be punished," said Qari Ghulam Mustafa, a top cleric.[9]

Angry mobs descended on NATO bases all over Afghanistan. Some Afghan troops turned their weapons on their foreign allies. Within a week four NATO troops were dead at the protestors' hands, including two high-ranking officers killed execution-style inside the Ministry of Interior in Kabul. Washington was compelled to pull its advisers from Afghan ministries—and U.S. plans to transform the manpower-intensive counterinsurgency campaign into a Special Operations Forces–led shadow war were in danger of imploding.[10]

The goal was to reduce the American presence to a token force of a few thousand commandos responsible for training, advising, and, when necessary, leading an Afghan army hundreds of thousands strong. It was a shadow war strategy built on mutual respect. "If the trust, ability and willingness to partner falls apart, you are looking at the endgame here," warned Mark Jacobson, the former NATO deputy senior civilian representative in Kabul.[11]

In one sense, the U.S.-led coalition had itself to blame for the riots and killings. Too many U.S. troops habitually disrespected their Afghan trainees, according to some of the elite Special Operations Forces heading up those training sessions. And those small, tactical acts of cultural stupidity could lead to a strategic moment like the February riots.

The mishandling of the Koran was like a match on that explosive tinder and reflected an almost willful ignorance of Afghan sensitivities. "How after 11 years here is there no system in place for properly disposing of religious [documents]?" one sergeant attached to a Special Forces unit based in Kabul told me. "It's just fucking stupid."[12]

By time of the riots there had already been nearly forty incidents in which Afghan troops attacked their international trainers, resulting in some seventy coalition fatalities. In the past, some of these attacks have been blamed on Taliban infiltration. But the Afghan government worker suspected of murdering the two American officers inside the Ministry of Interior did not have Taliban ties, ministry spokesman Sediq Sediqi said.[13]

And the Laghman commandos believed that most of the incidents were sparked by cultural misunderstandings. David Sedney, the deputy assistant secretary of defense for Afghanistan, in a January Congressional testimony agreed, chalking up "the majority" of attacks by trainees to "personal motivation."[14]

The riots hit hard in Laghman, though the province thankfully was spared the murders that occurred elsewhere. "They stormed Mehtar Lam and broke through the wire," Tom told me a few days into the rioting. "Eventually, they tired of their own anger and retreated. We're expecting the same today: 2,000–3,000 people in total."[15]

At the behest of their commanders in Kabul, the Laghman team "took a couple steps back" from performing its mission, Tom said. The temporary suspension of training in Laghman echoed the temporary pullout of all U.S. advisers from Afghan government ministries. As long as the violence directed against the coalition continued, and as long as international trainers were at elevated risk of being murdered by their trainees, the commandos and other advisers would find it difficult, if not impossible, to prepare Afghans to secure their own country. The more widespread the anger, the less likely Afghans were to even want foreigners around.

The riots soon abated, but the insider killings did not. On August 28, 2012, a man wearing an Afghan army uniform opened fire on Australian soldiers in the southern province of Uruzgan, killing three and wounding two. That attack brought the total number of NATO personnel killed in so-called "green-on-blue" assaults to fifteen in August alone. It was official: rogue Afghan soldiers and police turning their weapons on their allies was now the leading cause of death for NATO troops in Afghanistan.[16]

The insider attacks revealed the darkest side of shadow war. Like mercenaries, proxy fighters had a bad habit of turning on their sponsors. In relying on the armies of other nations to do the fighting and dying in its expanding shadow wars, the United States took the chance that these armies would rankle, resist, revolt.

The U.S.-led coalition took steps to protect its trainers and advisers in Afghanistan. There would be more armed guards, more background checks on Afghan trainees, and new instruction to help coalition troops spot potential murderers. But most significantly, there would be less contact between the foreigners and Afghan troops. That meant less training, less oversight, less United States in its own proxy war.

As the Afghanistan war entered its twilight years, it was unclear how the frayed relationship between the Americans and their proxies would play out over the long term. After shadow war victories in Somalia and the Philippines, it was possible that Washington faced a sort of self-defeat in Afghanistan as the proxy strategy, meant to insulate the United States from the worst effects of its wars, backfired with bloody effect.

Calculus

There was widespread concern that similar backlash would occur in other shadow battlegrounds. The escalating use of armed drones, in particular, threatened to create more insurgents and terrorists than it eliminated. "When you kill one terrorist, you breed 10 terrorists," Ekmeleddin İhsanoğlu, head of the Organization of Islamic Cooperation—the international union of Muslim countries—told *The Daily Show with Jon Stewart*.[17]

By that reckoning, America's drones had created a *lot* of terrorists. In a speech before a Rotary Club in Easley, South Carolina, on February 19, 2013, U.S. Sen. Lindsey Graham said drones had killed 4,700 people.[18] A count by the UK Bureau of Investigative Journalism more or less corroborated Graham's figure. Based on news accounts, the investigative nonprofit estimated as many as 4,756 (and potentially hundreds fewer) had been killed just in Pakistan, Yemen, and Somalia.[19]

The bureau figured up to 1,200 of the dead were innocent civilians caught in the drones' blast radius. Graham admitted civilians had died, but said the robotic strikes were still worth it. "Sometimes you hit innocent people, and I hate that, but we're at war, and we've taken out some very senior members of Al Qaeda."

İhsanoğlu was less blasé. "In the short history of using drones against terrorists, there have been certain major mistakes by killing innocent people." That, too, fueled terror recruitment, according to some observers. "Drones have replaced [the U.S. terror prison in] Guantánamo [Bay, Cuba,] as the recruiting tool of choice for militants," Jo Becker and Scott Shane wrote in the *New York Times*.[20]

It was a popular notion, but one without much of an analytical backing. In 2012 Chris Swift, a fellow at the University of Virginia's Center for National Security Law, decided to test the theory. He was determined to see for himself whether drone strikes really created more militants than they eliminated. He chose Yemen as his test case.

In 2012 the rate of drone strikes in Yemen more than doubled, with around two dozen attacks in just the first six months of the year. By then no fewer than 329 people had died in the Yemen drone campaign, at least 58 of whom were innocent civilians, according to a count by the Bureau of Investigative Journalism.[21] Some Yemenis believe the civilian body count was much higher. "For every headline you read regarding 'militants' killed by drones in #Yemen, think of the civilians killed that are not reported," NGO consultant Atiaf Al Wazir tweeted.[22]

Another Yemeni Twitter user drew the link between the drone war's innocent victims in a Tweet directed at top U.S. counterterrorism adviser John Brennan. "Brennan do you hear us?!!! We say #NoDrones #NoDrones #NoDrones. You are killing innocent people and creating more enemies in #Yemen."[23]

"Across the vast, rugged terrain of southern Yemen, an escalating campaign of U.S. drone strikes is stirring increasing sympathy for al Qaeda–linked militants and driving tribesmen to join a network linked to terrorist plots against the United States," the *Washington Post*'s Sudarsan Raghavan reported.[24]

In late May 2012, Swift spent a week in the country's arid, rugged south, interviewing tribal leaders. To get to the sources that really mattered, Swift sensed he had to "get out of the . . . political elite" in the capital of Sana'a. He teamed up with an experienced fixer and slipped into heavily armed Aden in Yemen's south in the back of pickup trucks. "I always expected that my next checkpoint was going to be my last," Swift recalled.

Swift survived some close calls and brought back what was arguably the freshest and most relevant data on militant recruiting in southern Yemen. In southern Yemen "nobody really gets excited about drones," he explained. He said his sources were "overwhelming saying that Al Qaeda is recruiting through economic inducement." In other words, for the most part the terror group paid people to join. Swift concluded that the narrative embraced by Yemeni tweeters, the *Times*, and the *Post* originated in, and was sustained by, a comparatively wealthy, educated, and English-speaking community based in Sana'a. He called them the "Gucci jean-wearing crowd."

But cosmopolitan Sana'a wasn't breeding many terrorists, and popular opinions in the city didn't necessarily reflect the reality in Yemen's embattled south, Swift argued. "Nobody in my cohort [of interview subjects] drew a causal link between drones on one hand and [militant] recruiting on other," Swift told me.

Which wasn't to say Yemen's militants didn't fear the American killer robots. In fact, they were "terrified of drones," Swift said. "They make a big deal of surviving drones in their propaganda videos." The militants' fear of drones perhaps underscored the robots' effectiveness. It did *not* argue for widespread resentment among everyday people in southern Yemen that compelled them to join the terrorists' ranks. At least, that's what Swift believed.

Swift said he wasn't trying to defend drones on moral grounds. There were plenty of reasons for Americans or anyone else to object to the proliferation of robotic weapons. But it was important to separate that issue from Americans' understanding of militant recruiting in Yemen, he said. "Our drone debate is our drone debate."[25]

Drone Advocacy

In 2011 John Brennan, Obama's top counterterrorism adviser, started making the rounds to defend the drone war. "Going forward, we will be mindful that if our nation is threatened, our best offense won't always be deploying large armies abroad, but delivering targeted, surgical pressure to the groups that threaten us," Brennan said in a speech at the Johns Hopkins School of Advanced International Studies in Washington, D.C., in June.[26]

In an address at the Woodrow Wilson International Center for Scholars in Washington, D.C., in April 2012, Brennan continued the argument. "Compared against other options, a pilot operating this aircraft remotely, with the benefit of technology and with the safety of distance, might actually have a clearer picture of the target and its surroundings, including the presence of innocent civilians," Brennan said. "It's this surgical precision, the ability, with laser-like focus, to eliminate the cancerous tumor called an al Qaeda terrorist while limiting damage to the tissue around it, that makes this counterterrorism tool so essential," he added.[27]

It surprised no one when, in January 2013, Obama nominated Brennan to take over the CIA. For nearly two years Brennan had been steadily building the case for continuing the agency's lethal, covert drone war. Soon after the nomination the White House made it known that Brennan had been helping to craft a new set of policy guidelines for the use of robotic strike planes.

The "drone playbook" was meant to institutionalize what had once been ad hoc efforts run by the Pentagon and intelligence agencies. It established clearer and more rigorous procedures for the conduct of robotic attacks, imposing order on the existing, uncoordinated mix of U.S. drone initiatives.

While the rules appeared to restrict the UAV campaign, in fact they could *facilitate* the escalation of robotic attacks by providing clear processes for using drones in new places against new targets. Drone skeptics and civil libertarians were alarmed. The playbook represented "a step in exactly the wrong direction," Hina Shamsi, from the American Civil Liberty Union, told the *Washington Post*.[28]

But with more than a decade of strikes behind it, and with the alternative—large-scale land war—losing its luster, the drone war had momentum. The Obama administration had even sought advice from the Justice Department on justifying robotic attacks on U.S. citizens involved in terror plots overseas.[29] American citizen Anwar al-Awlaki, killed by a Predator in Yemen in 2011, was the test case. Brennan described him as a legitimate target.[30]

And new UAVs—plus upgrades to existing 'bots—were in development, adding enhanced artificial intelligence and firepower to the expanding legal and policy framework that was making permanent drones' elevation from niche surveillance system to the main weapon of U.S. shadow warfare.

Upgrades

In April 2012 General Atomics proposed a big upgrade to the MQ-9 Reaper drone, adding fuel pods, longer wings, and stronger landing gear. With all three enhancements, a Reaper's endurance jumped from twenty-seven hours to a whopping forty-two— almost two days of continuous flying.

The upgrade was just a company proposal with no government backing, but its merits were hard to ignore. The company offered three related upgrades. One added a new eighty-eight-foot-span wing, replacing the existing sixty-six-foot wing. The longer wing boosted lift and improved fuel efficiency.

Plus, Reaper users could add two new fuel pods in place of some of the drone's weapons, each carrying a hundred or so gallons of gas. The upgrades meant more weight on the airframe and required new heavy-duty landing gear that could support the nearly six-ton weight of the improved Reaper. The new wing, fuel pods, and landing gear could be installed by company reps at the Reapers' forward bases in Afghanistan, East Africa, and elsewhere.

The enhancements reflected "customers' emerging needs," said Frank Pace, the former drone engineer–turned–president of General Atomics' airplane division. To save money, the air force had proposed to cut its annual Reaper purchases in half, to just twenty-four a year. But the flying branch still wanted to be able to keep up to eighty-five armed drones in the air at all times.[31]

In 2012, that took two drones on the ground for each one in the air. Getting more flight time out of each aircraft might mean fewer were needed overall, as the increased endurance bought time for mechanics to fix, refuel, and re-arm the robots that weren't flying. If you had two days to prep the next drone, there might be less need for spare 'bots.

A few months after General Atomics offered the endurance upgrades, the air force still hadn't said whether it intended to buy them. But the flying branch did move ahead on a parallel series of enhancements. In May the first Reaper Block 5 took off from General Atomics' facility in Palmdale, California. The company kept the new Reaper's debut a secret until officially announcing the new model in September.

Compared to earlier editions of the Reaper, the Block 5 boasted "increased electrical power, secure communications, auto land, increased gross takeoff weight, weapons growth and streamlined payload integration capabilities," the company said.[32] The air force planned to introduce the new 'bot in 2014.[33]

The secure communications were arguably the most urgent of these improvements. They promised to finally eliminate drones' vulnerability to hacking that dated back to 1996—and which might have been a factor in Iran's capture of the stealthy Sentinel in late 2011.

In parallel to the upgrades, the Pentagon and CIA were developing brand-new drones with all these enhancements—plus radar-dodging stealth features even better than the Sentinel's—built in from the start.

Next Generation

In December 2012 *Aviation Week* journalist Bill Sweetman concluded that Northrop Grumman had been working on a large, armed UAV for the Pentagon and CIA—one with greater speed, payload, range, and stealth than the current Predators, Reapers, and Sentinels. Development began in 2008, Sweetman surmised, based on his analysis of company documents and interviews with industry insiders. "It is, by now, probably being test-flown at Groom Lake," Sweetman wrote of the new drone.

The purported location, at least, made total sense. The Air Force's secret facility in Groom Lake, Nevada, is part of the so-called Area 51 complex and previously was the test site for the U-2 and SR-71 reconnaissance planes and the F-117 stealth fighter.

If real, the in-development drone could help explain some peculiar moves by the air force in 2012 and 2013. The flying branch proposed to abandon almost all of its essentially brand-new Global Hawk UAVs while also cutting production of the smaller Reaper drones. Congress ultimately nixed both proposals, but the air force's willingness to part with some of its publicly acknowledged drones was possibly indicative of a brand-new 'bot preparing to enter service and take over from the older models.

There was plenty of precedent for covert drone development. The Sentinel, of course, was developed in total secrecy by Lockheed Martin and flew combat missions for around five years before breaking cover.

Likewise, Lockheed and rival Boeing both secretly designed and built large, stealthy, jet-powered UAV demonstrators for a navy effort to add drones to aircraft carrier decks—an initiative Northrop was also openly supporting with a drone prototype of its own. The new Boeing and Lockheed naval drones, which both bore a superficial resemblance to the Sentinel (as did Northrop's less secretive naval UAV prototype), were unknown to the outside world except as rumors until the companies unveiled them as part of their sales efforts.

Northrop's purported new UAV was probably meant to build on the concepts explored by the fast, radar-evading Sentinel. Sweetman estimated only around twenty Sentinels were built in the early 2000s as a stopgap measure pending the introduction of Northrop's more high-tech robot sometime in the mid-2010s. In 2008, the company's financial documents listed a $2-billion "restricted programs" contract that Sweetman believed was the development deal for the new drone.

Around the same time, Northrop Grumman hired as a consultant John Cashen, the man most responsible for designing the radar-defeating shape of Northrop's older B-2 Spirit stealth bomber. Not coincidentally, in 2009 Northrop filed patents for two variants of a new manned stealth bomber design, both sharing the same tailless flying-wing shape as the company's B-2 and Pegasus naval drone prototype.

Northrop's other efforts apparently influenced the secret drone design. "It is believed to be a single-engine aircraft with a wingspan similar to a Global Hawk," Sweetman wrote of the new UAV. A Global Hawk spans 116 feet, making it roughly as big across as a 737 airliner. Consistent with the three-year-old patents, Sweetman concluded that the secret UAV likely included radar, electronic surveillance systems and radar jammers, and, quite possibly, a bomb bay for carrying guided bombs.

Sweetman's conclusions were just speculation, albeit highly informed speculation. But with a classified budget of no less than $30 billion a year, the Pentagon—to say nothing of the even more opaque CIA—was undoubtedly working on a host of advanced drone designs. Northrop's new 'bot just had the most detectable paper trail. Whether and when this and other secret drones would be revealed to the public was, according to Sweetman, "anyone's guess."[34]

Possibly the first member of the public to glimpse Northrop's new robot—or something similar—did not realize what he was looking at. In mid-2011 a freelance photographer—I agreed to withhold his name—was visiting the air force's Tonopah Test Range in Nevada, a somewhat less secretive adjunct to Groom Lake, a.k.a. Area 51. While walking along the tarmac with an officer guide, the photographer spotted, some 150 yards away, what appeared at first to be a Sentinel drone parked in an open hangar.

But upon closer inspection, the photog noticed details inconsistent with the recently revealed Sentinel. The engine air intake was different. The skin material seemed less metallic. And the craft was apparently much bigger than the Sentinel, which by then had appeared only in grainy photos taken in Afghanistan. (Tehran's capture of a crashed Sentinel was still a few months off, but the photographer later said that the details revealed by Iranian footage of the wrecked UAV only confirmed his earlier impressions.)

Recalling the encounter, the photographer concluded he had seen a new variant of the Sentinel. He was not aware at that time that Northrop was developing, and the air force and CIA were testing in and around Area 51, a brand-new and larger UAV with outward similarities to the Sentinel.

It was clear the air force had not intended the photographer to see the new 'bot, whatever it was. The colonel leading the tour grew uncomfortable. "I was specifically asked not to photograph it and I complied," the photog said of the mystery drone.[35]

Artificial Intelligence

The new drone or drones would be orders of magnitude more "intelligent" than the Predators, Reapers, Sentinels, and Global Hawks, which were either directly steered by a remote operator or programmed to follow fairly uncomplicated paths marked by GPS waypoints. Human beings remained in direct control for much of a vehicle's flight, albeit at a great distance. People told the drones where to go, where to point their sensors, and, through a complicated series of checks and functions requiring multiple levels of approval, when to fire a missile or drop a bomb.

"Unmanned vehicles—even the most advanced in the military—are one step above remote control," Missy Cummings, a robot developer at the Massachusetts Institute of Technology, told me.[36]

As the Pentagon and CIA added drones, deployed them in more locations, and flew them longer, human resources were becoming a major constraint on the robotic force. A single Reaper on a twelve-hour mission could require the attention of four or six operators, dozens of maintainers, and a hundred or more imagery analysts—180 to 200 people per airborne robot, according to the air force.[37]

Multiply that by the nearly seven hundred medium and large drones the Pentagon copped to owning in 2012 plus possibly scores more in the CIA's arsenal or other secret holdings. Ironically, unmanned aircraft were becoming a major drain on manpower.[38] "The number one manning problem in our Air Force is manning our unmanned platforms," Gen. Philip Breedlove said in late 2010.[39]

That was about to change. "Advances in AI (artificial intelligence) will enable systems to make combat decisions and act within legal and policy constraints without necessarily requiring human input," the air force stated in its forty-year plan for drone development, published in 2009.[40] The next generations of armed UAVs, perhaps including Northrop's secret new drone, would be capable of navigating on their own, searching for targets on their own, and, in theory, using weapons without being told—although the latter was strictly against military and presumably CIA policy.

"Even though it's possible for a [UAV] to find a target, identify it, and give those coordinates electronically to a weapon, it won't do that unless it's told to," Carl Johnson, a Northrop vice president, told me. "The technology is there, but there is still a need for a human in the loop."

Withholding a license to kill was a mere caveat on burgeoning robot autonomy. "In the future we're going to see a lot more reasoning put on all these vehicles," Cummings said. For a machine, "reasoning" meant drawing useful conclusions from vast amounts of raw data—say, scanning a bustling village from high overhead and using software algorithms to determine who was an armed militant based on how they looked, what they were carrying, and how they were moving, all while the drone was maneuvering for the best view.

Robot developers were trying to build massive "what-if" software databases detailing out every possible scenario a future drone might face. Gathering the data was a painstaking effort that in 2012 was just getting underway, according to Stefanie Tellex, who worked alongside Cummings at MIT. "We're seeing the beginning of efforts to apply large data-sets to robots in order to increase their robustness and level of autonomy."

But as robot developers added autonomy, they ran into one huge problem. "We don't know a lot about how to tell a machine how to handle surprises," explained Randall Davis, another MIT roboticist.[41] In other words, drones just weren't creative. That was a huge problem as long as the machines were being asked to hunt highly imaginative and adaptive terrorists and insurgents.

In a former militant stronghold in the West African nation of Mali in early 2013, a reporter discovered a crude handbook for defeating drones. It advised militants to coat their vehicles in mud to foil heat sensors and cover themselves in carpets and grass mats to disappear from UAVs' view.[42]

Researchers were pretty much unanimous: only a human being could see through these tricks.

Human-robot teamwork was the solution. A drone would fly and scan on its own, calling for human assistance only rarely—when something unusual appeared in the terrain below or when it wanted permission to shoot. "Humans contribute the things humans are good at, and robots contribute what robots are good at," is how MIT's Seth Teller described the dynamic.[43] The result would be much more lethal flying robots requiring many fewer people to manage them. If the same number of operators were able to oversee a much larger number of robots, there could be a commensurate escalation of the scale and intensity of American drone campaigns. Say, two hundred armed robots in the air worldwide at any given moment instead of just eighty-five (the goal in 2012).

Washington welcomed the prospect of a bigger drone arsenal. "I think the American people expect us to use advanced technologies," John Brennan, the top counterterrorism adviser to President Barack Obama and future head of the CIA, said in an April 2012 speech. The United States was arming itself for the next two decades of shadow wars.[44]

Unwelcome

In February 2012, McClatchy reporter Alan Boswell and two journalists from *Time* arrived in Obo, a town in southern Central Africa Republic (CAR) where, it was rumored, U.S. Special Forces had set up a small base to help direct the hunt for Joseph Kony and the Lord's Resistance Army in CAR, South Sudan, and Congo.

President Barack Obama had announced the new U.S. intervention to the region the previous October, heralding it as "a significant contribution toward counter LRA efforts." Boswell and his colleagues were some of the first correspondents for American media to attempt to cover firsthand Washington's latest shadow war.[45]

They didn't get very far. U.S. Africa Command was working on a plan to showcase American military efforts in Central and East Africa—in essence, a small-scale embed, invitation only—but the command was not ready or willing to engage any reporters traveling on their own to the battle zone. Africom hadn't even sorted out its talking points.

"Twice in emails, a spokesman for the military said there was no U.S. base in Obo and that U.S. troops deployed here were staying at a Ugandan base," Boswell wrote. "But the Ugandan base is at an abandoned church on one side of town, while the newly constructed outpost where the Americans stay is near a police station on the opposite side. Locals say the American compound has its own helicopter pad."[46]

The obfuscation was the flipside of the military's eventual strategy for portraying the U.S. intervention in the media. A month later Africa Command invited select members of the local and international press on a four-day "event" in Uganda and CAR highlighting what the command later described as "the African-led counter-LRA mission."

"This visit resulted in extensive worldwide coverage of the story, which clearly articulated our advise and assist mission," Africom spokesman Tom Davis would write, as though articulating *Washington's* vision for covert warfare were the point of Boswell's reporting.[47]

Back in Obo, a new frontline in America's creeping shadow wars, the three journalists strolled up to the U.S. compound. "Two close-cropped white heads poked briefly above the wall," Boswell wrote. Whether he meant it or not, his article lent a single voice to an American shadow war strategy some two decades in the making. As Boswell recounted, one of the "close-cropped" heads turned to the journalists and yelled, "You are not allowed in here."[48]

Bemused

In 2012 Abraham Karem, the inventor of the Predator drone, was still developing warplanes. His new company Karem Aircraft, Inc., with offices in California and Texas, was working on a military transport with tilting rotors, able to take off and land like a helicopter and cruise like a regular airplane.

Now seventy-six, Karem—the "dronefather," as the *Economist* described him—was a frequent commenter in news reports about UAVs. He seemed amused at the way the Predator had changed warfare. "I just wanted UAVs to perform to the same standards of safety, reliability and performance as manned aircraft," he said. "I was not the guy who put missiles on the Predator."[49]

Epilogue

For years darkness had slowly been gathering over America's wars. U.S. involvement in armed conflict had never been so obscured. It was rarer by the day for large numbers of Americans to even do any direct fighting.

Building on a Cold War tradition and spurred by its reluctance to expend American lives—a fundamental impulse only underscored by the bloody departures from historical trends that were the Iraq and Afghanistan Wars—Washington had cultivated proxies and had encouraged its proxies to also enlist proxies of *their* own.

That layering was best expressed in Somalia, the cauldron of U.S. shadow warfare, where America's proxy Kenya employed Somali proxies of its own, thus avoiding the nationalist backlash that had defeated the United States' previous proxy effort with Ethiopia as the front.

Wars were being fought many degrees removed from their origins.

The shadows were cast by technology—the ever more sophisticated drones that flew from secret bases on secret missions over distant battlefields and did most of America's state-sponsored killing by remote control—and by the tradition of anonymity within the Special Operations Forces and mercenary groups that represented a growing proportion of the core shadow war manpower.

The government's approach to the press deepened the darkness. By the second decade of U.S. shadow wars in the 2010s, bureaucrats had successfully inverted the media's relationship to the government. Where once the free press expected the government to respond to its demands—and got results—now the government thoroughly dictated when, where, and how reporters covered U.S. wars. The press pool, and later the embed system, were the vehicles for this pernicious reversal of American norms.

The conflicts themselves were easier than ever to mask. Thanks in part to an expanding force of international peacekeepers deployed to more and more war zones, armed conflicts by and large had become smaller, shorter, and less bloody at the same time that the proxy strategy rendered their origins and aims more obscure to more people.

The darkness is chilling. But also comforting. It's harder to tell when, where, and why America takes up arms, but it's clear these shadow conflicts are a facet of warfare's evolution into something far less awful and destructive than the word "war" implies.

More and more, we're at peace. We shrink from even the most justified acts of state violence. We should not cease to pay attention to the places where, reasons why, and means by which we inflict violence.

Nor should we wish to return to a time when major warfare consumed the planet in broad daylight.

Addendum

As the initial deadline for this book passed, a long-running and highly secretive U.S. counterterrorism campaign in the African Sahel region emerged from the shadows, dragged into the sunlight by a French military operation that bore no small resemblance to the American-backed attacks by Ethiopia and Kenya in Somalia.

Washington's Sahel campaign, targeting al Qaeda in the Islamic Maghreb and other militant groups in the West African country of Mali, involved all the usual shadow war forces: commandos, drones, and proxy forces—the latter composed in part of Chadians long accustomed to fighting other people's wars for them.

On January 11, 2013, Islamic militants occupying northern Mali in West Africa advanced on a key town separating the government-controlled south from the northern part of the country, held by rebels since the spring of 2012. France, Mali's former colonial ruler, quickly deployed air and ground forces alongside Malian troops to first stop the advance, then recapture the north. French jet fighters bombed rebel positions scouted by Paris's tiny fleet of unarmed, Predator-style Harfang drones. In an echo of the U.S. invasion of Afghanistan twelve years prior, French army Special Forces organized Malian battalions and led them into battle. French armored vehicles, artillery, and attack helicopters arrived to reinforce the Malians.

In three months of fighting several hundred militants, a few score African troops, and just two French soldiers would die alongside potentially hundreds of civilians caught in the cross-fire. It wasn't a big war, but it grew to involve governments all over the world.[1]

As the fighting escalated, a host of Western and African countries pledged planes, people, and logistical support to the French-Malian troops. The Pentagon publicly expressed its wariness of a potentially drawn-out war. "The real question is, now what?" Army Gen. Carter Ham, Africom commander, said as the first French bombs fell.[2]

Washington ultimately sent C-17 airlifters to haul people and supplies between French air bases and Mali and KC-135 aerial tankers to refuel the French jet fighters on their long bombing sorties and pledged $50 million in cash, but it resisted a fuller commitment even as Chadian troops crossed the border into Mali to join the French and the West African economic union vowed to raise a UN-style peacekeeping force in the embattled country.

America's reluctance was a cover. In fact, the United States was playing—and had long played—a central role in counterterrorism efforts in Mali and across the Sahel. The deniability factor, however, was high.

In 2004 the U.S. State Department launched the Pan Sahel Initiative, a $500-million diplomatic and military program meant to help the region's governments defeat Islamic terrorists within their own borders. The initiative specifically targeted Algeria, Chad, Mali, Mauritania, Niger, Senegal, Nigeria, Morocco, and Tunisia, with Libya a candidate for involvement provided relations between it and the United States improved.

U.S. embassies in the Sahel added more military attachés as Special Forces and trainers and advisers drawn from the regular U.S. military—as many as a thousand at a time—fanned out across the region, training native soldiers and improving their technical capabilities. In Chad and Mali, U.S. commandos instructed the Chadian army in basic tactics.

A Special Forces sergeant expressed his frustration with the cultural gap between the Americans and their Chadian trainees. "It was like going to Mars," he told the *Washington Post*.[3] But a Special Forces officer deployed to Mali praised his students from the Malian army. "They're really a sharp unit, and they're picking it up quickly."[4]

The Pan Sahel Initiative changed names several times and, gradually, all but disappeared from the U.S. press. But the commandos remained. On March 22, 2012, Malian president Amadou Toumani Toure was ousted by U.S.-trained Malian army officers frustrated with Toure's leadership against Islamists in the country's vast, arid north. The coup, which Washington was swift to condemn, illustrated yet again the risks of covert U.S. military assistance. It was not uncommon for men trained by the United States to threaten the democratically elected governments that the United States publicly backed. Within a week of the coup the Defense Department had ceased all military training programs in Mali—or so the Pentagon claimed. Then on April 20 three Special Operations Command troops and three civilian women died in an early morning car accident in the southern city of Bamako, Mali's capital.

Pressed for details, the Pentagon eventually identified all the dead Americans. One of them, Master Sgt. Trevor Bast, worked for the little-known Army Intelligence and Security Command, which operated radio intercept gear in order to help find and target terrorists. Megan Larson-Kone, a spokesman for the U.S. embassy in Bamako, told the *Post* that the American commandos had remained in Mali to "wind down" the training program— and in hopes that the political chaos would be quickly resolved and American forces could resume working with the Malians.[5]

And that was the last specific information the U.S. government provided about American forces in Mali in the aftermath of the coup. But their presence continued to be felt. In mid-June a missile, possibly fired by a U.S. drone, killed seven militants in northern Mali. American sources contacted by journalist Bill Roggio declined to confirm or deny the drone attack.[6]

But American drones *were* apparently active over Mali, despite the Defense Department's silence. Amateur aviation enthusiasts monitoring air traffic control broadcasts via specialist websites could hear the drones' operators steering the robots from bases in Europe toward Mali, carefully avoiding civilian flights.[7]

And as French and Malian forces pushed the Islamists north in January and February 2013, quickly liberating all of Mali's major cities, Washington moved to expand its UAV operations in the region—this time openly. President Barack Obama announced the construction of a new drone base in Niger, placing Predator- and Reaper-class 'bots within quick flying distance of militant holdouts in Mali's desert fringe.

U.S.-led training efforts dating back to 2004 also bore fruit. In early March the Chadian government announced its troops in northern Mali had found and killed Moktar Belmoktar, a top militant affiliated with al Qaeda in the Islamic Maghreb whose plot against a natural gas facility in Algeria in April had resulted in the deaths of three dozen hostages, including several Americans.[8]

That the same Chadian army that had ineffectually chased me around the desert town of Abéché in 2009 amid a deadly flurry of friendly fire could, just three years later, hunt down and kill a top terrorist *in a foreign country* is clear testimony to the effectiveness of covert U.S. military assistance that, if anything, is expanding even as large-scale, overt warfare diminishes.

Shadow wars rage on.

Notes

1. Tinkerers, Dictators, and Soldiers of Fortune

1. Curtis Peebles, *Dark Eagles: A History of Top Secret U.S. Aircraft* (Novato, CA: Presidio, 1995), 207.
2. Peter Finn, "Rise of the Drone: From Calif. Garage to Multibillion-Dollar Defense Industry," *Washington Post*, December 23, 2011, http://www.washingtonpost.com/national/national-security/rise-of-the-drone-from-calif-garage-to-multibillion-dollar-defense-industry/2011/12/22/gIQACG8UEP_story.html.
3. Stephen Trimble, "A History of Predator from the Ultimate Insider," *The DEW Line*, March 17, 2011, http://www.flightglobal.com/blogs/the-dewline/2011/03/a-history-of-predator-from-the.html.
4. Steve Coll, *Ghost Wars: The Secret History of the CIA, Afghanistan, and Bin Laden, from the Soviet Invasion to September 10, 2001* (New York: Penguin, 2004), 528.
5. Trimble, "History of Predator."

6. Peebles, *Dark Eagles*, 209.

7. Trimble, "History of Predator."

8. Greg Goebel, "The General Atomics Predator," VectorSite.net, February 2, 2001, http://www.vectorsite.net/twuav_07.html.

9. Coll, *Ghost Wars*, 528.

10. Jon Lake, "The Unmanned Future," *Combat Aircraft* magazine, October 2012, 61.

11. Peebles, *Dark Eagles*, 212.

12. Ibid.

13. Trimble, "History of Predator."

14. Peebles, *Dark Eagles*, 212; Goebel, "General Atomics Predator."

15. Samantha Weinberg, *Last of the Pirates: The Search for Bob Denard* (New York: Pantheon, 1995), 64–67.

16. Simon Fraser University, *Human Security Report*, 201, http://hsr group.org/docs/Publications/HSR2012/Figures/2012Report_Fig_5 _3_WarTrends50-09.pdf.

17. Ibid., figure A.1, http://hsrgroup.org/docs/Publications/HSR2012/ Figures/2012Report_Fig_A_1_BDsSBConflict46-09.pdf.

18. Ibid., figures 8.2 and 8.1, http://hsrgroup.org/docs/Publications/ HSR2012/Figures/2012Report_Fig_8_2_CloseupOSVDeaths.pdf, http://hsrgroup.org/docs/Publications/HSR2012/Figures/ 2012Report_Fig_8_1_GlobalCampaignsOSV.pdf.

19. Ibid., figure 8.3, http://hsrgroup.org/docs/Publications/HSR2012/ Figures/2012Report_Fig_8_3_RegionalOSVCampaigns.pdf.

20. William Shawcross, *Deliver Us from Evil: Peacekeepers, Warlords and a World of Endless Conflict* (New York: Simon & Schuster, 2001), 48.

21. "Post Cold-War Surge," United Nations Peacekeeping, UN.org, http://www.un.org/en/peacekeeping/operations/surge.shtml (accessed February 2013).

22. "Saudis Treating Somali President for Crash Injuries," *Los Angeles Times*, May 25, 1986, http://articles.latimes.com/1986-05-25/news/ mn-7297_1_somali-saudis-president.

23. Jane Perlez, "300,000 Somali Refugees Flee Civil War in Sudden Exodus," *Sarasota Herald-Tribune*, August 13, 1988, http://news .google.com/newspapers?id=YzAcAAAAIBAJ&sjid=xnkEAAAAIBA J&pg=3442,2925281&dq=somali+national+movement&hl=en.

24. Jane Perlez, "Report for U.S. Says Somali Army Killed 5,000 Unarmed Civilians," *New York Times*, September 9, 1989, http://

www.nytimes.com/1989/09/09/world/report-for-us-says-somali
-army-killed-5000-unarmed-civilians.html.

25. "65 Reported Slain at Somali Soccer Game," *Los Angeles Times*, July
    11, 1990, http://articles.latimes.com/1990-07-11/news/mn-232_1
    _soccer-game.

26. Jane Perlez, "Unrest Fills Somalia's Capital as Rebel Groups Press
    Drive to City," *New York Times*, December 12, 1990, http://www
    .nytimes.com/1990/12/12/world/unrest-fills-somalia-s-capital-as
    -rebel-groups-press-drive-to-city.html.

27. Perlez, "Report for U.S. Says Somali Army Killed 5,000 Unarmed
    Civilians."

28. "Siad Barre Has Fled, Say Rebels," *New Strait Times*, January 13, 1991,
    http://news.google.com/newspapers?id=BhFZAAAAIBAJ&sjid=J5AD
    AAAAIBAJ&pg=6108,3113170&dq=siad+barre&hl=en.

29. Shawcross, *Deliver Us from Evil*, 85.

30. Ibid., 86.

31. Tom Zeller Jr., "Back in Somalia, With al Qaeda's Connection More
    Clear," *New York Times*, January 9, 2007, http://thelede.blogs
    .nytimes.com/2007/01/09/back-in-somalia-with-al-qaedas
    -connection-clear/.

32. Jon Mordan, "Press Pools, Prior Restraint and the Persian Gulf War,"
    Air & Space Power Journal, June 6, 1999, http://www
    .airpower.au.af.mil/airchronicles/cc/mordan.html.

33. Malcom W. Browne, "Reporting America at War," PBS, http://www
    .pbs.org/weta/reportingamericaatwar/reporters/browne/ap_09.html.

34. Mordan, "Press Pools, Prior Restraint and the Persian Gulf War."

35. Michael Mandel, "The Journalism Job Market: Part I, Looking Back,"
    Business Week, September 16, 2009, http://www.businessweek.com/
    the_thread/economicsunbound/archives/2009/09/the_journalism
    .html.

36. Greg Myre, "Comoro Islands Nation Tries to Oust Mercenary," *Pittsburgh Post-Gazette*, December 11, 1989.

37. Weinberg, *Last of the Pirates*.

38. Ibid., 36–38.

39. Ibid., 70–83.

40. Jamey Keaten, "Ex-French Mercenary Denard Dies at 78," *Washington Post*, October 14, 2007, http://www.washingtonpost.com/wp
    -dyn/content/article/2007/10/14/AR2007101400409.html.

41. "Bob Denard, 78; French Mercenary Fought Communism," *Los Angeles Times*, October 15, 2007, http://articles.latimes.com/2007/oct/15/local/me-denard15.

42. Myre, "Comoro Islands Nation Tries to Oust Mercenary."

43. Keaten, "Ex-French Mercenary Denard Dies at 78."

44. "Man Accused of Murder Wins Defamation Suit," IOL News, June 3, 2012, http://www.iol.co.za/news/crime-courts/man-accused-of-murder-wins-defamation-suit-1.1333109#.UYyOssr9dxM.

45. Jeffrey Gettleman, Mark Mazzetti, and Eric Schmitt, "U.S. Relies on Contractors in Somalia Conflict," *New York Times*, August 10, 2011, http://www.nytimes.com/2011/08/11/world/africa/11somalia.html?pagewanted=all.

46. Peebles, *Dark Eagles*, 215.

47. Coll, *Ghost Wars*, 531.

48. Trimble, "A History of Predator."

49. Peebles, *Dark Eagles*, 215.

50. Lake, "The Unmanned Future," 61.

51. Peebles, *Dark Eagles*, 215.

52. Trimble, "A History of Predator."

53. Shawcross, *Deliver Us from Evil*, 28.

54. "First Strike: Global Terror in America," FBI.gov, February 26, 2008, http://www.fbi.gov/news/stories/2008/february/tradebom_022608.

55. "Terrorism," National Institute of Justice, September 13, 2011, http://www.nij.gov/topics/crime/terrorism/.

56. "22 USC § 2656f—Annual Country Reports on Terrorism," Cornell University Law School, http://www.law.cornell.edu/uscode/text/22/2656f (accessed March 2013).

57. Philip Keefer, Norman Loayza, eds., *Terrorism, Economic Development, and Political Openness* (New York: Cambridge University Press, 2008), 93.

58. Shawcross, *Deliver Us from Evil*, 239.

59. Ibid., 31.

60. Ibid., 46.

61. Ibid., 35.

62. Ibid., 21.

63. Ibid., 28.

2. Disillusioned

1. "United Nations Operations in Somalia I (UNISOM I)," UN.org, http://www.un.org/en/peacekeeping/missions/past/unosom1back gr2.html.

2. "Ambush in Mogadishu: Interview with General Thomas Montgomery," PBS.org, http://www.pbs.org/wgbh/pages/frontline/shows/ ambush/interviews/montgomery.html.

3. "2-year Mission of Peacekeeping Ends in Somalia," *Gainesville Sun*, March 3, 1995, http://news.google.com/newspapers?id=5fZQAAAAI BAJ&sjid=leoDAAAAIBAJ&pg=1847,485456&dq=somalia+pakistan is+killed+peacekeeping+june+5+1993&hl=en.

4. "Ambush in Mogadishu."

5. "2-year Mission of Peacekeeping Ends in Somalia."

6. "26 U.N. Troops Reported Dead in Somalia Combat," *New York Times*, June 6, 1993, http://www.nytimes.com/1993/06/06/ world/26-un-troops-reported-dead-in-somalia-combat.html.

7. Kevin Sites, "Black Hawk Ground: Cactus and Bitterness Grow Where American Chopper Was Downed," Kevin Sites (blog), September 18, 2005, http://kevinsites.wordpress.com/2009/09/11/ hello-world/.

8. "Dan Eldon," Committee to Protect Journalists, http://cpj.org/ killed/1993/dan-eldon.php.

9. "The United States Army in Somalia," U.S. Army Center of Military History, http://www.history.army.mil/brochures/Somalia/Somalia .htm.

10. "400 Rangers Headed to Bloody Somalia," *Rochester Sentinel*, August 24, 1993, http://news.google.com/newspapers?id=cshUAAA AIBAJ&sjid=mTsNAAAAIBAJ&pg=6033,5925710&dq=day+of+the+ rangers+somalia&hl=en.

11. "3 Killed as U.S. Chopper Is Shot Down in Somalia," *New York Times*, September 25, 1993, http://www.nytimes.com/1993/09/25/world/3 -killed-as-us-chopper-is-shot-down-in-somalia.html.

12. Clifford Day, "Critical Analysis on the Defeat of Task Force Ranger," research paper, U.S. Air Force Air Command and Staff College, Montgomery, Alabama, March 1997, http://www.gwu.edu/ ~nsarchiv/NSAEBB/NSAEBB63/doc10.pdf.

13. Sites, "Black Hawk Ground."

14. "United States Army in Somalia."

15. Matt Welch, *McCain: The Myth of a Maverick* (New York: Palgrave Macmillan, 2008) 161–62.

16. "U.S. to Pull Out of Somalia by Mid-September," *Deseret News*, August 26, 1994, http://news.google.com/newspapers?id=nRtOAA AAIBAJ&sjid=huwDAAAAIBAJ&pg=6996,4767783&dq=us+pulls +out+somalia&hl=en.

17. "U.S., Italy Secure Beach Perimeter," *Daily Courier*, February 28, 1995, http://news.google.com/newspapers?id=kScOAAAAIBAJ&sji d=unoDAAAAIBAJ&pg=6591,3900699&dq=us+pulls+out+somalia &hl=en.

18. Robert Young Pelton, "Black Hawk Down Redux?: Another Famine, Another War. What Did America Learn from 1993?" *SomaliaReport*, July 21, 2011, http://www.somaliareport.com/index.php/post/1196/ Black_Hawk_Down_Redux.

19. "Ambush in Mogadishu."

20. James McKinley Jr., "How a U.S. Marine Became a Warlord in Somalia," NomadNet, August 12, 1996, http://www.netnomad.com/ aydiidyounger.nyt.html.

21. Armando Ramirez, "From Bosnia to Baghdad: The Evolution of U.S. Army Special Forces from 1995 to 2004," Naval Postgraduate School thesis, September 2004, https://docs.google.com/ viewer?a=v&q=cache:zPKFvnm-aasJ:www.fas.org/man/eprint/ ramirez.pdf+&hl=en&gl=us&pid=bl&srcid=ADGEESjf2xUoX5FN SDIHIFosWZRGx2moscwOQuixoRFxXbvdwsm14BjFxIzXcyuY ap9orjhjz3oDdahB1vXXCivn8qqu7nDtR96lYi5f3TCUPkvjDk3Imh RXsUG_EMB5xzrnTg6HhFoK&sig=AHIEtbTCjTLdLws6a4LqvDx tHCMNUeMYpg.

22. Presidential Decision Directive 25, "United States: Administration Policy on Reforming Multilateral Peace Operations," The American Society of International Law, Washington, D.C, May 1994, http:// www.kentlaw.edu/academics/courses/admin-perritt/pdd-25.html.

23. "Rwanda: How the Genocide Happened," BBC News, December 18, 2008, http://news.bbc.co.uk/2/hi/1288230.stm.

24. Bill Clinton, *Giving: How Each of Us Can Change the World* (New York: Knopf, 2007), 96.

25. "Unamir: International Tribunal of Rwanda," UN.org, 1999, http:// www.un.org/en/peacekeeping/missions/past/unamirS.htm.

26. "Monthly Summary of Military and Civilian Police Contribution to United Nations Operations," UN.org, http://www.un.org/en/peace keeping/contributors/documents/Yearly_Summary.pdf.

27. "Unamir: International Tribunal of Rwanda," UN.org.

28. "Post Cold-War Surge," United Nations Peacekeeping.

29. "Monthly Summary of Military and Civilian Police Contribution to United Nations Operations."

30. Garth Myers, Thomas Klak, and Timothy Koehl, "The Inscription of Difference: News Coverage of the Conflicts in Rwanda and Bosnia," *Political Geography* 15, no. 1 (1996): 21–46, http://www.colorado .edu/geography/class_homepages/geog_2002_s06/laptop_s06/ current%20projects/Cox_Low%20Robinson%20Book%20chapter/ Cox_Low%20Book%20chapter/media%20war%20Bosnia%20 and%20DRC%20in%20PG.pdf.

31. P. W. Singer, *Corporate Warriors: The Rise of the Privatized Military Industry* (New York: Cornell University Press, 2007), 9.

32. Pete Sawyer, "Who's Who in Executive Outcomes," *NewsConfidential*, http://newsconfidential.com/FS/FS_Story.php?RequestID=32925 (accessed July 2013).

33. James Davis, *Fortune's Warriors: Private Armies and the New World Order* (Vancouver: Douglas & McIntyre, 2002), 132.

34. Jim Hooper, "Executive Outcomes," *World Air Power Journal* (Spring 1997): 38–49; Scott Fitzsimmons, "Adapt or Die: The Cultural Foundations of Military Performance in the Sierra Leonean Civil War," Department of Political Science, University of Calgary, http://www .cpsa-acsp.ca/papers-2009/Fitzsimmons1.pdf.

35. Singer, *Corporate Warriors*, 11.

36. Ibid., 257.

37. Ibid., 118.

38. "Former South African Policeman Died in Uganda Plane Crash: Report," *Xinhua*, March 11, 2009.

39. Rowland Evans and Robert Novak, "Somali Holds U.S. Ship for Spy Activities," *Lodi News Sentinel*, August 4, 1970, http://news.google .com/newspapers?id=-CY_AAAAIBAJ&sjid=sE8MAAAAIBAJ&pg=7 056,2785939&dq=somali-coast-guard&hl=en.

40. "Oceans Victories," Greenpeace, http://www.greenpeace.org/usa/ en/campaigns/victories/oceans-victories/.

41. Shashank Bengali, "Somalis Say Illegal Fishing by Foreign Trawlers

Drove Them to Piracy," McClatchy, April 29, 2009, http://www
.informationclearinghouse.info/article22522.htm.

42. Michael Phillips, "Clan Leaders to Defend Fish Beds from Raids by
Foreign Fishermen," *Star-News*, February 3, 1994, http://news
.google.com/newspapers?nid=1454&dat=19940203&id=pKksAAAAI
BAJ&sjid=IBUEAAAAIBAJ&pg=7055,861058.

43. Bengali, "Somalis Say Illegal Fishing."

3. Balkanization

1. Paul Kaminski, U.S. Senate testimony, LexisNexis, March 19, 1997.

2. "Timeline: Siege of Srebrenica," BBC News, June 9, 2005, http://
news.bbc.co.uk/2/hi/675945.stm.

3. Goebel, "The General Atomics Predator."

4. Jacques Gansler, U.S. Senate testimony, March 12, 1998.

5. Linda Shiner, "Predator: First Watch," *Air & Space*, May 2001, http://
www.airspacemag.com/military-aviation/predator.html?c=y&page=2.

6. Sheila Widnall and Ronald Fogleman, U.S. Senate testimony, Lexis-
Nexis, May 21, 1997.

7. Linda Kozaryn, "Predators Bound for Bosnia," American Forces
Press Service, February 8, 1996, http://www.defense.gov/news/
newsarticle.aspx?id=40516.

8. Kaminski, U.S. Senate testimony.

9. Kozaryn, "Predators Bound for Bosnia."

10. Robert Leonard, *Global Hawk and DarkStar in the HAE UAV ACTD*
(Arlington, VA: Rand, 2002), http://www.rand.org/content/dam/
rand/pubs/monograph_reports/MR1474/MR1474.chap2.pdf.

11. "Global Hawk (CONV HAE UAV) Program," Federation of American
Scientists, https://www.fas.org/irp/agency/daro/uav96/20-21
.html (accessed March 2013).

12. "Factsheets: RQ-4 Global Hawk," U.S. Air Force, January 27, 2012,
http://www.af.mil/information/factsheets/factsheet.asp?id=13225.

13. "Factsheets: DarkStar," U.S. Air Force, August 26, 2009, http://www.
nationalmuseum.af.mil/factsheets/factsheet.asp?id=616.

14. "Patent D382851—Unmanned Aircraft," U.S. Patent Office, August
26, 1997, http://www.ptodirect.com/Results/Patents?query=PN/
D382851.

15. "Clinton: Strike Sends Message to Saddam," CNN, September 3,
1996, http://www.cnn.com/WORLD/9609/03/iraq.clinton/.

16. Ian Urbina, "This War Brought to You by Rendon Group," *Asia Times*, November 13, 2002, http://www.atimes.com/atimes/Middle _East/DK13Ak01.html.

17. James Bamford, "The Man Who Sold the War: Meet John Rendon, Bush's General in the Propaganda War," *Rense*, November 21, 2005, http://rense.com/general68/sold.htm.

18. "Operation Determined Falcon," Globalsecurity.org, http://www .globalsecurity.org/military/ops/determined_falcon.htm.

19. "Nato Poised to Strike," BBC, March 23, 1999, http://news.bbc .co.uk/2/hi/europe/301900.stm.

20. "NATO Operation Allied Force," U.S. Defense Department, June 21, 1999, http://www.defense.gov/specials/kosovo/.

21. Frank Fernandez, U.S. Senate testimony, LexisNexis, March 21, 2000.

22. Daniel Haulman, "U.S. Unmanned Aerial Vehicles in Combat, 1991-2003," U.S. Air Force, June 9, 2003, http://www.afhra.af.mil/ shared/media/document/AFD-070912-042.pdf.

23. Shiner, "Predator: First Watch."

24. Lt. Gen. Marvin Esmond, U.S. House of Representatives testimony, LexisNexis, October 19, 1999.

25. Goebel, "General Atomics Predator."

26. Robert McCabe, "Virginia Beach Company in Legal Battle over Boots," *Virginian-Pilot*, April 29, 2012, http://hamptonroads .com/2012/04/virginia-beach-company-legal-battle-over-boots.

27. "Bancroft Global Development," Guidestar, http://www.guidestar .org/organizations/54-1955545/bancroft-global-development.aspx.

28. Mary Riddell, "A Glimmer of Hope in the Dark Heart of Africa?" *Telegraph*, March 22, 2009, http://www.telegraph.co.uk/comment/ columnists/maryriddell/5033434/A-glimmer-of-hope-in-the-dark -heart-of-Africa.html.

29. Mark Bowden, "The Truth about Mogadishu No, the Battle Was Not an al-Qaeda Ambush. Yes, President Clinton Could Have Done More," *Philadelphia Inquirer*, October 8, 2006, http://articles.philly .com/2006-10-08/news/25417846_1_al-qaeda-mogadishu-bin.

30. "Profile: Fazul Abdullah Mohammed," BBC News, June 11, 2011, http://www.bbc.co.uk/news/world-africa-13738393.

31. Ben Snowdon and David Johnson, "Primer on the Embassy Bomb-ings and the U.S. Strikes on Sudan and Afghanistan," Information

Please Database, 2007, http://www.infoplease.com/spot/newsfacts
-sudanstrikes.html#ixzz2I7xYrfCp.

32. Bill Roggio, "Al Qaeda names Fazul Mohammed East African Commander," *Long War Journal*, November 11, 2009, http://www
.longwarjournal.org/archives/2009/11/al_qaeda_names_fazul.php
#ixzz29ACndWjl.

33. *9/11 Commission Report* (New York: W. W. Norton, 2004).

34. Ibid., 190–91.

35. Ibid., 364.

36. Richard Whittle, "Predator's Big Safari," Mitchell Institute for Airpower Studies, August 2011, http://www.afa.org/mitchell/reports/
MP7_Predator_0811.pdf.

37. Ibid.

38. "Big Safari," Federation of American Scientists, July 30, 1997,
http://www.fas.org/irp/program/collect/big_safari.htm.

39. Thomas P. Ehrhard, *Air Force UAVs: The Secret History*, Mitchell
Institute, July 2010, http://www.afa.org/mitchell/reports/MS
_UAV_0710.pdf.

40. Whittle, "Predator's Big Safari."

41. Coll, *Ghost Wars*, 549.

42. Whittle, "Predator's Big Safari."

43. Ibid.

44. *9/11 Commission Report*, 210.

45. Ibid., 211.

46. Ibid., 213.

47. Whittle, "Predator's Big Safari."

48. Author interview with "Tom" in Laghman, Afghanistan, February
2012.

49. "Obama's Warfare: 'From Power to a Policy,'" NPR, August 26,
2012, http://www.npr.org/2012/08/26/160077178/obamas-warfare
-from-power-to-a-policy.

50. Whittle, "Predator's Big Safari."

51. Doug Stanton, *Horse Soldiers: The Extraordinary Story of a Band of
US Soldiers Who Rode to Victory in Afghanistan* (New York: Scribner,
2009).

52. Jim Garamone, "Wolfowitz Shares Special Forces' Afghanistan Dispatches," American Forces Press Service, November 15, 2011, http://
www.defense.gov/News/NewsArticle.aspx?ID=44448.

53. *Human Security Report 2012*, Figure 5.2, http://hsrgroup.org/docs/Publications/HSR2012/Figures/2012Report_Fig_5_2_GlobalSBBDs46-08.pdf.

54. Ibid., Figure 7.1, http://hsrgroup.org/docs/Publications/HSR2012/Figures/2012Report_Fig_7_1_GlobalNSConflictsBDs.pdf.

55. Ibid., Figure 5.8, http://hsrgroup.org/docs/Publications/HSR2012/Figures/2012Report_Fig_5_8_DeathsIntraIntlizedIntra89-09.pdf.

56. Steven Pinker, "Violence Vanquished," *Wall Street Journal*, September 24, 2011, http://online.wsj.com/article/SB10001424053111904106704576583203589408180.html.

4. Backwaters

1. Thom Shanker and Eric Schmitt, "U.S. Moves Commandos to East Africa to Pursue Qaeda in Yemen," *New York Times*, September 18, 2002, http://www.nytimes.com/2002/09/18/international/middleeast/18MILI.html.

2. "Fact Sheet: Combined Joint Task Force—Horn of Africa," U.S. Africa Command, December 2012, http://www.hoa.africom.mil/pdfFiles/Fact%20Sheet.pdf.

3. Michael Gordon, "Threats and Responses: The Operations; U.S. Turns Horn of Africa into a Military Hub," *New York Times*, November 17, 2002, http://www.nytimes.com/2002/11/17/world/threats-and-responses-the-operations-us-turns-horn-of-africa-into-a-military-hub.html?pagewanted=all&src=pm.

4. James Bamford, *The Shadow Factory: The NSA from 9/11 to the Eavesdropping on America* (New York: Anchor Books, 2009), 135, 136.

5. Sean Naylor, "The Secret War: How U.S. Hunted AQ in Africa," *Army Times*, October 30, 2011, http://www.armytimes.com/news/2011/10/military-seals-horn-of-africa-al-qaida-terrorists-103011w/.

6. Jeremy Scahill, "Obama's Expanding Covert Wars," *Nation*, June 4, 2010, http://www.thenation.com/blog/obamas-expanding-covert-wars#.

7. Dana Priest and William Arkin, "'Top Secret America': A Look at the Military's Joint Special Operations Command," *Washington Post*, September 2, 2011, http://articles.washingtonpost.com/2011-09-02/world/35273073_1_navy-seal-joint-special-operations-command-drones.

8. "Too Much is Enough," Strategy Page, January 18, 2012, http://www.strategypage.com/htmw/htsf/articles/20120118.aspx.

9. Ramirez, "From Bosnia to Baghdad."

10. Scahill, "Obama's Expanding Covert Wars."

11. "Jemaah Islamiyah (a.k.a. Jemaah Islamiah)," Council on Foreign Relations, June 19, 2009, http://www.cfr.org/indonesia/jemaah-islamiyah-k-jemaah-islamiah/p8948.

12. "Joint Special Operations Task Force – Philippines," Globalsecurity.org, http://www.globalsecurity.org/military/agency/dod/jsotf-p.htm; Katherine Evangelista, "Fisherman Dead, Son Hurt as US Speedboat Slams into Fishing Boat off Basilan," Global Nation, April 20, 2012, http://globalnation.inquirer.net/34069/fisherman-dead-son-hurt-as-us-speedboat-slams-into-fishing-boat-off-basilan.

13. "Drone Aircraft in Philippines," Star-News, March 12, 2002, http://news.google.com/newspapers?id=QdFOAAAAIBAJ&sjid=mR8EAAAAIBAJ&pg=4743,3438049&dq=drone+philippines&hl=en.

14. Goebel, "General Atomics Predator"; "General Atomics Gnat," Directory of U.S. Military Rockets and Missiles, http://www.designation-systems.net/dusrm/app4/gnat.html.

15. "Drone War over the Sulu Sea," Malaysia Flying Herald, June 5, 2012, http://malaysiaflyingherald.wordpress.com/2012/06/05/drone-war-over-the-sulu-sea/.

16. Al Jacinto, Esther Schrader, and Richard Paddock, "Army Helicopter Crashes in the Philippines; 10 Aboard," Los Angeles Times, February 22, 2002, http://articles.latimes.com/2002/feb/22/news/mn-29313.

17. "Operation Enduring Freedom Casualties—Afghanistan," iCasualties.org, http://www.icasualties.org/OEF/Fatalities.aspx.

18. "2 U.S. Troops Killed in Philippines Blast," CBS News, September 29, 2009, http://www.cbsnews.com/2100-202_162-5348332.html.

19. "Two Special Forces Soldiers Killed in the Southern Philippines," Joint Special Operation Task Force–Philippines, October 2, 2009, http://jsotf-p.blogspot.com/2009/10/two-special-forces-soldiers-killed-in.html.

20. Sol Jose Vanzi, "Soldiers Take over Major MILF Base," Philippine Headline News Online, May 31, 2000, http://www.newsflash.org/2000/05/hl/hl012186.htm.

21. Antonieta Lopez, "The Heroine Comes Home," Philippine Star, March 30, 2001, http://www.philstar.com/headlines/90237/heroine-comes-home.

22. AFP Modernization Program, "Sustaining the Movement: Annual Accomplishment Report 2005," Philippines Air Force, http://adroth.ph/afpmodern/wp-content/uploads/2011/12/afpmp-annualrpt051.pdf.

23. "Drone Aircraft in Philippines," *Philippine Star*, March 12, 2002, http://news.google.com/newspapers?id=QdFOAAAAIBAJ&sjid=mR8EAAA AIBAJ&pg=4743,3438049&dq=drone+philippines&hl=en.

24. Roel Parentildeo, "Spy Plane Crashes in Zamboanga," *Philippine Star*, April 1, 2002, http://www.philstar.com/headlines/155626/spy-plane -crashes-zamboanga.

25. "Crashed U.S. Drone Held Hostage In Jolo Island," *Zamboanga Journal*, February 17, 2006, http://zamboangajournal.blogspot.com/2006/02/crashed-us-drone-held-hostage-in-jolo.html.

26. Mark Mazzetti, "The Drone Zone," *New York Times*, July 6, 2012, http://www.nytimes.com/2012/07/08/magazine/the-drone-zone .html?pagewanted=all&_r=0.

27. D. B. Grady, "Drone Warfare . . . in the Philippines?," *The Week*, July 18, 2012, http://news.yahoo.com/drone-warfare-philippines-063000794 .html.

28. Mazzetti, "The Drone Zone."

29. Kamran Sadaghiani, "Silver Fox UAV Flies in the Philippines for the 31st MEU," *Space War*, November 5, 2007, http://www.spacewar .com/reports/Silver_Fox_UAV_Flies_In_The_Philippines_For_The _31st_MEU_999.html.

30. "MILF Shoots Down U.S. Spy Plane in Mindanao," GMA News, November 14, 2008, http://www.gmanetwork.com/news/story/133562/news/regions/milf-shoots-down-us-spy-plane-in-mindanao.

31. Al Jacinto, "Military Spy Plane Shot Down in Maguindanao," GMA News, June 20, 2009, http://www.gmanetwork.com/news/story/165394/news/regions/military-spy-plane-shot-down-in-maguindanao.

5. Distracted

1. "Former Aide: Powell WMD Speech 'Lowest Point in My Life,'" CNN, August 23, 2005, http://articles.cnn.com/2005-08-19/world/powell. un_1_colin-powell-lawrence-wilkerson-wmd-intelligence? _s=PM:WORLD.

2. Colin Powell, speech to U.N., *Washington Post*, February 5, 2003, http://www.washingtonpost.com/wp-srv/nation/transcripts/powell-text_020503.html.

3. George W. Bush, press conference, March 6, 2003, http://
georgewbush-whitehouse.archives.gov/newsreleases/2003/03/
20030306-8.html.

4. Bill Moyers, "Buying the War," PBS, April 25, 2007, http://www.pbs
.org/moyers/journal/btw/transcript1.html.

5. Bamford, "The Man Who Sold the War."

6. Kim Hume, "Birth of the Embed," *Weekly Standard*, March 28, 2003,
http://www.weeklystandard.com/author/kim-hume.

7. Bill Katovsky and Timothy Carlson, eds., *Embedded: The Media at
War in Iraq* (Guilford, CT: Lyons Press, 2004), x.

8. Katovsky and Carlson, *Embedded*, xi.

9. Hume, "Birth of the Embed."

10. Whittle, "Predator's Big Safari."

11. David Fulghum, "A Classified Lockheed Martin Unmanned Reconnaissance Aircraft Was Used in Iraq," *Aviation Week*, July 6, 2003,
http://sgforums.com/forums/1164/topics/51320.

12. Steve Fainaru, *Big Boy Rules* (Philadelphia: Da Capo Press, 2008), xi.

13. William Solis, Government Accountability Office, House of Representatives testimony, June 13, 2006, http://www.gao.gov/new
.items/d06865t.pdf.

14. Government Accountability Office, "Rebuilding Iraq: Actions Still
Needed to Improve the Use of Private Security Providers," June
2005, http://www.gao.gov/new.items/d05737.pdf .

15. Fainaru, *Big Boy Rules*, 179.

16. Ryan Devereaux, "Blackwater Guards Lose Bid to Appeal Charges
in Iraqi Civilian Shooting Case," *Guardian*, June 5, 2012, http://
www.guardian.co.uk/world/2012/jun/05/blackwater-guards-lose
-appeal-iraq-shooting.

17. Spencer Ackerman, "Blackwater Wins Piece of $10 Billion Merce-
nary Deal," *Wired*, October 1, 2010, http://www.wired.com/danger
room/2010/10/exclusive-blackwater-wins-piece-of-10-billion
-merc-deal/.

18. Singer, *Corporate Warriors*, 220–21.

19. "Operation Iraqi Freedom Casualties," iCasualties.org, http://
icasualties.org/iraq/index.aspx.

20. "Iraqi Deaths," iCasualties.org, http://icasualties.org/iraq/Iraqi
Deaths.aspx.

21. Charlie Reed, "Journalists' Recent Work Examined Before Embeds,"

Stars and Stripes, August 24, 2009, http://www.stripes.com/news/journalists-recent-work-examined-before-embeds-1.94239.

22. David Martin, "Holding a Story Is a Judgment Call," CBS News, February 20, 2006, http://www.cbsnews.com/8301-500486_162 -1330945-500486.html.

23. Author interview with Monte Morin, Iraq, 2006.

24. "History of 30th Reconnaissance Squadron (Beast of Kandahar Handlers)," *Deep Blue Horizon* (blog), December 8, 2009, http:// deep bluehorizon.blogspot.com/2009/12/history-of-30-reconnaissance -squadron.html.

25. Keith Rogers, "Predator Spy Planes: Aircraft in High Demand," *Las Vegas Review-Journal*, March 4, 2006, http://www.reviewjournal .com/lvrj_home/2006/Mar-04-Sat-2006/news/6183518.html.

26. "Fact Sheet: 30th Reconnaissance Squadron," U.S. Air Force, July 17, 2007, http://www.afhra.af.mil/factsheets/factsheet.asp?id=10193.

27. "Mystery UAV Operating in Afghanistan," *Shephard*, April 10, 2009, http://www.shephardmedia.com/news/uv-online/mystery-uav -operating-in-afghanistan/.

28. Ibid.

29. Graham Warwick, "Beast of Kandahar Stealthy UAV," *Aviation Week*, May 13, 2009, http://www.aviationweek.com/Blogs.aspx ?plckBlogId=Blog:27ec4a53-dcc8-42d0-bd3a-01329aef79a7&plckC ontroller=Blog&plckScript=blogscript&plckElementId=blogDest& plckBlogPage=BlogViewPost&plckPostId=Blog%253A27ec4a53 -dcc8-42d0-bd3a-01329aef79a7Post%253A25afdd9c-786a-483f -95ae-23cc9f365167.

30. Bill Sweetman, "Gotcha! Desert Prowler Unveiled," *Aviation Week*, December 1, 2009, http://www.aviationweek.com/Blogs.aspx?plck BlogId=Blog:27ec4a53-dcc8-42d0-bd3a-01329aef79a7&plckCon troller=Blog&plckBlogPage=BlogViewPost&newspaperUserId=27 ec4a53-dcc8-42d0-bd3a-01329aef79a7&plckPostId=Blog%253a27e c4a53-dcc8-42d0-bd3a-01329aef79a7Post%253a3a3730f4-c5f9-475c -be42-1fdc18846c1b&plckScript=blogScript&plckElementId=blog Dest.

31. David Fulghum, "U.S. Air Force Reveals Operational Stealth UAV," *Aviation Week*, December 4, 2009, http://www.aviationweek.com/ Blogs.aspx?plckBlogId=Blog:27ec4a53-dcc8-42d0-bd3a-01329aef79

a7&plckController=Blog&plckBlogPage=BlogViewPost&news
paperUserId=27ec4a53-dcc8-42d0-bd3a-01329aef79a7&plckPostId
=Blog%253A27ec4a53-dcc8-42d0-bd3a-01329aef79a7Post%253A
649e3cf4-8c07-4739-82cf-322c6c56ccd5&plck.

32. "Factsheet: RQ-170 Sentinel," U.S. Air Force, December 2, 2010, http://www.af.mil/information/factsheets/factsheet.asp?id=16001.

33. Sweetman, "Gotcha! Desert Prowler Unveiled."

6. Empowered

1. Author interview with Kennedy Mwale, Mombasa, Kenya, 2008.

2. "Profile: Somalia's Islamic Courts," BBC News, June 6, 2006, http://news.bbc.co.uk/2/hi/5051588.stm.

3. U.S. Diplomatic Cable, June 26, 2006, http://wlstorage.net/file/frazer-somalia-memo-2006.pdf.

4. David Axe, "Behind the Ethiopian Blitz," *Ares*, January 16, 2007.

5. Ibid.

6. David Axe, "WikiLeaked Cable Confirms U.S.' Secret Somalia Op," *Wired*, December 12, 2010, http://www.wired.com/dangerroom/2010/12/wikileaked-cable-confirms-u-s-secret-somalia-op/.

7. "About the Command," U.S. Africa Command, http://www.africom.mil/about-the-command.

8. "Bush: No New US Bases in Africa," Agence-France Presse, February 20, 2008, http://afp.google.com/article/ALeqM5hxW3qPqxijg wKjcGZjhCmNNoP3YQ.

9. "U.S Africa Command Denies Plans of Establishing in Bases in Botswana," U.S. Africa Command, August 21, 2012, http://www.africom.mil/getArticle.asp?art=8199&lang=0.

10. "Bush: No New US Bases in Africa."

11. Thomas P. M. Barnett, "The Americans Have Landed," *Esquire*, June 27, 2007, www.esquire.com/features/africacommand0707.

12. Aweys Osman Yusuf, "Islamists Vow a Rebellious War as Ethiopian Troops Head to Kismayu," Shabelle Media Network, December 30, 2006, http://web.archive.org/web/20070106221717/http://allafrica.com/stories/200612300075.html.

13. "Timeline of the War in Somalia," Wikipedia, http://en.wikipedia.org/wiki/2007_timeline_of_the_War_in_Somalia.

14. "AU Wants UN Role in Somalia," Reuters, January 20, 2007, http://tvnz.co.nz/view/page/411319/964109.

15. "AMISOM Background," AMISOM.org, http://amisom-au.org/about/amisom-background/.

16. *International Financing Investments*, Global Humanitarian Assistance: Somalia (February 21, 2012), http://www.globalhumanitarian assistance.org/wp-content/uploads/2012/02/gha-somalia-briefing -paper-feb-2012-final.pdf.

17. "50 Journalists Killed in Somalia since 1992/Motive Confirmed," Committee to Protect Journalists, http://cpj.org/killed/africa/ somalia/ (accessed July 2013).

18. "Canadian Journalist Reported Abducted in Somalia," CBC News, August 23, 2008, http://www.cbc.ca/news/world/story/2008/08/23/ somalia-journalists.html.

19. "50 Journalists Killed in Somalia," Committee to Protect Journalists.

20. Jeffrey Gettleman, "U.N. Voices Concern on Child Soldiers in Somalia," *New York Times*, June 16, 2010, http://www.nytimes .com/2010/06/17/world/africa/17somalia.html?_r=0.

21. Author interviews with Somali journalists, Mogadishu, Somalia, 2007.

22. Robert Young Pelton, "Enter the Drones," *SomaliaReport*, July 6, 2011, http://www.somaliareport.com/index.php/post/1096.

23. Sean Naylor, "The Secret War: Tense Ties Plagued Africa Ops," *Navy Times*, November 28, 2011, http://www.navytimes.com/ news/2011/11/army-tense-ties-plagued-africa-ops-112811w/.

24. ICC International Maritime Bureau, *Piracy and Armed Robbery Against Ships, Annual Report, 1 January–31 December 2008* (January 2009).

25. Frank Nyakairu, "Pirates Off Somalia Get $18–30 Million Ransoms: Report," Reuters, October 1, 2008, http://www.reuters.com/article/ 2008/10/01/us-somalia-piracy-idUSTRE48T14Y20081001.

26. Reuben Kyama, "Seychelles Official Warns of Threats to Country's Tuna Industry," Voice of America, February 15, 2010, http://www .google.com/url?sa=t&rct=j&q=&esrc=s&source=web&cd=4&ved =0CFAQFjAD&url=http%3A%2F%2Fwww.voanews.com%2F content%2Fseychelles-official-warns-of-threats-to-countrys-tuna -industry-84478922%2F159779.html&ei=6fQWUfyjIoaE8AT1_oDA Dg&usg=AFQjCNFyJ4Yc9glOOAJGuy6Tv53JZ1Xt2g&sig2=Bxg4 --LE9hW73i1xRI92Tg&bvm=bv.42080656,d.eWU.

27. Author interviews with Jemma Lembere and Edward Kalendero, Mombasa, Kenya, 2008.

28. David Axe, "Why the Somali Pirates Are Winning," *Guardian*, April 9, 2009, http://www.guardian.co.uk/commentisfree/cifamerica/2009/apr/09/piracy-somalia-alabama-us-navy.

29. Terry McKnight, *Pirate Alley: Commanding Task Force 151 Off Somalia* (Annapolis, MD: Naval Institute Press, 2012).

30. John Keller, "DOD Plans to Spend $5.78 Billion for Unmanned Vehicles Procurement and Research in 2013," *Military & Aerospace Electronics*, February 14, 2012, http://www.militaryaerospace.com/articles/2012/02/dod-unmanned-vehicle-spending-requiest-for-2013-announced.html.

31. Author interview with James Curry, Kandahar, Afghanistan, October 2009.

32. "Democrats Prepare to Launch National Convention," CNN transcript, July 26, 2004, http://transcripts.cnn.com/TRANSCRIPTS/0407/26/lt.04.html.

33. Craig Whitlock and Greg Miller, "U.S. Assembling Secret Drone Bases in Africa, Arabian Peninsula, Officials Say," *Washington Post*, September 20, 2011, http://www.washingtonpost.com/world/national-security/us-building-secret-drone-bases-in-africa-arabian-peninsula-officials-say/2011/09/20/gIQAJ8rOjK_story.html.

34. U.S. State Department diplomatic cable, Cable reference id: #09PORTLOUIS292, http://www.cablegatesearch.net/cable.php?id=09PORTLOUIS292&q=seychelles.

35. Chris Greenwood and Daniel Bates, "Seven Held Over Smuggling of a Banned Stimulant from England to U.S. to Fund Terror," *Daily Mail*, May 1, 2012, http://www.dailymail.co.uk/news/article-2138143/Seven-held-smuggling-banned-stimulant-England-U-S-fund-terror.html.

36. "Somali Rebels Detain Several Pirate Gang Leaders," Reuters, February 17, 2011, http://ca.reuters.com/article/topNews/idCATRE71G6KN20110217.

37. U.S. State Department diplomatic cable.

38. "Bancroft Global Development," Guidestar.

39. Robert Young Pelton, "Contractor's Paradise—Part One," *SomaliaReport*, September 10, 2011, http://www.somaliareport.com/index.php/post/1548/Contractorrsquos_Paradise_-_Part_One.

40. "Rouget Convicted Under SA Mercenary Laws," IOL News, May 20, 2005, www.iol.co.za/news/south-africa/rouget-convicted-under-sa-mercenary-laws-1.241764#.UIZFKobze5w.

41. Gettleman, Mazzetti, and Schmitt, "U.S. Relies on Contractors in Somalia Conflict."

7. Backlash

1. Dan Browning, "Alleged Minneapolis Somali Terror Recruiter Is Back in Jail," *Minneapolis Star-Tribune*, October 24, 2012, http://m.startribune.com/local/?id=175697051.
2. Author interviews with Somali-American residents of Minneapolis, 2009.
3. Richard Stanek, "It Can and Does Happen Here: Somali Youth with Terrorist Ties in the Twin Cities," *Police Chief*, February 2011, http://www.policechiefmagazine.org/magazine/index.cfm?fuseaction=display_arch&article_id=2313&issue_id=22011.
4. James Walsh, Richard Meryhew, and Allie Shah, "2 Somali Men Indicted in Terror Plot," *Star Tribune*, http://www.startribune.com/printarticle/?id=50654962.
5. Brooke Janssens, "Two Rare Lion Cubs Saved in Somalia," *Earth Times*, March 28, 2011, http://www.earthtimes.org/conservation/two-rare-lion-cubs-saved-somalia/612/.
6. Jeremy Scahill, "The CIA's Secret Sites in Somalia," *Nation*, August 1–8, 2011, http://www.thenation.com/article/161936/cias-secret-sites-somalia.
7. Gettleman, Mazzetti, and Schmitt, "U.S. Relies on Contractors in Somalia Conflict."
8. Pelton, "Contractor's Paradise — Part One."
9. Katharine Houreld, "U.S. Relies on Contractors in Somalia Conflict," *Huffington Post*, August 10, 2011, http://www.huffingtonpost.com/2011/08/10/bancroft-global-development-somalia_n_923531.html.
10. Gettleman, Mazzetti, and Schmitt, "U.S. Relies on Contractors in Somalia Conflict."
11. Robert Young Pelton, "Does the U.S., U.N. and AMISOM Supply Al Shabab," *SomaliaReport*, July 30, 2011, http://somaliareport.com/index.php/post/1253.
12. *United Nations Peace Operations 2009: Year in Review*, United Nations, https://www.un.org/en/peacekeeping/publications/yir/yir2009.pdf.
13. *Human Security Report 2012*, figure 6.5, http://hsrgroup.org/docs/Publications/HSR2012/Figures/2012Report_Fig_6_5_BDsTermTypesRecurringIntra.pdf.

14. Ibid., Figure 5.8, http://hsrgroup.org/docs/Publications/HSR2012/ Figures/2012Report_Fig_5_8_DeathsIntraIntlizedIntra89-09.pdf.

15. Ibid.

16. David Axe, "Is the U.N. Making Things Worse in Darfur?," *American Prospect*, July 14, 2008, http://prospect.org/article/un-making -things-worse-darfur.

17. David Axe, "The Limits of Smart Power," *American Prospect*, November 5, 2010: http://prospect.org/article/limits-smart-power-0.

18. *The Christmas Massacres: LRA Attacks on Civilians in Northern Congo*, Human Rights Watch (2009), http://www.hrw.org/sites/default/ files/reports/drc0209webwcover_1.pdf.

19. David Axe, "Congo Peacekeepers Always a Step Behind LRA," *World Politics Review*, September 22, 2010, http://www.worldpolitic- sreview.com/articles/6471/war-is-boring-congo-peacekeepers -always-a-step-behind-lra.

20. Author interview with Marc Dillard, Kinshasa, Democratic Republic of Congo, October 2010.

8. The American Way of War

1. John Vandiver, "GIs Retrain Congo Troops Known for Being Violent," *Stars and Stripes*, May 2, 2010, http://www.stripes.com/news/ gis-retrain-congo-troops-known-for-being-violent-1.101774.

2. Nicole Dalrymple, "U.S. and DRC in Partnership to Train Model Congolese Battalion," U.S. Army, February 20, 2010, http://www .army.mil/article/34756/U_S_and_DRC_in_partnership_to_train _model_Congolese_battalion/.

3. Author interviews with U.S. Army soldiers, Kinshasa, Democratic Republic of Congo, October 2010.

4. "Letter from the President to the Speaker of the House of Representatives and the President Pro Tempore of the Senate Regarding the Lord's Resistance Army," White House, October 14, 2011, http:// www.whitehouse.gov/the-press-office/2011/10/14/letter-president -speaker-house-representatives-and-president-pro-tempore.

5. Axe, "The Limits of Smart Power."

6. Craig Whitlock, "U.S. Drone Base in Ethiopia Is Operational," *Washington Post*, October 27, 2011, http://articles.washingtonpost .com/2011-10-27/world/35276956_1_drone-flights-drone-operations -reaper-drones.

7. Bill Roggio, "U.S. Reapers Flying from Ethiopia," *Long War Journal*, October 27, 2011, http://www.longwarjournal.org/threat-matrix/archives/2011/10/us_reapers_flying_from_ethiopi.php.

8. Noah Shachtman, "Is This the Secret U.S. Drone Base in Saudi Arabia?," *Wired*, February 7, 2013, http://www.wired.com/dangerroom/2013/02/secret-drone-base-2/.

9. "Drones by Country: Who Has All the UAVs?," *Guardian*, August 3, 2012, http://www.guardian.co.uk/news/datablog/2012/aug/03/drone-stocks-by-country.

10. Ryan Grim, "Robert Gibbs Says Anwar al-Awlaki's Son, Killed by Drone Strike, Needs 'Far More Responsible Father,'" *Huffington Post*, October 25, 2012, http://www.huffingtonpost.com/2012/10/24/robert-gibbs-anwar-al-awlaki_n_2012438.html.

11. Craig Whitlock, "Remote U.S. Base at Core of Secret Operations," *Washington Post*, October 25, 2012, http://articles.washingtonpost.com/2012-10-25/world/35499227_1_drone-wars-drone-operations-military-base.

12. Spencer Ackerman, "New Bird of Prey Hunts Somali Terrorists: Raven Drones," *Wired*, June 27, 2011, http://www.wired.com/dangerroom/2011/06/new-bird-of-prey-hunts-somali-terrorists-raven-drones/.

13. Clark Piece, "MQ-8B Fire Scout Training Facility Unveiled at Naval Air Station Jacksonville," Jax Air News, July 11, 2012, http://www.navy.mil/submit/display.asp?story_id=68333.

14. *UN Monitoring Group on Somalia and Eritrea Report* (2012), http://www.somaliareport.com/downloads/UN_REPORT_2012.pdf.

15. Ibid.

16. "U.S. Small Plane Crashes in Mogadishu," IOL News, March 28, 2008, http://www.iol.co.za/news/africa/us-small-plane-crashes-in-mogadishu-1.394523#.UCRo8aN8GSo.

17. "Executive Summary: Aircraft Accident Investigation MQ-1B, 'Predator,' T/N 07-3183 at a Forward Operation Location," U.S. Air Force, May 13, 2009, http://usaf.aib.law.af.mil/ExecSum2009/MQ-1B_AOR_13May09.pdf.

18. "Class A Aerospace Mishaps: Fiscal Year 2011," ibid., http://usaf.aib.law.af.mil/indexFY11.html.

19. Lauren Gambino, "U.S. Drone Crashes at Seychelles Airport," *Telegraph*, April, 5, 2012, http://www.telegraph.co.uk/news/worldnews/

africaandindianocean/seychelles/9188548/US-drone-crashes-at
-Seychelles-airport.html.

20. *UN Monitoring Group on Somalia and Eritrea Report.*

21. "Surveillance Drone Crashes in Somali Capital," Associated Press, February 3, 2012, http://news.yahoo.com/surveillance-drone -crashes-somali-capital-134652928.html.

22. *UN Monitoring Group on Somalia and Eritrea Report.*

23. Covert Drone War category, Bureau of Investigative Journalism, http://www.thebureauinvestigates.com/category/projects/drones/ (accessed March 2013).

24. Noah Shachtman, "Drone, Copter Team Kills 2,400 Bombers in Iraq," *Wired*, January 21, 2008, http://www.wired.com/dangerroom/ 2008/01/drone-copter-te/.

25. "U.S. Airstrikes in Pakistan Called 'Very Effective,'" CNN, May 18, 2009, http://www.cnn.com/2009/POLITICS/05/18/cia.pakistan .airstrikes/.

26. "Introduction," *Air Combat Command Concept of Operations for Endurance Unmanned Aerial Vehicles*, Federation of American Scientists, December 3, 1996, http://www.fas.org/irp/doddir/usaf/ conops_uav/part01.htm.

27. Ibid.

28. "U.S. to Base New Unmanned Spy Plane in Korea," *Korea JoongAng Daily*, December 19, 2009, http://koreajoongangdaily.joinsmsn .com/news/article/article.aspx?aid=2914210.

29. Stephen Trimble, "Report: RQ-170 Spied Over Osama bin Laden's Bed Last Night," *Flight*, May 2, 2011, http://www.flightglobal.com/ blogs/the-dewline/2011/05/report-rq-170-spied-over-osama.html.

30. "Introduction," *Air Combat Command Concept of Operations for Endurance Unmanned Aerial Vehicles.*

31. "Insurgents Intercepted Drone Spy Videos," CBS News, December 17, 2009, http://www.cbsnews.com/2100-202_162-5989077.html.

32. Siobhan Gorman, Yochi Dreazen, and August Cole, "Insurgents Hack U.S. Drones," *Wall Street Journal*, December 17, 2009, http:// online.wsj.com/article/SB126102247889095011.html.

33. Jeff Glor, "Drone 'Hijackings' in U.S. Raise Security Concerns," CBS News, July 4, 2012, http://www.cbsnews.com/8301-505263 _162-57466342/drone-hijackings-in-u.s-raise-security-concerns/.

34. Dave Majumdad, "Anti-access/Area Denial Challenges Give

Manned Aircraft Edge Over UAVs," *Flightglobal*, July 25, 2012, http://www.flightglobal.com/news/articles/anti-accessarea-denial-challenges-give-manned-aircraft-edge-over-uavs-374745/.

35. Author interview with Khalif Ibrahim Noor via e-mail, June 2011.

36. Malkhadir Muhumed, "Young Somali Soldier: I Killed Top al-Qaida Operative," NBC, June 14, 2011, http://www.today.com/id/43399631/43492289#.USANUmfQDqs.

37. Jeremy Scahill, "Blowback in Somalia," *Nation*, September 26, 2011, http://www.thenation.com/article/163210/blowback-somalia#.

38. Robert Young Pelton, "Kenya Modified Invasion to Suit U.S. Concerns," *SomaliaReport*, November 14, 2011, http://www.somaliareport.com/index.php/post/2028/Kenya_Modified_Invasion_to_Suit_US_Concerns.

39. "The Smiling Warlord Who Controls Ras Kamboni," *Daily Nation*, June 12, 2012, http://somalilandpress.com/the-smiling-warlord-who-controls-ras-kamboni-30249.

40. "The Commander of the Ras Kamboni Brigade, Sheikh Ahmed Madobe, Said the Final Push to Take the City Was Very Imminent," *Daily Nation*, September 28, 2012, http://puntlandi.com/the-commander-of-the-ras-kamboni-brigade-sheikh-ahmed-madobe-said-the-final-push-to-take-the-city-was-very-imminent/.

41. Peter Ng'etich, "KDF: We Have Killed 700 Militants," *Daily Nation*, January 7, 2012, http://www.nation.co.ke/News/KDF-We-have-killed-700-militants-/-/1056/1301746/-/nutdiqz/-/index.html.

42. David Axe, "Somali Abduction Squad Takes American; How Will the U.S. Respond?," *Wired*, October 27, 2011, http://www.wired.com/dangerroom/2011/10/somali-abduction-squad/.

43. "Kidnapped French Woman Dies in Somalia," ABC News, October 20, 2011, http://www.abc.net.au/news/2011-10-19/kidnapped-frenchwoman-dead-in-somalia/3580026.

44. Kelly Gilblom, "Somalia Challenges Kenya Over Oil Blocks," Reuters, July 6, 2012, http://www.reuters.com/article/2012/07/06/kenya-somalia-exploration-idUSL6E8I63IM20120706.

45. Jeffrey Gettleman and Josh Krohn, "Kenya Reportedly Didn't Warn U.S. of Somalia Incursion," *New York Times*, October 20, 2011, http://www.nytimes.com/2011/10/21/world/africa/americans-given-no-warning-of-kenyas-march-into-somalia-officials-say.html.

46. Ibid.; Gabe Joselow, "Is Kenya Battling al-Shabab Alone?," Voice of America, October 25, 2011, http://www.voanews.com/content/is -kenya-battling-al-shabab-alone-132640988/159075.html.

47. "Foreign Military Financing Account Summary," U.S. State Department, June 23, 2010, http://www.state.gov/t/pm/ppa/sat/c14560 .htm; Daniel Volman, "U.S. Military Activities in Kennya," African Security Research Project, January 2008, http://concernedafrica scholars.org/african-security-research-project/?p=3.

48. Jason Straziuso, "Former 2-star Resigns as Ambassador to Kenya," *Air Force Times*, June 29, 2012, http://www.airforcetimes.com/news/ 2012/06/ap-air-force-former-2-star-resigns-kenya-ambassador -062912/.

49. "US Air Force, Kenyan Maintainers Turn Wrenches Together," U.S. Central Command, http://www.dvidshub.net/news/9786/us-air- force-kenyan-maintainers-turn-wrenches-together#.UK3ljoYWmH8.

50. Jim Fisher, "Air Forces Africa Commander Visits Kenyan Air Force," U.S. Air Force, August 26, 2009, http://www.af.mil/news/story .asp?id=123164973.

51. Emmanuel Chirchir, Twitter, November 1, 2011, https://twitter .com/MajorEChirchir/status/131394603067777024.

52. Fred Oluoch, "U.N. Unveils New Look Amisom as Kenya Joins Up," *East African*, February 11, 2012, http://www.theeastafrican.co.ke/ news/UN+unveils+new+look+Amisom+as+Kenya+joins+up/-/ 2558/1324660/-/gtn01k/-/index.html.

53. "Kenyans Enter Kismayo, Mopping Up Begins," *SomaliaReport*, September 29, 2012, http://www.somaliareport.com/index.php/ topic/47.

54. "Allied Forces Target Kismayo, Civilians Killed," *SomaliaReport*, August 11, 2012, http://www.somaliareport.com/index.php/ post/3582/Allied_Forces_Target_Kismayo_Civilians_Killed.

55. "Somali Militants Hold Kismayo under Kenyan Force Attack," BBC, September 28, 2012, http://www.bbc.co.uk/news/world-africa -19765225.

56. Patrick Mayoyo, "How KDF Used Spy Planes to Seize Kismayu," *Daily Nation*, September 30, 2012, http://www.nation.co.ke/News/ How+KDF+used+spy+planes+to+seize+Kismayu+++/-/1056/ 1521630/-/1ub6cm/-/index.html.

57. "Kenyans Enter Kismayo, Mopping Up Begins."

58. "Explosions Rock Somalia's Kismayo," Al Jazeera, October 2, 2012, http://www.aljazeera.com/news/africa/2012/10/201210253950687 422.html.

59. Author interview with Derek Granger, aboard the USS *Donald Cook*, 2009.

60. Author interview with Martin Murphy, via e-mail, 2009.

61. "Pictured: Desperate Chinese Sailors Fight Off Somali Pirates with Beer Bottles and Molotov Cocktails," *Daily Mail*, December 23, 2008, http://www.dailymail.co.uk/news/article-1098125/Pictured-Desperate-Chinese-sailors-fight-Somali-pirates-beer-bottles-Molotov-cocktails.html.

62. Author interview with John Dalby, via e-mail, 2011.

63. Author interview with Claude Berube, via e-mail, 2011.

64. "Blackwater's Pirate-Fighting Navy Has Sunk!," U.S. Naval Institute, January 4, 2010, http://blog.usni.org/2010/01/04/blackwaters-pirate-fighting-navy-has-sunk.

65. Author interview.

66. Steven Carmel speech transcript, "Pirates vs. Congress: How Pirates Are a Better Bargain," Information Dissemination, August 11, 2011, http://www.informationdissemination.net/2011/08/pirates-vs-congress-how-pirates-are.html.

67. Author interview with Paul Gibbins, via e-mail, 2011.

68. Author interview with "Dave," via e-mail, 2011.

69. Author interview with Martin Murphy, via e-mail, 2009.

70. Spencer Ackerman, "Somali Pirate Kingpin Calls It Quits as Hijackings Plummet," *Wired*, January 10, 2013, http://www.wired.com/dangerroom/2013/01/pirate-kingpin/.

71. Nasongo Willy, "Somalia: Puntland Signed an Agreement with Sarecen Company to Train Its Marine Forces," Al Shahid, http://english.alshahid.net/archives/15361.

72. Robert Young Pelton, "Erik Prince, an American Commando in Exile," *Men's Journal*, November 2010, http://www.mensjournal.com/magazine/erik-prince-an-american-commando-in-exile-20121016.

73. Mark Mazzetti and Eric Schmitt, "Private Army Formed to Fight Somali Pirates Leaves Troubled Legacy," *New York Times*, October 4, 2012, http://www.nytimes.com/2012/10/05/world/africa/private-army-leaves-troubled-legacy-in-somalia.html?pagewanted=all &_r=0.

74. "Did the U.N. Shut Down Anti-Piracy Program?," *SomaliaReport*, February 28, 2011, http://www.somaliareport.com/index.php/ post/141/Did_The_UN_Shut_Down_Anti-Piracy_Program.

75. Mazzetti and Schmitt, "Private Army Formed."

76. *UN Monitoring Group on Somalia and Eritrea Report.*

77. Mazzetti and Schmitt, "Private Army Formed."

78. Maria Ressa, "U.S. Smart Bombs Used in Sulu Attack," *Rappler*, March 22, 2012, http://www.rappler.com/nation/2910-us-smart -bombs-used-in-sulu-attack.

79. "Operation Enduring Freedom Casualties—Afghanistan."

80. Julie Alipala, "RP Terror Campaign Cost Lives of 11 U.S., 572 RP Sol- diers — Military," *Inquirer Mindanao*, October 2, 2010, http://global nation.inquirer.net/news/breakingnews/view/20101002-295567/ RP-terror-campaign-cost-lives-of-11-US-572-RP-soldiersmilitary.

81. Jim Gomez, "AP Enterprise: Philippines Using U.S. Smart Bombs," Associated Press, March 21, 2012, http://news.yahoo.com/ap -enterprise-philippines-using-us-smart-bombs-142048159.html.

82. Simon Tisdall, "Philippines Peace Deal Is Far from a Done Deal," *Guardian*, October 7, 2012, http://www.guardian.co.uk/world/2012/ oct/07/philippines-peace-deal-terror-challenge.

83. Simon Tisdall, "Philippines Moves Close to Historic Peace Deal with Islamist Rebels," *Guardian*, February 13, 2013, http://www .guardian.co.uk/world/2013/feb/13/philippines-peace-deal-islamist -rebels.

9. Full Circle

1. Jessica Stone, "Afghanistan's Troop Killers," *Daily Beast*, March 23, 2010, http://www.thedailybeast.com/articles/2010/03/23/ afghanistans-troop-killers.html.

2. "Obama Calls Situation in Afghanistan 'Urgent,'" CNN, July 20, 2008, http://articles.cnn.com/2008-07-20/politics/obama .afghanistan_1_presumptive-democratic-presidential-nominee -afghanistan-afghan-president-hamid-karzai?_s=PM:POLITICS.

3. "Obama's Warfare."

4. Spencer Ackerman, "Military's Own Report Card Gives Afghan Surge an F," *Wired*, September 27, 2012, http://www.wired.com/ dangerroom/2012/09/surge-report-card/.

5. David Axe, "Insider Attacks Now Biggest Killer of NATO Troops,"

Wired, August 30, 2012, http://www.wired.com/dangerroom/2012/08/insider-attacks/.

6. Robert M. Gates, February 25, 2011, speech, West Point, New York, U.S. Defense Department, http://www.defense.gov/speeches/speech.aspx?speechid=1539.

7. "Obama's Warfare."

8. Author interviews with "Tom" and "Red," Laghman, Afghanistan, February 2012.

9. Kevin Sieff, "Afghans Protest Burning of Korans at U.S. Base," *Washington Post*, February 21, 2012, http://www.washingtonpost.com/world/asia_pacific/afghans-protest-improper-disposal-of-koran-at-us-base/2012/02/21/gIQAjhBqQR_story.html?wprss=rss_war-zones.

10. "Man in Afghan Army Uniform Kills 3 NATO Troops," *Army Times*, August 29, 2012, http://www.armytimes.com/news/2012/08/ap-man-in-afghan-army-uniform-kills-3-nato-troops-082812/.

11. Greg Jaffe, "Violence in Wake of Koran Incident Fuels U.S. Doubts about Afghan Partners," *Washington Post*, February 26, 2012, http://www.washingtonpost.com/world/national-security/violence-in-wake-of-koran-incident-fuels-us-doubts-about-afghan-partners/2012/02/26/gIQAgc3qcR_story.html.

12. Author interview with Special Forces sergeant, via e-mail, February 2012.

13. Bill Roggio and Lisa Lundquist, "Green-on-Blue Attacks in Afghanistan: The Data," *Long War Journal*, August 23, 2012, http://www.longwarjournal.org/archives/2012/08/green-on-blue_attack.php.

14. David Sedney, Congressional testimony, 112th Congress, February 1, 2012, http://armedservices.house.gov/index.cfm/files/serve?File_id=682a1b43-0f21-4c1f-84ce-75202f733258.

15. Author interview with "Tom," via e-mail, February 2012.

16. Roggio and Lundquist, "Green-on-Blue Attacks in Afghanistan."

17. Jon Stewart, interview with Ekmeleddin İhsanoğlu, *The Daily Show with Jon Stewart*, February 15, 2012.

18. Micah Zenko, "How Many Terrorists Have Been Killed by Drones?," Council on Foreign Relations, February 20, 2013, http://blogs.cfr.org/zenko/2013/02/20/how-many-terrorists-have-been-killed-by-drones/.

19. Covert Drone War, Bureau of Investigative Journalism.

20. Jo Becker and Scott Shane, "Secret 'Kill List' Proves a Test of Obama's Principles and Will," *New York Times*, May 29, 2012, http://

www.nytimes.com/2012/05/29/world/obamas-leadership-in-war
-on-al-qaeda.html?pagewanted=all&_r=0.

21. Covert Drone War, Bureau of Investigative Journalism.

22. Atiaf Alwazir, Twitter, May 14, 2012, https://twitter.com/Woman
fromYemen/status/202020016680468481.

23. NoonArabia, Twitter, May 13, 2012, https://twitter.com/Noon
Arabia/statuses/201659270381580288?tw_i=201659270381580288
&tw_e=details&tw_p=tweetembed.

24. Sudarsan Raghavan, "In Yemen, U.S. Airstrikes Breed Anger, and
Sympathy for al-Qaeda," *Washington Post*, May 29, 2012, http://www
.washingtonpost.com/world/middle_east/in-yemen-us
-airstrikes-breed-anger-and-sympathy-for-al-qaeda/2012/05/29/
gJQAUmKI0U_story.html.

25. Author interview with Chris Swift, via e-mail, July 2012.

26. "Remarks of John O. Brennan, Assistant to the President for Homeland Security and Counterterrorism, on Ensuring al-Qa'ida's Demise—
As Prepared for Delivery," The White House, June 29, 2011, http://
www.whitehouse.gov/the-press-office/2011/06/29/remarks-john-o
-brennan-assistant-president-homeland-security-and-counter.

27. John Brennan, "The Efficacy and Ethics of U.S. Counterterrorism
Strategy," The Woodrow Wilson International Center for Scholars,
April 30, 2012, http://www.wilsoncenter.org/event/the-efficacy-and
-ethics-us-counterterrorism-strategy.

28. Greg Miller, Ellen Nakashima, and Karen DeYoung, "CIA Drone
Strikes Will Get Pass in Counterterrorism 'Playbook,' Officials Say,"
Washington Post, January 9, 2013, http://www.washingtonpost.com/
world/national-security/cia-drone-strikes-will-get-pass-in-counter
terrorism-playbook-officials-say/2013/01/19/ca169a20-618d-11e2
-9940-6fc488f3fecd_story.html.

29. Jason Linkins, "John Brennan Ducks Drones in Confirmation Hear-
ing and We Stop Worrying About Extra-Judicial Killings," *Huffington
Post*, February 9, 2013, http://www.huffingtonpost.com/2013/
02/09/john-brennan-drones-confirmation_n_2649233.html.

30. Barbara Starr, Pam Benson, and Tom Cohen, "Brennan Defends al-
Awlaki Drone Strike as Part of War with al Qaeda," CNN, February 7,
2013, http://www.cnn.com/2013/02/07/politics/brennan
-confirmation-hearing.

31. "GA-ASI Unveils New Enhanced Endurance Designs for Predator B,"

General Atomics, April 18, 2012, http://www.ga.com/press
-releases/94-ga-asi-unveils-new-enhanced-endurance-designs-for
-predator-b.

32. "GA-ASI Introduces System-wide Enhancements for Predator B/
MQ-9," General Atomics, September 8, 2012, http://www.ga.com/
press-releases/492-ga-asi-introduces-system-wide-enhancements
-for-predator-b-mq-9.

33. "MQ-9 Reaper Unmanned Aircraft System (UAS)," Defense
Department, http://www.dote.osd.mil/pub/reports/FY2011/pdf/
af/2011mq9reaperuas.pdf.

34. Bill Sweetman, "Reading Secret USAF Bomber, ISR Plans," *Aviation
Week*, December 3, 2012, http://www.aviationweek.com/Article
.aspx?id=/article-xml/AW_12_03_2012_p04-520329.xml.

35. Author interview with freelance photographer, via e-mail, late 2012.

36. Author interview with Missy Cummings, late 2011.

37. Marc Schanz, "The Reaper Harvest," *Air Force*, April 2011, http://
www.airforce-magazine.com/MagazineArchive/Pages/2011/
April%202011/0411reaper.aspx.

38. "Drones by Country: Who Has All the UAVs?" *Guardian*, August
3, 2012, http://www.guardian.co.uk/news/datablog/2012/aug/03/
drone-stocks-by-country.

39. Schanz, "Reaper Harvest."

40. "United States Air Force Unmanned Aircraft Systems Flight Plan,
2009-2047," U.S. Air Force, 2009, http://www.fas.org/irp/pro-
gram/collect/uas_2009.pdf.

41. Author interview with Carl Johnson, by phone, September 2011.

42. Spencer Ackerman, "DIY Drone-Proofing: Militants Use Carpet,
Grass Mats, Mud to Hide From Robots," *Wired*, February 21, 2013,
http://www.wired.com/dangerroom/2013/02/diy-droneproofing/.

43. Author interview with Randall Davis, via e-mail, early 2012.

44. "The Efficacy and Ethics of U.S. Counterterrorism Strategy," The
Woodrow Wilson International Center for Scholars, April 30, 2012,
http://www.wilsoncenter.org/event/the-efficacy-and-ethics-us
-counterterrorism-strategy.

45. "Letter from the President to the Speaker of the House of Representatives and the President Pro Tempore of the Senate Regarding the
Lord's Resistance Army."

46. Alan Boswell, "African Villagers Embrace U.S. Role in Hunt for

Lord's Resistance Army Leader," McClatchy, February 13, 2012, http://www.mcclatchydc.com/2012/02/13/138737/african-villagers -embrace-us-role.html#storylink=cpy.

47. "Letter to the Editor, TomDispatch — Response to 'Secret Wars, Secret Bases, and the Pentagon's "New Spice Route" in Africa,'" U.S. Africa Command, July 27, 2012, http://www.africom.mil/Newsroom/ Article/9094/letter-to-the-editor-tomdispatch--response-to--34.

48. Boswell, "African Villagers Embrace U.S. Role."

49. "The Dronefather," *Economist*, December 1, 2012, http://www .economist.com/news/technology-quarterly/21567205-abe-karem -created-robotic-plane-transformed-way-modern-warfare.

Addendum

1. Spencer Ackerman, "French Troops Target Terrorists in Mali as Newest Shadow War Begins," *Wired*, January 11, 2013, http://www .wired.com/dangerroom/2013/01/mali/.

2. Tyrone C. Marshall Jr., "AFRICOM Commander Addresses Concerns, Potential Solutions in Mali," U.S. Africa Command, January 24, 2013, http://www.africom.mil/Newsroom/Article/10234/ general-ham-at-howard-university.

3. Ann Scott Tyson, "U.S. Pushes Anti-Terrorism in Africa," *Washington Post*, July 26, 2005, http://www.washingtonpost.com/wp-dyn/ content/article/2005/07/25/AR2005072501801.html.

4. Phillip Ulmer, "Special Forces Support Pan Sahel Initiative in Africa," U.S. Defense Department, March 8, 2004, http://www .defense.gov/News/NewsArticle.aspx?ID=27112.

5. Craig Whitlock, "Mysterious Fatal Crash Offers Rare Look at U.S. Commando Presence in Mali," *Washington Post*, July 8, 2012, http:// articles.washingtonpost.com/2012-07-08/world/35488661_1 _malian-counterterrorism-commando.

6. Bill Roggio and Lisa Lundquist, "Did the U.S. Launch a Drone Strike on AQIM in Northern Mali?," *Long War Journal*, June 24, 2012, http://www.longwarjournal.org/threat-matrix/archives/2012/06/ did_the_us_launch_a_drone_stri.php#ixzz2NA0cviE8.

7. Author interview with David Cenciotti, via e-mail, early 2013.

8. "Veteran Jihadist Moktar Belmoktar Is Killed in Mali, Chadian Forces Say," CNN, March 3, 2013, http://www.cnn.com/2013/03/02/ world/africa/mali-unrest/index.html.

Index

Abdallah, Ahmed, 14–17
Abdiner, Mustafa Haji, 101
Abizaid, John, 96
Abu Sayyaf, 67, 161, 162
Ackerman, Spencer, 167
Afghanistan, 58, 163
    drone attacks in, 140
    drone surveillance in, 43
    insider attacks in, 165–68,
        172–75
    Obama's promise to escalate
        war in, 166–67
    post–9/11 training of troops in,
        169–172
    Predators' use in, after 9/11,
        54–56

African Union Mission in Somalia
    (AMISOM), 98–99, 114, 121–25,
    139, 144–45, 151, 157, 160
Agolla, Francis, 151
Ahmed, Salah Osman, 121
Ahmed, Sharif Sheikh, 97–98, 147
Ahmed, Shirwa, 119–120
Aidid, Mohamed Farah, 25–28, 29, 30
Air & Cosmos magazine, 88
Al Nahyan, Sheikh Mohammed
    bin Zayed, 96, 159
al Qaeda
    recruiting in Yemen, 177
    Somalia and, 49–50, 64, 66, 93
    World Trade Center bombing,
        1993, 20–21

al Qaeda in the Islamic Maghreb (AQIM), 191, 194
Al Qaeda Network Execute Order (AQN ExOrd), 66
Al Shabab, 93, 96–98, 100–103, 113–14, 119–121
    Kenyans in Somalia and, 149–152
    Somalis turn away from, 144–48
    U.S. mercenaries and, 123–25
Al Wazir, Atiaf, 176
al-Awlaki, Anwar, 137, 179
al-Bashir, Omar, 129
al-Haideri, Adnan Ihsan Saeed, 75–76
al-Harethi, Qaed Salim Sinan, 50, 62–63
Ali, Abdullah, 102
Ali, Muhamda, 161–62
Amber drone, 4–5
Ambinder, Marc, 142
AMISOM. *See* African Union Mission in Somalia (AMISOM)
Angola, 35–36
Ankunda, Paddy, 100
Annan, Kofi, 22, 33
Aquino, Benigno, 162
Aviation Week magazine, 88–89
Ayro, Aden Hashi Farah, 50, 120

Baloyo, Mary Grace, 69
Bamford, James, 45, 63, 76
Bancroft Global Development, 37, 47, 114–15, 121–24
Barlow, Eeben, 35–36
Barre, Mohamed Siad, 9–11, 25, 37
Bast, Trevor, 193–94
Beaver, Sean, 166

Becker, Jo, 175
Belmoktar, Moktar, 194
Benin, Denard and, 7, 15
Berube, Claude, 155
Big Boys Rule (Fainaru), 80–81
Big Safari engineering team, of U.S. Air Force, 51–52, 78
bin Hir, Zulkifli, 161–62
bin Laden, Osama, 50, 112, 142, 145, 147
Black, Cofer, 53
Blackwater, 81–82, 154–55, 158–59
Blaser, Virginia, 113–14
Boeing, 43, 181
Bosnia, 33, 41–42
Boswell, Alan, 186, 187
Bourgeaud, Gilbert. *See* Denard, Bob (Gilbert Bourgeaud)
Boutros-Ghali, Boutros, 26
Breedlove, Philip, 184
Brennan, John, 176, 177–78, 186
Brennan, Nigel, 100
Burns, John, 85
Bush, George H. W., 26
Bush, George W., 73–74, 97, 167

Carmel, Stephen, 155
Carroll, Jill, 85
Carson, Johnnie, 122, 148–49, 150
Carter, Ashton, 138
Cashen, John, 182
Castellano, Frank, 107–9
Central African Republic (CAR), 129, 135–36, 186
Chad, 125, 127–29, 193, 194–95
Chalabi, Ahmad, 75–76
Cheney, Dick, 12
Chirchir, Emmanuel, 150, 151

CIA (Central Intelligence
Agency), 23, 112–13, 136–38, 140–
41, 144–45, 178, 180–84
Gnat drones and, 5–6, 18–19
Iraq and, 45, 73–76
Predator drones and, 52–55,
62–64, 68
Special Operations Forces and,
65–66
Clark, James, 78
Clinton, Bill, 31–32, 44
Clinton, Hillary, 131–32
Comoros, 8, 14–17, 34
Congo, Denard in Belgian, 6–7.
See also Democratic Republic of
Congo (DRC)
Cuéllar y de la Guerra, Javier
Pérez de, 25–26
Cummings, Missy, 183–84, 185
Curry, James, 111–13

Dalby, John, 154, 155
Darfur, refugees from, 127–29
Dark Star drone prototype, 43–44,
80, 88, 141
Davis, Randall, 185
Davis, Tom, 187
Day, Clifford, 28
Defense Advanced Research Proj-
ects Agency (DARPA), 4, 43
Democratic Republic of Congo
(DRC), 32, 48–49, 129–132
U.S.-led military training and
health clinic in, 133–36
Denard, Bob (Gilbert Bourgeaud),
6–8, 14–17, 34
Dijme, Hawa Mamhat, 127–28
Dillard, Marc, 132

Djibouti, 63, 137–38, 140
Djohar, Said Mohamed, 17
Donovan, John, 77
Dory, Amanda J., 138
Dostum, Abdul Rashid, 55
Drones. *See also specific drones*
addition of laser designators,
weapons, and communica-
tion to, 50–54
Brennan's advocacy of, 177–78
civilian deaths and creation of
terrorists, 175–77
detection tasks, 110–14
development of in 1990s,
43–44
early versions, 3–6
hacking risk, 143–44
locations in 2009, 113
locations in 2010, 136–37
upgrades in size, stealth and
artificial intelligence of, 179–
186
uses of, generally, 17–24

Ehrhard, Thomas, 52
Eid, Farah Ismail, 38, 39
Elmi, Abdifatah Mohammed, 100
Eritrea, 61, 94–96, 139
Esmond, Marvin, 47
Ethiopia, 10, 93–99, 136, 144
EUFOR, 128–29
Executive Outcomes PMC, 35–37,
159, 160

Fainaru, Steve, 80–81
Fall, François Lonseny, 98
Farah, Aden Hashi, 103
Farmajo, Mohamed Abdullah, 145
Fire Scout robo-copters, 139

Fogleman, Ronald, 42
Forces Armées de la République Démocratique du Congo (FARDC), 129–130, 133–36
Franks, Tommy, 55
Frazer, Jendayi, 94–95
Fulghum, David, 80

Garvelink, William, 134
Gates, Robert, 168
General Atomics, 5–6, 19, 41, 42, 51, 68, 78, 179–180
Gettleman, Jeffrey, 123
Global Hawk drones, 43, 111, 139, 141, 181, 182
Gnat 750 drones, 5, 6, 18–19, 67–70
Gobbi, Ferruccio, 130
Goebel, Greg, 5, 47
Graham, Lindsay, 175
Granger, Derek, 153

Ham, Carter, 192
Harfang drones, 192
Hassan, Abdi, 146
Hassan, Mohamed Abdi, 157
Helmi, Mohamed Mohamoud, 140
Hersi, Mohamud "Adde" Muse, 119
Hirabe, Moqtar, 101–3
Holbrooke, Richard, 46
Huddleston, Vicki, 94–95
Hughes, Christian, 166
Hume, Kim, 76
Humphreys, Todd, 143–44
Hunt, Richard, 94–95
Hussein, Mohamed Omar, 101, 120–21

Hussein, Qusay, 45
Hussein, Saddam, 44–45, 73–74, 79

İhsanoğlu, Ekmeleddin
Iran
    capture of U.S. drone, 142–44
    limitations of drones and, 141
Iraq, 58, 63, 140, 162, 166–67
    drone surveillance in, 43
    insurgency and deaths in, 82–83
    intelligence prior to U.S. invasion of, 73–75
    media embed system and government management of information, 74–77, 83–87
    Predator drones armed with Stinger missiles, 77–79
    press coverage of invasion of Kuwait, 12–13
    security contracts and mercenaries in, 80–82
    stealth drone and, 79–80, 87–89
    U.S. propaganda in, 44–45
Iraqi National Congress (INC), 75–76
Islamic Courts Union (ICU), in Somalia, 61, 93–94, 95, 97–98, 113–14
Ismail, Ali, 38
Isse, Abdifatah Yusuf, 121
Isse, Mahad, 100
Italy, Mohamed Farah, 101–2

Jacobson, Mark, 173
Jaffar, Said Mohammed, 14, 17
Jamal, Omar, 120–21
Jemaah Islamiyah, 67, 161, 162
Johnson, Carl, 184

Jonah, James, 26
Jumdail, Gumbahali Umbra, 161–62
Jumper, John, 50–52
Juppé, Alain, 150

Kabila, Joseph, 49, 132
Kabila, Laurent, 36, 48–49
Kalendero, Edward, 105–6
Kaminski, Paul, 41, 43
Karem, Abraham, 3–6, 18–19, 41–42, 186–87
Katovsky, Bill, 76, 77
Kenya, 148–152, 189
Klak, Thomas, 33
Koehl, Timothy, 33
Kony, Joseph, 129, 135, 186
Koran, U.S. mishandling of copies of, 172–73
Kurth, Tyler, 165–66

Lake, Darren, 88
Landmine Clearance International, 47, 114
Larson-Kone, Megan, 194
Le Roy, Alain, 125
Le Sage, Andre, 160
Leading Systems, Inc., 3–5
Lembere, Jemma, 105
Letterman, David, 75
Lindhout, Amanda, 100
Lockheed Martin, 43, 80, 88, 181
Lord's Resistance Army (LRA), in Congo, 129–131, 135–36, 186
Luitingh, Lafras, 159

Madobe, Sheikh Ahmed, 149
Maersk, 155
Maersk Alabama, 107–10, 153

Malé, Serge, 128–29
Mali, 185, 191–95
Martin, David, 86
Martineau, Geoffrey, 97
Maxwell, David, 71
Mboligikpele, Fidel, 130
McCain, John, 29–30
McKnight, Terry, 107–10
McVay, Justin, 87–88
media reporting
    historic attempts to censor, 11–13
    increasing U.S. secrecy and, 190
    Iraq and government management through embedding, 74–77, 83–87
    U.S. media's support of non-intervention in Rwanda, 33–34
mercenaries
Denard and, 6–8, 13–17
in Iraq, 80–82
in Somalia, 114–15
Michel, James, 113–14
Miller, Judith, 76
Mills, John, 62
Milošević, Slobodan, 46
Mission de l'Organisation de Nations Unies en République Démocratique du Congo (MONUC), 131–32
Mladić, Ratko, 41
Mobutu Sese Seko, 7, 36, 48–49
Mogadishu. *See* Somalia
Mohamed, Ali Mahdi, 25
Mohammed, Fazul Abdullah, 49, 146

Montgomery, Thomas, 27, 28, 30
Moran, Paul, 75–76
Mordan, Jon, 13
Morin, Monte, 86–87
Moro Islamic Liberation Front
   (MILF), in Philippines, 67–72,
   161, 162
Murphy, Martin, 153, 154, 157, 158
Mustafa, Qari Ghulam, 172
Mwale, Kennedy, 91–92
Myers, Garth, 33

Naylor, Sean, 64
Nelson, Mitch, 55
New York Herald, 12
NFD, 36–37
9/11 Commission Report, 50
Noor, Khalif Ibrahim, 144–46
North Korea, 141
Northrup Grumman, 43, 180–81,
   184

Obama, Barack
   Afghanistan and, 163, 166–68
   Central African Republic and,
      186
   Congo and, 135
   drones and, 178–79
   Mali and, 194
   Somali pirates and, 108–9
   Special Operations Command
      and, 66
Omar, Mullah, 55
Operation Lightning Thunder, in
   Congo, 135–36
Osman, Maria, 28–29
OV-10 Bronco attack planes, in
   Philippines, 68–69, 72, 160–62
Owens, Brandon, 166

Pace, Frank, 4–6, 18–19
Pakistan, drone attacks in, 140
Panetta, Leon, 140
Patek, Umar, 70
Peltier, Isaac, 172
Pelton, Robert Young, 30, 115, 124–
   25, 158–59
Petraeus, David, 167
Philippines, 67–70, 140, 160–62
Phillips, Richard, 107–10, 153
Pioneer drones, 6
pirates, off Somalia, 37–39, 91–92,
   104–10, 150, 153–60
Powell, Colin, 73–75
Predator drones, 6, 19
   al-Awlaki and, 137
   costs in 1996, 43
   detection tasks, 110–11
   in Iraq, armed with Stinger
      missiles, 77–79
   limitations of, 46–47
   loses of, 41–42, 46
   in Philippines, 70–71
   in Somalia, 103–4, 140
   strike on al-Harethi, 63
   vulnerability of, 141
Predator's Big Safari (Whittle), 52,
   54
Prince, Erik, 158–59
private military companies
   (PMCs), 34–37
Protected Vessels International
   (PVI), 155, 156

Rage, Sheik Ali Mohamed, 152
Raghavan, Sudarsan, 176
Ramirez, Armando J., 31, 65–66
Rather, Dan, 75

Raven drones, 138–39, 140
Reaper drones, 136, 140, 181, 184
    detection tasks, 110–12
    hacking of, 143–44
    upgrades of, 179–180
Rendon, John, 44–45
Rendon Group, 44–45, 75–76, 83–84
Reynolds number, 4–5
RG-8 relay plane, 18–19
Rice, Condoleezza, 53
Rogers, Keith, 88
Roggio, Bill, 136, 194
Rouget, Richard, 17, 37, 115, 124
RQ-4 Global Hawks. *See* Global
    Hawk drones
RQ-170 Sentinel. *See* Sentinel
    drones
Rumsfeld, Donald, 66, 76, 77
Rwanda, 31–34, 48
Rykaart, Duncan, 36–37, 124

Saracen International, 158, 159
Scahill, Jeremy, 66, 147
Scan Eagle drones, 107, 110, 139,
    140, 161, 162
Schmitt, Eric, 55, 168
Schramme, Jacques, 7
Schwartz, Norton, 144
SEAL Team Six, Somali pirates
    and, 108–10
Sediqi, Sediq, 173
Sedney, David, 173
Sentinel drones, 87–89, 111, 181
    Iran's capture of, 142–44, 180
    U.S. surveillance reach and,
    141–42
September 11 2001 attacks, Preda-
    tor's use in Afghanistan after,
    54–56

Serbia, 45–46
Sethna, Zaab, 75
Seychelles, 105, 113–14
Shachtman, Noah, 137
Shadow Factory, The (Bamford), 63
Shalikashvili, John, 22
Shamsi, Hina, 178
Shane, Scott, 175
Shapi, Khalid, 105
Shawcross, William, 11, 20, 22–23
Sherman, William Tecumseh, 12
Sholtis, Tadd, 79
Short, Michael, 46
Siad, Yusuf Mohamed (Indha
    Adde), 147
Silver Fox drone, 71
Simon Fraser University's Human
    Security Report Project, 125–26
Singer, P.W., 34–35, 36, 82
Sites, Kevin, 29
Smith, Aaron, 166
Soilih, Ali, 14–16
Somalia
    al Qaeda and, 49–50, 64, 66, 93
    dangers for journalists in,
        99–103
    downing of U.S. Blackhawk
        helicopters in, 28–31
    drones and, 64, 103–4, 138–140
    end of Barres' government,
        9–11
    Kenya as U.S. proxy in, 148–
        152, 189
    mercenaries in, 114–15, 121–25
    pirates and, 37–39, 91–92, 104–
        10, 150, 153–60
    residents turn away from Al
        Shabab, 144–48

Somalia (*continued*)
sale of U.S. arms to, 124–25
Somali-American "travelers"
and, 119–121
Special Operations Forces in,
64–66, 95–98, 108–10
UN peacekeepers and, 25–30,
61
U.S. shadow war in 2006, 93–98
South Africa, 34–35, 48–49, 56
South Sudan, 127, 135–36, 186
Spain, 154
Special Operations Command
(SOCOM), 31, 65
Special Operations Forces (SOF),
in Somalia, 64–66, 95–98, 108–
10
Stanek, Richard, 121
Starr, Barbara, 112
Sterling, 159–160
Stock, Michael, 47–48, 114–15,
124–25, 160
Stone, Jessica, 165
Sweetman, Bill, 88–89, 180–81
Swift, Chris, 176–77
Synthetic Aperture Radar (SAR),
on Reaper drones, 112

Tajir, Ahmed, 101–3
Teller, Seth, 185
Tellex, Stephanie, 185
Tenet, George, 73
terrorism, changing face of war
and, 20–24
30th Reconnaissance Squadron,
87–89
Tom (U.S. Army Special Forces
Officer), 169–172, 174

Toure, Amadou Toumani, 193
Transitional Federal Government
(TFG), in Somalia, 93, 95, 98,
124, 145–46, 152, 160
Tundok, Wahid, 72
Turkey, 5, 6

Uganda
Central African Republic and,
186–87
Congo and, 48, 129, 135–36
Somalia and, 98, 100–101, 104,
115, 123–24, 139–40, 148
United Arab Emirates (UAE), 11,
79, 139, 158, 159
United Nations High Commis-
sioner for Refugees (UNHCR),
23, 128–29
United Nations, peacekeeping
operations of, 9, 18, 22–23, 25–30,
32–33, 98, 125–29, 131–32
Unmanned Vehicles magazine, 88
Urban, Jesse, 71
USS *Bainbridge*, 107–9
USS *Chafee*, 104, 106
USS *Cole*, 50, 56, 62, 63
USS *Donald Cook*, 153
USS *Mount Whitney*, 62

Vincent, Steve, 85

wars, decline in number and
intensity of, 8–9, 57
Wetangula, Moses, 148–49
Whittle, Richard, 52, 54, 78, 79
Widnall, Sheila, 42
Wilkerson, Lawrence, 73, 74
Wilson, E. K., 120
Woodruff, Bob, 85, 86

Woolsey, James, 5, 18

World Trade Center bombing, 1993, 20–21

Wurster, Donald, 70

Yemen, 50, 62–63, 140, 176–77

Yugoslavia, 18

Zeender, Rocky, 67

Zenawi, Meles, 95

About the Author

David Axe is a freelance journalist based in Columbia, South Carolina. He is a regular contributor to *Wired*, Voice of America, and many other media outlets. A war correspondent since 2005, David has reported from Iraq, Afghanistan, Somalia, Congo, East Timor, Lebanon, and other conflict zones. He is the author and coauthor of several books, including the graphic novels *War Fix*, *War Is Boring*, *The Accidental Candidate*, and *Army of God*, plus the nonfiction books *Army 101*, *War Bots*, and *From A to B*. David blogs at https://medium.com/war-is-boring.